John Kennedy

Robert Morris and the Holland Purchase

John Kennedy

Robert Morris and the Holland Purchase

ISBN/EAN: 9783743321700

Manufactured in Europe, USA, Canada, Australia, Japa

Cover: Foto ©ninafisch / pixelio.de

Manufactured and distributed by brebook publishing software (www.brebook.com)

John Kennedy

Robert Morris and the Holland Purchase

ROBERT MORRIS

AND THE

HOLLAND PURCHASE

The Old Land Office at Batavia.

BATAVIA IS A comparatively new town, and yet it contains within its borders one of the most interesting historical landmarks in the world.

One cannot visit Concord Bridge, or Bunker Hill, or Saratoga, or Yorktown, or Mount Vernon, without being stirred to the very depths of his soul with memories of the great struggle for American independence. That great conflict decided not only the destinies of America, but the condition of mankind throughout the world. The sublime Declaration of Independence voiced the yearnings and aspirations of humanity everywhere; and the success of the American people in throwing off despotic power and enthroning the popular will, has stirred all other people with hope and determination. Other nations have taken up the maxims that "governments derive their just powers from the consent of the governed," that "government is of the people, by the people, for the people." Under the operation of these maxims the thrones of earth are either disappearing entirely or are becoming the obedient servants of the popular will. Constitutional liberty is springing up everywhere, and human rights are becoming entrenched within laws of the people's own making. The world is going on fitting itself for freedom and habilitating itself with freedom, all because the American revolution was successful. It goes on doing so under the asuring adage that "What man has done, man can do." Such is the overpowering effect of example.

The revolutionary struggle was the great epoch in the history of the world, the turning point between the old order of things and the new.

The intelligence and courage of the colonial farmers will be the theme of song and story to the end of time. Their deeds will acquire only added lustre as the centuries slip away. "Those were the times that tried men's souls;" but the men of that day had souls equal to the occasion.

> " By the rude bridge that arched the flood,
> Their flag to April's breeze unfurled,
> There once the embattled farmers stood
> And fired the shot heard around the world."

And, Oh, what farmers they were! Their furious onslaught at Concord bridge was repeated in the death-grapple at Bunker Hill, where they thrice hurled back the advancing foe, and were beaten at last only by the exhaustion of their ammunition. They fell back in sullen retreat from Long Island only to seek new fighting ground. With shoeless feet and tattered garments they entered upon long retreats and famous forced marches; year after year added only to the intensity of their sufferings; until the horrors of Valley Forge expressed the high-water mark of human endurance. Yet, out of all this privation and suffering they could spring upon the enemy at Trenton and Princeton, and Saratoga, and Yorktown, and force him to the wall.

One visits the Old South Church and looks with reverence upon the mute but eloquent relics associated with those brave deeds ; and one is similarly affected in visiting the headquarters of the American commander at Newburg, the famous old house with the seven doors and one window, the house from which Washington gave his last orders to his army, the house in which he sternly refused a crown. There it is as he left it ; and it will be kept so for ages by the State of New York. The furniture is the furniture he used ; you see his inkstand, his autograph letters and orders, a lock of his hair ; you see articles that belonged to his Adjutant-General Hamilton, and to other distinguished officers of his household; you see nothing within or about the building but what was used in the Revolutionary struggle. In the midst of those objects with so great a history the imagination is stimulated to call up the men who used them and the times in which they were used. And in the midst of such material reminders one is stirred up to be a better citizen, a truer patriot.

Go a little farther South to Tappan, where Andre was condemned and executed. There is the church (or a restoration of it) in which the famous trial was held, where the intrepid bearing of the prisoner won the sympathies of the entire populace and almost melted his stern judges to clemency. But they were men who could perform a painful duty, and could visit a great crime with a great punishment. When the condemned man appealed to the Commander-in-Chief to modify his sentence, so that he might die the death of a soldier rather than that of a felon, the appeal had but a few yards to go, to another headquarters still preserved intact, in which sat the benevolent Washington with heart bleeding for the unfortunate man, but with the resolution to let the stern laws of war take their course. There is the chair in which he sat while sympathy wrestled with duty ; there is the old fireplace into which he gazed ; and around it are still the same beautiful tiles from Holland that recall at once the good taste of the period and the restful pleasure they must have given the last distinguished occupant of the dwelling. Here again the sacred precinct is surrounded with the protection of the law ; another shrine is preserved and reserved for the veneration of American patriotism. It is kept as nearly as possible as Washington would wish to see it; no profane speculation can pervert it to ignoble uses ; it is dedicated forever to the visualizing of the greatest period in history, or until slowly consuming time alone shall cause it to disappear from the sight of men.

All know that Mount Vernon is placed under the same protection, and nothing but long delayed decay may remove from the sight of men the appointments of Washington's home, and the tomb in which his remains lie buried.

The thousands that pay their tribute of veneration to those interesting spots will only be increased by other thousands upon thousands as the years roll by. But had the Revolution failed, how long would the interest in an unsuccessful rebel have survived ? or how much interest would there have been felt in places associated with unsuccessful rebellion ?

That the Revolution was menaced with failure is a truth most appalling to the student of history. The courage and determination of the American farmers did not fail; but the brave American soldiers could not win battle with starved, and debilitated, and frozen bodies, and with empty hands. The provisions, the clothing, the pay, the ammunition, the equipments, the *materiel* of war of the American soldiers did fail. They failed not until the treasury was empty ; they failed not until the credit of the country was exhausted, until the notes of the government were so depreciated that the pay of a colonel would not buy oats for his horse ; they failed not until the substance of the colonies was consumed by forced loans. This was their last resource, and this failed; the next inevitable step was the failure of the Revolution itself. The colonists' learned the bitter lesson that help comes not to the losers: it comes to the winners. Help finally came from a friendly nation ; but it came to the victors of Saratoga, not to the vanquished of Long Island and Brandywine, not to the shivering martyrs of Valley Forge.

The Roman Curtius leaped into the chasm that his country might be saved; the American Curtius, the renowned Robert Morris, leaped into the chasm of his country's distress; the chasm closed, and his rescued country marched over him to victory. He threw his wealth and credit into the scale of his country's wants, and he sent to Holland and successfully negotiated there a series of loans backed by his own private credit. This Holland money relieved the situation; it turned a new and unlooked for stream into the exhausted treasury ; food, and clothing, and arms, and ammunition, and equipments, and weapons, were bought ; the sad stories of Long Island, and Brandywine, and Germantown, and Valley Forge were changed to the pæans of Bennington, Saratoga, Monmouth, and Yorktown. The Revolution did not fail. An indirect result of all these transactions was the Holland Land Purchase made from Robert Morris himself.

On the banks of the Tonawanda there is situated a beautiful and thriving town called Batavia. It is well-known that Batavia is another name for Holland, just as Britannia is another name for England, just as Caledonia is another name for Scotland, just as Hibernia is another name for Ireland, just as Gaul is another name for France, just as Iberia is another name for Spain, just as Helvetia is another name for Switzerland, just as Hellas is another name for Greece.

The town of Batavia was so called because it was made the local headquarters of the Holland Land Company, the investors in the Holland Purchase. In the town of Batavia on the very bank of its winding and gently flowing Indian stream, stands a stone building, which has stood for nearly a century. This building is famous throughout Western New York as the Old Land Office of the Holland Purchase.

If ever a building deserved preservation, it is that same old Land Office. If Mount Vernon, and Tappan, and Newburgh are shrines, the old Land Office should be a shrine of shrines ; for the man who made the sale to the Hollanders saved the other buildings from being regarded as so many worn-out barns. This great landmark in our history should be saved from ignoble uses, and from needless wear and tear, it should be put into a condition to tell its silent but eloquent story to as many generations as possible. Over the portals of Mount Vernon, and Tappan, and Newburgh, and Faneuil Hall, and the Old South Church, the appropriate legend might be inscribed :

"Heroism did its best to win Independence;" over the portals of the old Land Office should be written in letters of gold, "The Revolution did not fail."

The flag of a nation redeemed should float above this hallowed structure; the portrait of Robert Morris should be hung upon its walls; it should be his monument; and its fac-simile should appear on the pedestal of every statue erected to him by his admiring and grateful countrymen. It should be reserved to no other purpose than to contain mementoes of the settlement, growth, struggles, and triumphs of this fair land. As an object lesson in patriotism and statesmanship it could have a most uplifting effect upon each growing generation.

The Hollanders made the purchase not because it was land, but because it was fine land. When one travels among the fertile lands west of the Genesee, when he sees the waving grain, the luxuriant meadows, the fat pastures, and the mammoth barns, he thinks of Robert Morris and the Revolution that did not fail. And he congratulates each prosperous farmer that the title deed of his estate runs back to such a distinguished name as that of Robert Morris.

It is true that Robert Morris did not come into possession of the Holland Purchase until 1791, a few years subsequent to the closing of the Revolutionary war, that the transfer to the Holland Land Company was made the following year, and that the village of Batavia was founded and named at the very beginning of this century.

Still the founding of Batavia is an incident in the preservation of the Revolutionary war. It was a part of the great transactions by which that war, so important to the destinies of this nation and all mankind, was saved from disastrous failure.

Robert Morris procured the money that saved the Revolution; he negotiated several loans in Holland, and he backed all his transactions with his own private credit.

It was mainly Holland money that supplemented the private purse of one of the most remarkable men in history. Ruined in fortune by his responses to his country's needs, we find him at last selling to the Holland capitalists, whose money with his won the war, the noble tract known as the Holland Purchase.

The founding of Batavia was the last act in the great private tragedy by which the Revolutionary war was saved.

"That the government had in any way been able to finish the war, after the downfall of its paper-money, was due to the gigantic efforts of one great man—Robert Morris.—*John Fiske, The Critical Period of American History, p. 167.*

"Except for the sums raised by Robert Morris, of Philadelphia, even Washington could not have saved the country."—*Fiske, American Revolution, p. 244.*

"In the single campaign of 1781 gave notes for $1,400,000.—*American Encyclopædia.*

"In this emergency Robert Morris sent to camp 3,000,000 rations.—*Barnes' Centenary History.*

"By freely using his private credit he succeeded in restoring confidence in the promises of Congress to pay its honest debts."—*Ibid. p. 307.*

"More than once he prevented its (the army's) dispersion and the failure of the glorious achievement of independence."—*Turner's History of the Holland Purchase, p. 336.*

"Came forward with his princely fortune to the support of his distressed countrymen."—*Ridpath, p. 310.*

"The balance has been obtained by those Dutch loans."—*Hildreth, Vol. III., p. 544.*

"Brought to poverty by a vain attempt to support the government. For three years after the treaty of peace public affairs were in a condition bordering on chaos."—*Ridpath, p. 358.*

After signing the transfer of the Purchase the Atlas of the Revolution disappeared into a debtor's prison ; and we have no word of complaint from his patient lips against the ingratitude of that country that needed him no longer. Curtius had voluntarily sprung into the chasm. He could not complain if the chasm closed over him and his country moved on to its destiny.

But on the Holland Purchase where Robert Morris last appeared, wrestling like a Titan with his self-imposed burdens, his name should be ever kept green; and suitable honors should be there accorded to his memory.

The old Land Office should be preserved with religious veneration; its walls should be graced with his portrait; and his statue should adorn its grounds.

Every man on the Holland Purchase should deem it not only his privilege but his right to contribute to these honors. Every piece of real estate on this favored purchase has at the basis of its title one of the greatest names in history. Every farm recalls the life and fortunes of one of the purest of patriots and one of the greatest of men.

Let the Purchase do its duty to this grand and neglected man, and it may be that then the indifferent nation will wake up to a becoming sense of shame for its disgraceful neglect of it greatest hero and martyr. He gave all; the country took his all, and took it ravenously, and then—left him to poverty and oblivion !

I would not detract from the glory of Washington, and Franklin, and Lincoln, and Grant; they all deserve to stand out in heroic proportions before the imaginations of all generations. And we all rejoice that while they were great historical characters, they were also good men. But in the Pantheon of fame where their figures stand immortal I see an empty pedestal. On that empty pedestal I would place a figure fitted in every way to stand in their company; nor would I have its proportions reduced one whit below those of the others. Need I say that I would fill that empty pedestal with the figure of the Atlas of the Revolution, the unapproachable Robert Morris ?

"There were giants in those days." But some men are more than giants; they are demigods. You cannot measure them by ordinary standards; admiration is not enough; you must revere them.

There were many giants in the Revolution ; but that struggle revealed three Titans fighting in the van; those three were Washington, Franklin and Robert Morris.

There is no need of invidious comparisons. It is, perhaps, sufficient meed of honor to our hero to say that none of the others out-measured him.

Like all the others he was utterly free from selfish ambition, and, like them, he was willing, when his work was done to sink gently back into obscurity.

A kind fortune has preserved the others from an oblivion which they did not dread; let us here on the Purchase endeavor to resuscitate and rehabilitate their glorious compeer, the Curtius of American History, the Atlas of the Revolution, the man that seemed of all others providentially born for his time, the gentle Robert Morris.

The criticism has been made that the attempt to secure and preserve the old land office of the Holland Purchase is an appeal to sentiment, and that such an appeal cannot succeed in this practical age. It is true that the appeal is made to a sentiment—to the great sentiment of patriotism; and I am not sure that this age and nation have yet become so practical as to let such an appeal go forth unheard. Our people are certainly very busy in the acquisition of property, and it is both proper and commendable that they should be so. Industry, frugality, thrift, are virtues which redound not only to the independence, comfort, success, and happiness of their individual possessors, but they also make the aggregate prosperity of the nation as a whole. The public hive is stored and enriched by the activity of each individual busy bee.

We may well be proud of our country when we see every individual striving honestly and zealously after a competence; but we may well despair of our country whenever we see that its citizens have no aim in life beyond the acquisition of some extra dollars. Whenever our people descend to the making of money for its own sake, for the sake simply of having and hoarding it; whenever a proper and even a glorious means is perverted into an end, then the beginning of the end has come.

There are great uses for a competency; and great souls are struggling to get it in order to make those great uses of it. The grasping hand of avarice may be among our busy bees; but I believe that the silent ambitions, the unexpressed purposes of the great majority of American toilers would bear the most rigid scrutiny. They are planning not only how to get the money, but also the uses that they will put it to; and those plans of use are all centering around some cherished sentiments. The very soul of sentiment is at the bottom of our business world. If it were not so, we might well despair of the future. Those silent workers are reaching out to the discharge of some ultimate duties; the wolf is to be kept from the door; the leisure and means for improving the mind are to be secured; the children are to be educated and provided for; the condition of the unfortunate classes is to be ameliorated; the spread of the gospel and of good works is to be promoted; matters of import to the general weal are to be forwarded. All these sentiments are to be gratified, all these duties to be performed, when competency or affluence arrives.

The toilers are simply working to become free—free to exert their will—free to reveal the sentiments that dominate their dreams.

But the man with his mind on ultimate duties is always ready for the nearest duty. He is a man with a soul; but that is only another way of saying that he is a man super-charged with sentiment. Let the public peace be menaced, let the national life be imperiled, then, like Putnam, he forgoes all his plans, leaves his horses in the furrow as it were, and springs to his country's call. We have just seen two-and-a-half millions of American toilers spring from their vocations to put down a gigantic rebellion; and, having done it well, the survivors are now toiling again as if nothing had happened. O, there is plenty of sentiment yet in the breast of the average silent, practical American citizen! When you appeal to it in the right cause you never appeal in vain.

It is not to the idlers of a nation that any generous appeal can be made —not to the hungry waifs that have lost all manhood but its mere physical proportions—not to those who use an ample fortune in the worthless business of killing time; it is made to those who have a calling, a serious business in life; it is made, in short, to this very practical element; and it is not made in vain.

The practical men of the country are the nation's treasury in reserve, the nation's reserve of patriotism, and the nation's hope of glory. If you want a thing done that needs to be done, go to the practical men with it; if you want a thing done that ought to be done, go to the practical men with it. To say that an age is practical is only to say that it is readiest for great emotions, that it is ripest for great deeds. It takes a practical age to put millions into monuments, as our age has done; to fight down the cholera, the yellow fever, famine, fire, and floods. This practical age has a pocket to go into on such occasions; and no one will say that the hand ever goes into the pocket grudgingly when responding to such calls. Such occasions convince the practical people that it is not the best end in life to "put money into your purse," but rather to take it out of the purse.

In the moral education of children it is not a difficult thing to train them to put money into their purse; they are all acquisitive by nature. The main task is to train them to open their little purse and let its contents flow forth in generous deeds. Nothing delights the thoughtful parent or teacher more than to find the child becoming a discriminating giver. The child's mite, when freely given in response to a generous feeling, is even more precious than the widow's mite; for in the child the instinct of acquisition is the stronger, and the battle with selfishness the greater. Yes, it is more precious to give than to receive; and this is never more truly felt than among a people who are really prosperous, never more truly felt than in a practical age.

There is a wide difference between an age that is practical and one that is sordid. When every generous impulse is stifled, when selfishness runs riot, when all are remorselessly straining after money for the sake of personal indulgence or lavish display or the forwarding of unholy ambitions, when greed of gain has become a general disease, then has the dry-rot entered into the national life, and the collapse of that nation cannot be long deferred. There have been such ages, and there have been such awful examples; Greece, Rome, Venice, Florence, Genoa, all collapsed under the cankerous action of national avarice.

> "Ill fares the land to hastening ills a prey,
> Where wealth accumulates and men decay."

Empires are built upon sentiment; they disappear when the people become too calm, when they become imperturbable and boast that they are never stirred with emotions. The emotion is the wholesome storm that dispels the insidious fog and the deadly stagnation of the waters.

It is a compliment to a people to address to them an appeal on the line of sentiment; for you assume that they are ready to give to that appeal a suitable response.

But there is, after all, nothing more practical than sentiment. We expend untold millions to make the masses good citizens. What, then, could be more practical than to exspend a few hundreds in an endeavor to stir within those masses the noble sentiment of patriotism, the love of country and admiration of its history?

We do this by placing the flag of our country above each school house, and by carefully preserving the landmarks of the past. Nothing could be more impressive or effective than the recent indignation of our veterans over the desecration of Gettysburg battlefield. See the numerous monuments dotting that field of triumph, and note the snug little sum wisely given to the fostering of a great sentiment.

> "How sleep the brave who sink to rest
> By all their country's wishes blessed!
> When Spring, with dewey fingers cold,
> Returns to deck their hallowed mould,
> She there shall dress a sweeter sod
> Than Fancy's feet have ever trod.
>
> By fairy hands their knell is rung;
> By forms unseen their dirge is sung;
> There Honor comes, a pilgrim grey,
> To bless the turf that wraps their clay;
> And Freedom shall awhile repair
> To dwell a weeping hermit there."

Yes, it is practical all around. The parent who is planning the education of his children could not do a more practical thing than to surround them with an atmosphere in which they could breathe in the spirit of loftiest sentiment and devotion. Who could be at Bunker Hill without being stirred to heroic self-sacrifice? Who could look at Bunker Hill Monument without being at Bunker Hill?

And so with every landmark associated with a great past. The Old Land Office of the Holland Purchase bridges over the entire interval back to the Revolutionary struggle. It touches hands with Robert Morris himself, and carries us back to the critical moment when he alone, as if inspired by the Almighty Ruler of nations, saw the way through. The old building recalls the man, the cause, the intervening time. It recalls the struggle for liberty, the making of the nation, the preservation of the nation, and the growth of empire.

Such a landmark should be preserved with religious veneration, and I believe that there is sufficient sentiment in Western New York to ensure its preservation.

I cannot close this passage without another word about the original owner of the Holland Purchase, that peerless baron of short possession, but a possession long enough to make the region holy ground.

Robert Morris embodied in his personality the possibilities of human nature—the practical element and the sentimental, each in the highest degree. As a practical man he accumulated a fortune of eight millions. He doubtless had ulterior plans as to its use—such a man must have had his benevolent plans—but when the struggling Revolution was on he saw his opportunity, and he flung his millions in. Though he was thrown into a debtors prison, and died in abject poverty, yet I doubt whether he ever regretted the sacrifices he had made. I think he would have done it again. A great opportunity had come to him; and he had met it greatly. What more could a great-souled man wish? It is true that he was disowned and discredited, while lieutenant-colonels and captains were the heroes of the hour, the Great Heart of the Revolution pined forgotten in a loathsome prison; he died without any assurance that his country would ever utter his name with any emotions of gratitude.

But he had the consolation of all the greatest natures, the consolation that alone can satisfy a truly great soul—the consciousness of having done his duty, and of having made his life serviceable to mankind. Such a nature can, if necessary, dispense with the sound of popular applause. He saved the Revolution; he forced it to succeed; yet in his dire extremity he read the story of the Revolution with his name left out; and he gave no sign. He died as greatly as he had lived; we have no record of a single complaint passing from his lips; he sank gently to his rest

"Like one who wraps the drapery of his couch
About him and lies down to pleasant dreams."

But his farm will redeem him from oblivion, that mournful barony of his, the Holland Purchase, will do honor to his name, and will force that name to its proper position in American annals. There is sentiment enough for that.

With such a spirit hovering over the Old Land Office, and with all the associations of the intervening century clustering around it, who can doubt the propriety, yea, the imperative duty, of saving that great landmark from obliteration?

"Breathes there a man with soul so dead
Who never to himself has said
This is my own, my native land?
Whose heart has ne'er within him burned,
As home his footsteps he has turned
From wandering on a foreign strand?
If such there breathe go mark him well;
For him no minstrel raptures swell;
High though his titles, proud his name,
Boundless his wealth, as wish can claim;
Despite those titles, power, and pelf,
The wretch, concentred all in self,
Living, shall forfeit fair renown,
And, doubly dying, shall go down
To the vile dust from whence he sprung,
Unwept, unhonored, and unsung."

A contemporary writer thinks it sufficient meed of praise for Robert Morris to compare him with Jay Cooke. He more than intimates that Morris was a mere self-seeker who over-reached himself and came to grief. I regret to see one of the noblest and greatest characters in American History or in the history of the world, disposed of in such an off-hand and unjust manner. Jay Cooke was a mere banker who handled and disposed of the securities of our government during the War of the Rebellion. He handled them as a mere matter of business; and, while he may have helped the government, he did what he did solely for his own interest.

Morris, on the contrary, was a patriot who labored with might and main from first to last to win American Independence, and to establish the American government upon the firmest foundations. To achieve those great ends he put everything in peril—his good name, his life, his fortune. It was with no selfish aim that he signed the Declaration of Independence, and thus voluntarily placed a halter above his neck. The signers took all the chances of martyrdom; and it was many years before they knew that they would not be martyred. They took the chances of death; but it was the disgraceful death of a felon, a death on the gibbet, branded with the odium of treason.

It was with no selfish aim that Morris came to the rescue of Washington in 1777 and prevented the dispersion of the patriot army by instantly raising $50,000 on his own private credit. It was with no selfish aim that he assumed the burden of the whole expense of the war after the means and credit of the government had completely failed. He was not speculating in the securities of a strong government; he was simply bolstering up with his own private means the weakest and most desperate of causes. He simply added his labor, his thought, and his money to his life, and said with a persistency nothing short of sublime: "The Revolution must not fail?"

Will history say that this was a case of Robert Morris working for Robert Morris? History will perpetrate no such sublime injustice; though history has as yet been too silent in regard to his great deeds. The children of this generation can speak with familiarity of the subordinate officers of the Revolutionary army; but the men of this generation have to ask about the man who held that army together, who fed and clothed and supplied it, who pointed out its way to victory, and who hurled it on the foe. Yes, the men of this generation have no answer when Robert Morris is characterized as a mere financial adventurer, who somewhat miscalculated his opportunities, and chanced to land in a debtor's prison. History has done Robert Morris the wrong of silence, but not the wrong of actual slander. History has not written him down; but it has failed as yet to write him up. When it gets around to him it will have the grandest theme that ever called forth the tones of

. the man must not be known as a mere generous and enthusiastic .ey-bags; he revealed throughout the contest an intellect of imperial qual-.y and a prevision that was little short of inspiration. Much as his money did, his thought won the Revolution even more than his money. It was he who brought in the aid of the outside world, in the form of men and money. It was he who dissuaded Washington in 1781 from making an abortive assault upon New York, and who suggested in the place of such a blunder the glorious campaign of Yorktown.*

*See Turner's History of the Holland Purchase.

Had Morris not appeared on the scene, or had Morris died during the struggle, the Revolution would have collapsed. Who can say this of any other man? If it can not be said of any other man, then Morris was pre-eminently the man of the Revolution. We shudder to think what might have been had Washington not appeared, or had he been called away; we know what would have been had Morris disappeared; the history of the Revolution would have been the history of glorious despair, the history of gibbets, the history of the wreck of human hopes.

The life that was so recklessly exposed on the occasion of Braddock's defeat, that was put into frequent peril during the battles of the Revolution, might have encountered one of the dying bullets which it so bravely dared. The loss would have been terrible; it might have cost us victory, but who will say that it must have done so? The loss of Morris would have been sure ruin. A Jay Cooke sitting back and fattening upon his country's tribulations! Out on the thought! Shame on such profanation! The man of the Revolution, the one life on which all our destinies turned, the man admired for his intelligence and revered for his probity by all his contemporaries to be characterized within a century as a mere unsuccessful speculator! *O tempora! O mores!*

When we see Robert Morris languishing in a debtor's prison in the United States of America within a few years after the adoption of the Constitution which he helped to frame, and when we see him within a century characterized as a mere unlucky speculator, the proverbial ingratitude of republics comes home to us with its fullest force and in all its bitterness. He signed the Declaration of Independence; he held the armies together by the use of his princely fortune, his great integrity, and his mighty ability; he brought in aid from abroad; he literally pushed the Revolution through. When others despaired he said: "It can go on, and it must go on."

It did go on. But while he never lost his push he never lost his head; he also never pushed blindly; he always pushed toward definite results. Though not always seeing his way clearly as to means he was yet always clear as to the ends to be attained. He never blundered and he never failed. When the aggregate wisdom of the country lost the fight, it then became Morris's fight; and Morris won.

To see the man in all his aspects at once, the concentration of judgment, energy, resourcefulness, push, and determination, take the campaign of 1781. Washington felt that a blow must be struck; he would strike New York. Morris said no; the assault would be of doubtful issue, and would be made in any event at too great a cost of men and money; even if successful the British could with their great naval resources retake it; and things would be worse than they had been. Better, he said, swing the army around to Virginia and crush Cornwallis. Washington said he could not move so great as into Virginia; he had not the means of transportation. Morris said he would provide transportation. "How will you do it?" "I don't know; but I pledge my head that when you get to Philadelphia I will have the transportation." "Then we go."*

The transportation was ready on time; Cornwallis was crushed; and the war was ended.* Whose fight was it? Who won the fight? A mere finan-

*See Turner's History of the Holland Purchase.

cial adventurer unlucky enough to be jailed for being behind with his payments! O no; it was won by the most remarkable man that has ever appeared at any time in any country—by a man who will yet be honored by a full recognition of his great, disinterested, and beneficient services. This great land will find room in its affection for the man to whom it owes so great a debt; and it will pay that debt by a recognition commensurate with his service, though too long delayed. It will do justice not only to his services but to his character. His name among his contemporaries was the synonym of probity; any movement was half won when it had the countenance of Robert Morris. That we have a Constitution and a Union is largely due to the fact that Washington, Franklin and Morris sat in the convention that devised our great organic law.

We are living here on his beautiful farm, the famous Holland Purchase, more famous still by having had for its first owner the patriot Robert Morris. It is peculiarly appropriate that a movement should originate here to vindicate his name, a name in which we all feel a local interest, as well as the interest common to all citizens of the United States. No; compare him not with Jay Cooke, with all due respect to the latter; compare him rather with Solon and Epaminondas, with Alfred and Charlemagne.

And now as to the movement to preserve the old Land Office of the Holland Purchase. We feel deeply interested in the matter at Batavia—not as Batavians, but as residents of the Holland Purchase. We hope that all residents of the Holland Purchase, or further still, that all residents of land once owned by Robert Morris, will feel the same interest. If they do, then the care and preservation of the venerable building will be as light as a feather on the surface of the water.

We have started the movement for the preservation because we think that the reasons for its preservation are numerous and weighty. We have started the movement now because we think it is not a moment too soon. In a growing town such an old building is imperiled in many ways. The march of improvement sweeps up to the immediate premises. There is no sentiment in ordinary real estate transactions; the order for demolition is precipitated both by the onward sweep of improvements and by the last uses to which such a building is applied. It is rented to anybody for any purpose whatever, and it is rented by those who have no interest in its care. If it escape actual calamity in the form of fire or winds, it is nevertheless rendered constantly more decrepit, and so more and more out of keeping with its surroundings. Should demolition wait, it would only wait until ruin should make demolition not only inevitable but necessary. But demolition does not wait such an extreme age; the old Land Office had reached a point where it was in positive danger.

Hence the movement was not a moment too soon, if the building merited preservation. The Old South Church and Faneuil Hall as structures are sadly out of keeping with the imperial blocks with which they are flanked to-day; but their glorious associations shed around them a halo that more than overbalances their modest proportions and their faded material. Let real estate rise as it will—a thousand dollars a foot—ten thousand dollars a foot—patriotic remembrance says to the mighty wave of commerce: "Thus far shall thou go, and no farther; here shall thy proud waves be stayed. These are the altars at which civic devotion shall pay its homage; these are the altars at which civic devotion shall be fired. Men, after all, are higher than merchants and merchandise; and here we train up men—patriotic citizens."

The same devotion has seized upon Mount Vernon, upon Carpenters' Hall, upon the Headquarters at Newburg, and upon the Headquarters at Tappan, and has seized upon them for the same identical uses.

The Old Land Office is a great land-mark in the history of the United States; and to be a land-mark in the history of the United States is to be a land-mark in the history of mankind; for the United States in its brief existence has reversed the tides of history, has made itself the fountain instead of the receptacle, a fountain from which waves of mighty and benificent influence have steadily rolled back upon all the old communities of the world. But besides being involved in the making of the United States, the Old Land Office was involved to the very core in the making of Western New York. This great region of unapproachable scenery, and of unexampled fertility, fruitfulness, resources, and prosperity, is a little world in itself—and not such a very little world at that. It takes a dozen counties to hold it. It has one city of three hundred thousand inhabitants—ten times as large as the New York that wrestled with Howe and Clinton; it has another city of over one hundred and fifty thousand; and it is simply alive with corporations and communities that would be regarded as great towns by our Revolutionary fathers. Could they have had its present resources to draw upon it would have increased their fighting power at least one-half. So it is no small matter that has sprung directly from and grown up around the Old Land Office which we now seek to save.

When the colonists engaged in the deadly struggle, Western New York was a wilderness, broken only by the Indian trails, and by an occasional patch of Indian clearing. It could apparently respond to no calls for men or means; and so it was not called upon. Yet if the transaction with the Hollanders involved any question of settling accounts, Western New York did contribute to the struggle; and it contributed in such a way as to turn the fight when hope was gone. It contributed its own fertility; and that was something in a time when something was scarce, and when it needed something to win. The attempt to win on nothing had been tried with great dash; and it ended in egregious, in depressing, in ruinous failure.

Washington fell back in masterly retreat before the victors of L̲ ̲ ̲ ̲ land, and before the treason of Lee. In the dead of winter he la r̲d remnant of his army in safety beyond the Delaware river. Howe st̲ go home, after duly garrisoning the country he had conquered. Wasl̲. conceived the great idea of springing back upon the secure foe, and of t' the victory out of his hands. In this audacious project he had the ap[1] and co-operation of just one man in the country, a kindly gentleman of adelphia. This gentleman saw what was right and wise; and he appla̲ it. To the end of the struggle, to the adoption of the Constitution, to̲ launching of the nation, he never failed to see what was right and wise, he never failed to champion it with all his might and main. To champ what was right and wise was often to fly in the face of popular prejudices an ignorance, and to bring down about one's devoted head a whirlwind of obloquy. But this remarkable man never counted the cost; he never hesitated to burn bridges; it was enough for him that the matter was right and wise to induce him to "go in" like a very incarnation of pertinacity. Washington got through; but it was because he always had this good genius by his side, with his unerring intellect and intuitions, with his unswerving loyalty to the lonely chief, with his mighty influence, and with his unyielding pertinacity. Damon was never very far away, when Pythias had need of him.

Washington recrossed the river, crushed the unsuspecting garrison at Trenton, slipped away from Cornwallis' front, destroyed his reserves at Princeton, and got safely into winter quarters at Morristown. Howe did not go home; the Revolution was decidedly on instead of off. But now came the real crisis of the war. The soldiers realized that they had been doing all this on nothing; and they could not stand that. The children must have something to eat; and they must go home. Washington's strategy was not equal to the enemy that struck him now. To check Burgoyne, to bring on the dilatory French, the armies must keep the field, and not go home. But the soldiers were determined to relieve their children first, and if possible the country afterwards. Washington knew that it was bootless to turn to Congress. That honorable body was rich in what it had been using all along—*nothing*. But it needed *something* now. He turned to Damon. Damon had something—a matter of a few millions—as a result of his prudence and his attention to business. "Robert, the country has failed me. If I am not now extricated by you, all is lost." "You shall be extricated." Day and night Robert banged the knockers of Philadelphia capitalists. All were opportunely out of funds; for they had nothing to invest in a hard-pressed rebellion. At last a shrewd old Quaker asked what security he had to offer? "My note and my honor." "Robert, it is enough; thee shall have the money." And so on the third day Robert was able to put $50,000 hard shiners into the empty treasury chest of the commander-in-chief. Disintegration was arrested; and the war went gloriously on to Saratoga and Monmouth. At last Congress learned that it could not do something with nothing; so it asked Robert Morris, who had something and who knew how to get something, to take up the job. He took it up; and the war went gloriously on to Yorktown and Independence. Then, and not till then, did he lay the burden down. He was still destined, however, to help make our Constitution, to launch our new Ship of State, and to build our National Capitol.

In '77 he banged the doors of Philadelphia for money and got it; so in nd onward he banged the doors of all Europe for money, and got it. he was asked for his security; and again he offered his note and his r; and again he was able to fill the empty treasury. Coriolanus, on de ng for the last time from the walls of Rome, said to his mother: "Mother, have saved Rome; but you have destroyed your son." Robert Morris ht have said to himself: "Robert, you have saved your country; but you e destroyed yourself." There is a limit even to the strength of a Titan. e long and devoted use of that note and honor never affected the latter; it it took the foundation from under the former. The millions vanished into the maelstrom of the extraordinary Revolutionary finances, and Robert Morris emerged a ruined man. He endeavored to retrieve his fortunes; but the exhausted giant had to succumb. One of his first ventures was to buy Western New York. But he could not hold it. The larger part went in bulk to the very men who had advanced money on his note and honor in the time of his country's greatest need; and thus the famous Holland Purchase became one of the interesting facts in the history of New York State and the nation. I do not aver that the Hollanders paid him for the land with his own obligations; but there is a strong probability that something of that kind entered into the transactions. His affairs were so involved in the end that no one could get track or trace of them. More pathetic than his incarceration in a debtors' prison was his constant attempt while there to get through the labyrinth of his accounts, and to find, what he truly expected, a surplus sufficient to satisfy his creditors and clear that precious "honor" from any imputation of fraud. But it is a fact that Robert Morris owned the Holland Purchase; and it is a fact that he signed the deed that made the Holland Purchase. It is a fact that every piece of real estate in Western New York has at the basis of its title one of the greatest names in history—the name of a patriot of spotless integrity and of unexampled devotion—the name of a man of peerless intellect—the name of a man with such a will as makes history, by making all the world bend to it.

These facts alone are sufficient in my eyes to make the Old Land Office a monument of the Revolutionary struggle and to make the Holland Purchase almost holy ground. It should be saved if for these considerations alone. It should be put into a condition to carry its sturdy walls through a decade of centuries and tell the coming generations of the good and great deeds of a thousand years ago.

The relation of the Holland Purchase to the Revolution may be briefly summarized as follows. There was a time when Independence had nothing to uphold it but sums of money advanced by Hollanders. They sent the needed omething to needy America. They sent it not through their faith in a weak Congress and jarring foolish States, but through their faith in a capable and honorable business man, who pledged his private credit to the re-payment of the accommodations which he sought. They sent something to America at the call of Morris, and they came and got something out of America. They got the fertility of Western New York; and they got it from the hands of Robert Morris. America proved no bad investment to them.

Everybody was paid in one way or another except the great Curtius of the awful time, whose eight millions were but his armor, when he sprang full-panoplied into the yawning gulf of his country's terrible need.

But I will descend from the greater argument and take up the nearer and perhaps more palpable reasons for the preservation of this historic building.

The preservation of family heirlooms does credit to human nature. It is an answer to the appeal of the past not to be forgotten.

"To live in hearts we leave behind,
Is not to die."

Grandfather's chair may be a very humble piece of furniture; but it is prized beyond all price because it is grandfather's chair. He used it while he as winning an honorable name for his descendants. He left them his integrity and this chair. Incidentally he left them provision for their maintenance. They forget his dollars; but they remember him and the chair. They remember him through the chair. Each house has its particular heir-loom. The Old Land Office is a common reminder of all the grandfathers and great-grandfathers of Western New York. The frequent pilgrimages to the Land Office was a feature of their lives. They viewed again and again its sturdy walls; they stepped in and out again and again over its threshold; they found it the center of all their interests; the topic of much of their discourse. It was to them a social, religious and political headquarters, while they felled the trees and let the sunlight down through the woods to invite production in the fertile soil. There it stands, the same identical structure. That grandfather and great-grandfather could wish it so, is in itself sufficient reason to Western New York to save that building from destruction.

It speaks not only of past lives, but also of most wonderful vicissitudes. When it was planted at the junction of the Indian trails and began shedding the seeds of civilization into the wilderness, it was then a great and imposing edifice. As its seed bore fruit its consequence as an architectural triumph paled before the greater elegance and magnificence of its own prosperous offspring. It is a Sabine grad father walking the streets of imperial Rome. A Scaurus or a Mecenas may smile at the plain old gentleman; yet, but for the plain old gentleman, Scaurus and Mæcenas would not have been there. Scaurus and Mæcenas were able to look below the surface; and I am sure that they would have suppressed the rising amusement at the old gentleman's "style," and have welcomed the Great Past to their bosom. As to style, I doubt whether John Starke, or General Green, or Benjamin Franklin would be entirely at ease to-day in the country which they saved. Their's was not bad style; it was only an old style—a somewhat sober style, in perfect keeping with the conditions of life at that period. Men are mercifully spared from projection into a generation to which they do not belong. Buildings, on the contrary, being more enduring, have to suffer the progressive pressure of contrast.

But it is well that it is so. An old thing should look old. An old thing among the new is, in itself, presumptive evidence that it has a claim to preservation. It has ceased to be a factor in affairs; it has become a guest. Western New York is very bright; it is spank span new. The only old thing in it is this famous old building on the bank of the Tonawanda; and I believe that Western New York will act toward that venerable structure as a generous and cherishing host. For the sake of its great associations, its plain garb will be forgiven; and I trust that it will not only be tolerated, but that it will be made the guest of honor.

But the building will not be entirely without a function. It will gather to itself and shelter within its spacious interior, all manner of relics relating to the settlement and growth of this interesting region. As a school of instruction in history, it need not blush for its uses among the more ambitious modern buildings.

It has tasted the bitter dregs of degredation; it has fully exemplified the old ejaculation:

"To what base uses do we come at last!"

But it is to be rehabilitated, and to gain a higher respectability than it ever before possessed. A person of refinement may become reduced, but he never becomes vulgar. Let prosperity get around to him again, and he puts it on with the ease of an every day garment. He can bear a new prosperity because he is "to the manner born." The Old Land Office has known misfortune, but it has never known a vulgar hour. It had its birth in the very essence of refinement and culture. It was long the magnet to which all refinement in this region gravitated; it was long the luminary from which all refining influences were shed abroad over this region. Americans cannot stand a formal aristocracy; but they can stand all the true gentility that they can get among them. It is said by good thinkers that the best education must flow from the university downward, rather than that the primary schools should be trusted to evolve their own development. The Old Land Office has been the university to this entire region. Intelligence and refinement would unfold in the woods if you give them time enough. The Old Land Office made the woods intelligent and refined at once. It has waited in patience for its brilliant students to get around to it; and when they get around to it the decent old edifice will never express a false note, will never drop a single solecism. It has done a great work; it can do a greater; it is to the interest of Western New York as well as its duty to start this old seminary on its second and greater career.

"While stands the Coliseum, Rome shall stand;"
"When falls the Coliseum, Rome shall fall."

While stands the Land Office the Holland Purchase shall stand; for while that structure is in sight it carries its old boundaries with it. It stands for a domain. It preserves the unity of Western New York; though arbitrary county lines have cut it up into fragments. The Land Office preserves the autonomy of the region, the real unity, the unity of common origin, common conditions, common toils and triumphs. Let it stand, if only as a common bond of amity among all these brethren of the west.

I desire to say a few words about the recent "Life of Robert Morris," written by Professor William G. Sumner, of Yale college. Professor Sumner is a very distinguished scholar; and when I learned that he had written a biography of Robert Morris I expected to enjoy a rare treat. About twenty years ago it began to dawn upon me that a very great man had passed across the horizon of our affairs and that the historians had almost overlooked him. My subsequent reading and reflection have tended only to confirm that dawning conviction and to bring out more and more clearly to my mind the colossal personality of that neglected and forgotten man. I have awaited with eagerness the American Plutarch who would seize with avidity upon such a fine overlooked subject, and give us another immortal classic. Angelo was seized with a fury of attack at sight of a fine piece of marble; I was sure that the coming Plutarch would glow with creative energy at sight of the neglected Morris. I was prepared to find the longed-for Plutarch in Professor Sumner. I regret to say that I have been both extremely disappointed and deeply pained by the perusal of his book. The disappointment I might waive; but the pain compels me to speak out. I am disappointed with the literary qualities of the book ; but I do not intend this as a critique. I am pained with the doctrine of the book ; and I do intend this as a protest. If Professor Sumner should choose to give us a book as bald in style as the Saxon Chronicle, as disjointed as a dictionary, and as colorless as a brick of manufactured ice, I might be sorely disappointed, but I would not say a word. That is a question of taste, and the world takes care of such matters. I would not say a word, but I might have my preferences in the matter ; I might prefer the artistic structure and fervid style of Macaulay, or the masterly analyses of Plutarch. But furthermore I am often charitable as to form, even though I may not like the form. Men have a right to strike out on new lines, and make experiments. I don't like Walt Whitman's style for example ; but I am quite willing to give it a trial. It is not without its admirers ; and we know not yet what the final verdict may be in regard to it. Nor would I be understood as condemning Saxon Chronicles and dictionaries. On the contrary I consider them very valuable books in their respective spheres.

Professor Sumner could do his country a great service by making new Saxon Chronicles. They would be excellent data from which literature could be made. But after an experience with his present book I would advise him not to draw any conclusions. Just leave the facts strung along to speak for themselves.

I did not know but that Professor Sumner had hit upon a new form of biography. Michael Angelo said that the sculptor does not create ; he simply sees the angel in the stone and hastens to knock away the superfluous pieces, so that the angel may emerge. I did not know when I began reading this extraordinary book but that Professor Sumner was about to pursue the Angelo method ; and that if we followed him carefully we would see the angel emerge. Sumner could then have the triumph of bringing truth to light, rather than of simply stating what truth is. Sure enough the angel began to emerge. But I thought that this emergency was a little disturbing to the professor ; it was not just what he expected ; it was not what he wanted ; he hurried away from those spots where the emergence was dangerously imminent (or rather eminent); he hastened to the other side of the stone, and there chipped away bravely. At last he throws off the mask and positively declares that it is not an angel that he is looking for at all, but some other kind of character. But the angel emerged all the same. Bad as the book is, with all its omissions, with all its inuendoes, with all its insinuations, with all its open attacks, with all its unjust construction of facts, with all its cruel lack of sympathy, with all its pitiless pursuit of a man in dire extremity, yet, if there had never been another word written on the subject of Robert Morris than this book, if there should never be another word written hereafter about him, this book alone would place him in the fore-front of all the great, the wise, the good, the pure, the gentle, the noble, that this world has ever produced. The angel has emerged from the stone this time in spite of the sculptor. Baalam went on one mission ; he performed another. With no other basis than Sumner's book Washington, Franklin, Lincoln, and Grant need not blush for the fifth compeer that has stepped to their side. The words have been said and cannot be recalled. In that book enough has been said (more or less grudgingly) to sketch one of the greatest and best of characters—a character strong, symmetrical, consistent, true. I am pained because the young will not see the character which Professor Sumner has unwittingly drawn, but rather the character which he has tried to draw. May I ask the patience of the reader to follow him a little? He does not look for the fruit in the seed; he skips over the whole question of antecedents and training, merely stating the date and place of his birth, that his father was a merchant, and that the son was sent to Philadelphia at the age of 14 years and placed in the house of the Willings. The boy was the head of the house at 20; and yet this does not strike the professor as being anything remarkable. Yet it is the most remarkable thing of the kind on record. Hired boys do not usually get to the rear end of such firms until they are in the forties; they do well if they get to the head of them in the sixties. What an implied story of good antecedents and careful nurture, of brilliant abilities, steady habits, and strict attention to business! "The reconstruction of the firm indicates an infusion of youth and enterprise." That word "youth" seems to me an inadequate and altogether misleading description of the case. Another great genius said when taunted with his youth: "The atrocious crime of being a young man I will not attempt to palliate, nor do I deny." It could not be wealth that placed him at the head of the firm. In his father's estate "the personal property was nearly $7,000"—a mere drop in the bucket in a great shipping business. It might pay the office rent for a single year. True, "mention was made in his father's will of some real estate;" but it was all a small matter; it was brains and character that won, not money. By strict attention to business he was able twenty years later to lose eight millions in the Revolution.

His sterling character and abilities gained him the respect not only of his employers but of the best people of the time; he was able to marry into the best family of Pennsylvania, his wife being a sister of Bishop White, and the most cultivated woman of her time. These things are very significant to ordinary historians. They carry their own comment, even if the historian should slide over them. "Morris signed the non-important agreement of 1765;" and therefore, for the sake of his country, struck a deadly blow at his own business. Yet we are asked later on to believe that he had an insane desire for wealth. While his ships were rotting at the idle wharf "he was on a committee of citizens who forced the stamp distributor of Pennsylvania to desist from the administration of his office;" and thereby became especially obnoxious to the government eleven years before any one thought that it would cease to rule in America. Hampden and Elliot could do no more. "In June, 1775, he was appointed on the committee of safety for Pennsylvania"—a pestiferous nest of traitors, in the eyes of the government. He had already imperiled his business and his life, and made no ado about it. There was certainly nothing to pose for in all this; there was nothing in it to feed any of the forms of vanity with which he is charged. It just marks ten years of consistent and steady defiance by one who had much to lose and nothing to gain except his country's liberty. "Being a member of these three bodies at one time, we are not surprised to find him declaring that his time was occupied with public affairs to the injury of his private business." "Declaring," mind you, but not complaining. How does this concession of our author that Robert Morris performed his public duties at great private loss, tally with the intimations further on that he was in office "for revenue only." "After he became a member of congress he was absorbed in the work of that body." That is the kind of patriot he was; no half measures with him if business went to the canines. "He was appointed a member of the secret committee of correspondence." More deadly treason. But the people knew their man, if Professor Sumner does not. What sterling patriotism, what ability, what judgment, what tact, what delicacy, what discretion, did membership on those committees require! These qualities were conceded by his appointment; and we never hear that the masters of the time or the public had to recast their estimate of him. Not only in the business but in it to the very core—at the very root of the matter—"absorbed," as though he had no private business. He had given the latter a momentum in the previous twenty years that kept it going somewhat. He had made a success of the former by being "absorbed" in it; he was destined to make just as complete a success of history by the exercise of the same traits of character, the same qualities of mind. Is there any hint of the peculator, the speculator, or the Dives in all this? Far from it. Shame on the thought!

"Morris was one of those who hesitated about the Declaration of Independence." Washington was another; and every other man in the country, except Samuel Adams, was a third. They were fighting for rights; the idea of independence came later. "He voted against the resolution in favor of independence on the 2d of July;" because he wanted to learn first what the Howes had to offer. "He signed the Declaration, however, on the 2d of August;" after the chances of hanging for doing so had very much improved. It was but a few drys prior to the disastrous defeat on Long Island. "We can clearly see that Washington, for the manœuver that he executed at Trenton, really had no support from anybody but Morris." What praise! The whole world can see the wisdom of the manœuver after it was made. What praise for Morris that he could see the wisdom of it beforehand! What comfort to Washington that in that moment of dire extremity, with an enemy triumphant, with a country despairing, with treason in the camp, with friends falling away from him, with cabals forming around him, that he had one loyal heart to whom he could unbosom himself, one capacious mind that could understand him! "The three great crisis of the Revolution—the attack on Trenton, Burgoyne's surrender, and Cornwallis's surrender." Yes, and we see that at the first Morris alone was present to help the deserted chieftain through. But for Morris the other two crises never would have been passed. The short, sharp campaign of Trenton and Princeton made Washington one of the great military captains of history. He was just as great on his masterly retreat; but people do not understand retreat as well as victory. When Fabius became a Marcellus then even Fabius was understood. All could see that the war was on instead of over. The British redoubled their efforts and prepared to break the colonies in two. The real crisis came after Princeton. The terms of the veteran troops were expiring; and they were resolved to go home. Had they gone home what would have become of the campaign of 1777, the decisive campaign of Burgoyne? Had they gone home what would have become of the war? It would have ended in the defeat of the patriots, the revolution would have collapsed; Washington said so. That fatal disintegration was arrested by a man who never lost his head in a crisis—the great second genius of the war. Nothing but hard money would hold the soldiers; the military chest contained nothing but "Continental pasteboard." Robert Morris hurried to Philadelphia and, after vain appeals to patriotism, he pledged his private credit. At this the money flowed into his hands, and he was able to bring back fifty thousand shining dollars. The soldiers remained; Burgoyne fell; the French came in—all through the devotion and standing of one private citizen. If I were to select the man who has established a pre-eminent claim to write our annals, I would select John Fiske. This is his judgment on the matter: "Except for the sums raised by Robert Morris, of Philadelphia, even Washington could not have saved the country." This is one of the points at which Professor Sumner seems in a hurry to get to the other side of the stone. It is now twelve years since Morris ordered his own business to wither; and since he began to put all kinds of halters about his neck. And he has been flying night and day ever since. For what? To pose? To feed on avaricious maw? The army remained; the sequel was Saratoga and Monmouth. It was well for this country that Robert Morris in his youth "never applied hot and rebellious liquors to his blood;" for it needed the physical strength of a giant, as well as the intellect and heart of a Titan, to meet the demands which were now upon him, and which were never for a moment off him to the end of the war—the demands of a self imposed devotion to his struggling country. Had he even been stricken with temporary illness we were lost. Stronger language than this has flowed from pens having far better claims than mine to speak of American history. Who will say that this is not a great man? It may be urged in reply that it was generous to get the money, though not particularly great. We will see later. But where is the flaw in the character up to the present? It was the "honor" of Robert Morris that controlled, and was to control for years yet to come, the forces of the world. The revolution was won by character; men trusted Washington and his inseparable Damon, Robert Morris. But to return to the chipping. "He had begun to urge, from the first year of the war, that congress should employ competent executive officers upon proper salaries. He urged this as a measure of economy and efficiency in administration." Could anything better be urged, after a hundred years to think it over?

It is noticeable that no recommendation of Robert Morris ever needed to be modified; it is noticeable that every one of his recommendations has become incorporated into our civil polity; it is noticeable that scarcely a single great feature of our present government was not at some time recommended by Robert Morris. Does the great man appear yet? Or is it only a fussy money-bags? Lowell speaks of "men with empires in their brains." "His large head seems as well adapted for the government of an empire as that of most men;" I quote from our author the words of Prince de Broglie. But how were the above recommendations received? "We do not know of any one at that time who seconded his efforts in this direction." How lonely is a man who is a century ahead of his time!

"Congress was under the influence of a number of prejudices;" Robert Morris was under the influence of conviction alone from first to last. It was almost amusing to see this grand man time and again put down his solitary cane, and say to congress, and the country, and the world; "Thus far will I go; and that is the end of it; you must meet me there." They met him. Is is a great man yet? An intellect to see the way amid all the fogginess of the times; a will to force things along the way amidst all the obstructions of the times! And those were the "times that tried men's souls;" and those were the times that tried men's bodies; and those were the times that tried men's intellects. I don't know how you can get any better tests of greatness than those which Robert Morris triumphantly withstood at every moment of his public career. I have already shown, through our author, that his private career was phenomenal beyond all precedent. "He thought that all else should be laid aside in order to devote all available strength to an energetic prosecution of the war;" and he ever practised what he preached. The trimmers who were spreading their sails to catch the popular breeze would have left the Revolution stranded; this man with his cane going down from point to point, forced the Revolution through.

"It seemed to him that the quarrels about liberty and rights could be settled after peace and independence had been won." And it seems to us that everything that seemed right to him was right, is right, and always will be right. His extraordinary intelligence penetrated at once to the laws of everything that he had anything to do with; and his conscience always compelled him to follow the strict letter of the law. He was never without the courage of his convictions; he was always ready, if need be, to stand alone. Even according to our author he stood alone time and again, with his toe at the line and his lip set, waiting for the world to get around to him. It always got around to him when he took that attitude. Any nonentity can be obstinate; it takes the greatest of the great to know when to be wisely obstinate, to know when the time for concessions is past. Robert Morris could rule; but he could not ruin; none knew better than he when it was safe and wise to give way. In that age of jealousies and compromises there was no man more tactful. But never did a concession of his carry with it a suggestion of craven fear; never was a concession of his other than a master stroke in the interest of the public good.

In all his sublime and timely obstinacy he never crossed wills with Washington but once. They saw things alike; and together they pulled all along; like knew its like by instinct, and cleaved to it; no wedge of separation could enter between them; it was Damon and Pythias; it was Castor and Pollux; and before those Dioscuri the enemies of freedom, of sound economy, and of good government fell back in ignominious defeat. The whole Revolutionary period was the constant battle of Lake Regillus, in which those God-like youths continued to infuse into mere corporals' guards the spirit and power of conquering hosts. The benignant countenance of Pythias is seen all over the land—in marble, in bronze, in print, in paint—an inspiration to succeeding generations of patriots. But we look in vain, as yet, for the mild countenance of the unobtrusive Damon. I say as yet; for I have faith that the Plutarch will yet appear who will resuscitate the forgotten Damon, and re-introduce him to his much indebted countrymen. Castor has his shaft of marble shooting five hundred feet into the blue sky, and overtopping all other works of man as much as his character over-topped that of all other mortals. Pollux, according to our author, lies in a dark and chilly enclosure, with nothing above him but a horizontal slab inscribed with the dates of his birth and death, and stating incidentally that he had been the "Financier of the United States during the Revolution." "His resting place is therefore a damp and dark corner." No comment. Castor was true to the last to his more mortal brother; and in the last year of his life he sends the "affectionate regards of General and Mrs. Washington to Robert Morris." The message went to a man old and poor, and who had been for two years languishing in a debtors' prison, shut up with the yellow fever, and submitting with the meekness of a second Job to the direst blows that cruel fortune could devise. I believe that Job once cried out in his anguish; Morris never uttered a sound nor gave a single sign. The sage of Athens did not sip the hemlock more calmly than did Morris take the bitter dregs that came to him in the evening of his existence out of his glorious and beneficent life. Mark Tapley saw one compensation in adversity cheerfully borne—an opportunity to get credit worth having. Morris maintained his cheerfulness without seeking any credit at all ; he simply did it on principle, that it was a philosopher's duty. There was one thing he yet could do, and he would do it ; he could avoid breeding snow storms to chill other lives. Our author is good enough to call this ' grim pleasantry and a desperate reconciliation to facts." I fear that he would see nothing but "grim pleasantry and desperate reconciliation to facts" in the cases of Socrates and Phocion.

"In April, 1779, (after he had suffered two years of imprisonment) Governeur Morris visited Robert Morris in the prison and dined with him and Mrs. Morris there." Rather a change from the mansion and table where princes and potentates and all worthy people partook of the friendly and tactful hospitality of this same Robert and Mrs. Morris ! Rather a change from the mansion and table which supplied their comforts to the elegant and fastidi-Washington on the occasion of every visit of his to Philadelphia. He trusted "Robert" always ; hy lived with him whenever he could. And when Washington came as President to live in Philadelphia, Robert succeeded in persuading him to occupy the house that had always been his home there. ' The latter two (Mr. and Mrs. Morris) kept up high spirits, and the visitor was distressed to see that Morris had made up his mind to his situation more than he could have believed possible." Mr. and Mrs. Morris did what they had always done—they entertained their guests as handsomely as their circumstances would permit The lady who smiled in prison was according to our author "the second lady at court ; as to taste, etiquette, etc., she is certainly the first." This hospitality in prison has its counterpart in that of General Marion who graciously entertained the visiting British officer with a share of his solitary sweet potato. The officer on his return said to his superiors: "you can never conquer a people who take adversity like that. I fear that Professor Sumner would never enter fully into the spirit of these things ; for he seems to regard them all as "grim pleasantry." At Fort Sumter the soldiers ate their last crust amid exploding magazines and falling walls; they would have starved if that would have saved the fort ; as it was they demanded and obtained the "honors of war." At Bunker Hill the soldiers stayed till their last shot was fired ; they would still have stayed, if that would have held the hill. I take it that true heroism consists in rising superior to circumstances, and in maintaining an equable spirit and an exalted demeanor in the last extremity. The Roman sages used the expression "equal mind" to denote this supreme test of character.

> "The man resolved and steady to his trust,
> Inflexible to ill, and obstinately just,
> May the rude rabble's insolence despise,
> Their senseless clamors and unmeaning cries:—
>
> * * *
>
> Though the great frame of nature round him break,
> Into mad ruin and confusion hurled,
> He unconcerned would hear the mighty crack,
> And stand unmoved amid the crash of worlds."

Two years of apparently perpetual imprisonment without a single scowl, and without a single note of repining! And the cultured wife sharing it with him with the same high-bred resignation! Is not this literally

> "Patience sitting by a monument
> And smiling extremely out of act"?

It was worth all their losses and misfortunes to enable Robert Morris and his great-hearted wife to show their character under such supreme tests, to be photographed in such a setting. In looking into the countenance of Gouvernour Morris they looked into the face of their vanished affluence without a quiver. Greatness of soul could go no further. I know no picture in history that equals it.

But to return from the aged philosopher in prison, let us follow the strong man in the arena. We left him at the beginning of the glorious Burgoyne campaign. "During December and January he may be said to have carried on the work of the continent." Our author might have said something here about Atlas and Titans; but he didn't. I have already intimated that this seemed to be a ticklish spot with him; the angel seemed to be getting dangerously near the surface; so he judiciously hurries away to safer ground. Robert Morris was ruling the country, and was getting things round on time. —Saratoga. French Alliance. Monmouth. But he was not a usurper; he did not seize the government which he wielded; he simply accepted a government that in a manner slid onto him. It had been well for the country had congress continued to satisfy itself with the fiction of governing, and left the fact to Morris. But congress never ran away except when they scented some danger from afar; then they would carry the fiction with them and leave the fact behind. That was ever Morris's opportunity. When the Gauls were at the threshold the people were sent away and the Roman senate remained. The senate remained behind this time; but their aggregate number in the crisis was somewhat reduced. They numbered all told just one man. And he did not sit calmly at his door-way waiting to have his throat slit; he waited to spring like a Hercules upon the Nemæan lion and to strangle him in his arms.

Things were fairly safe after Monmouth: so congress took up the business again, and in the next two years succeeded in making a sorry mess of it. "The public men of the time truckled to public opinion to a degree modern men cannot understand,"—consequently they will soon need Morris again. "At the close of 1780 the leading public men almost despaired of the struggle." "Almost," but not quite ; for they had Robert Morris to fall back upon in the last extremi-y ; and they somehow felt that he might in some way pull them through. "To the public men in positions of responsibility, it seemed that everything might be lost." Naturally; for the job was manifestly too big for them. "Congress was driven . . . to supersede the board . . . of the treasury by a single competent officer." Exactly; just what Robert Morris wanted them to do four years earlier ; but there was too much "truckling" going on. They had at last to do a sensible thing or be totally shipwrecked. The breakers are just under the bow; the angry surf is roaring ; who will prevent the crash? "Robert Morris was regarded as the one man in the country for this office." Indeed! What, this peculator, this speculator, this fussy money-bags, this vain popinjay, this insanely avaricious man, the "only one" in a great nation that can save that nation from immediate destruction? Well, Mr. Sumner, I have heard of people who were compelled to use food that was not particularly appetizing to them; and when I come to look back upon that sentence of yours, and consider what a troublesome part of the stone you have reached, I must say that it is a brave one. It is a strong one ; the rhetorics would pass it ; I am now ready to say that there is literature in your book. "Morris was in command of the situation." He always was where things were as desperate as they could be; they never gave him anything but the worst kind of job. As long as there was a ghost of a chance of getting along without him they did not permit him to be "master of the situation." "It no doubt flattered his vanity." Oh, fie ' Mr. Sumner! You were brave a moment ago ; why did you not stay so? You seem to be panicky again, and to be making a wild dash to the other side of the stone. "No doubt," did you say? Well, I answer that there are men in the world, and there are men. "That all should turn to him at a moment of supreme crisis." Those were the only moments in which they did turn to him. They "all" always came to their senses when everything was almost lost. They stopped "truckling" just on this side of ruin. It was hardly giving Robert a fair chance ; but he did not split hairs. "As the one man who was indispensable to the country." You never spoke a truer word ; there was just "one indispensable" man in the Revolution ; and I am very glad to see that you know it. What surprises me is that it starts no reflections in your mind, except the entirely gratuitous and utterly unworthy one that "it no doubt flattered his vanity." We would like to get all that kind of vanity that is readily accessible. I believe that some one reported to Lincoln that General Grant had a weakness. The martyred president instantly asked where he bought it, that he might get a stock out of the same receptacle for all the rest of his generals. I think you said that they "all" knew it. They would all know it to-day if all the historians were as frank as you. Good things will keep; Robert Morris's character and career will keep; whether the historians think to write him up or not ; indeed, even if some historian should try to write him down.

"He had a clear idea of what he wanted and of what ought to be done." So clear, that when Adam Smith's book came out a few months later they "all" saw that Morris had told it all beforehand. "He also had very definite convictions." Just what I have been maintaining, thank you." "He therefore set his conditions;" in other words he put the cane down. Just so, you are giving me emphatic corroboration at every step. "He insisted, however, and carried his point;" in other words they always yielded when his lip took on the straight line. "Morris was one of the first to recognize the immense importance of union among the States." Great idea; what a pity the others couldn't see it then. They wouldn't give him a union to work with; they gave him the job and left him to grapple with a lot of loose recalcitrant States. He did not put the cane down on this point; and so when they would not let him get through in a sensible manner he pulled them through by hook and by crook (but never by ways that are crooked). I will allow our great historian, Professor Fiske, to voice this achievement: "That the government had in any way been able to finish the war after the downfall of the paper money, was due to the gigantic efforts of one great man—Robert Morris." Mr. Fiske is usually calm and judicial; the utterance in this passage is Demosthenic. And it leaves him in no panic; it is an angel that he is chipping for. I think that some allusions have been made to Titans. Well "gigantic" is not very far from it. But I beg especially to call attention to the last two words, "great man." There are great generals, great financiers, great sculptors, great historians, great biographers, etc.; but when you have run your gamut through you reach the climax of all in a great man. I have seen different appellations applied to Morris; but I have waited long for that happy and just characterization of Professor Fiske. I have seen the appellation "Great Financier" applied to him until I am nauseated with it. I could bear "great patriot," "great soul," or some other similar epithet; but nothing tells it all so well as great man."

"Who noble ends by noble means obtains,
Or, failing, smiles in exile or in chains,
Like good Aurelius, let him reign, or bleed
Like Socrates, that man is great indeed."

In the above spirited lines the poet allows alternatives. Morris needed none, he covered all the conditions, and is therefore in a manner doubly great. He "obtained the noblest ends" by only "noble means;" he "smiled in exile and in chains" without "failing;" "like good Aurelius" he did "reign;" and he reigned through crises, the like of which Aurelius never knew. "Like Socrates" he did "bleed" at every physical, mental, and moral pore; and he bled with the same lamb-like and saintly resignation.

He got the money and he got them through; that sums up the doings of 8 1-8 3. He got them out of Scylla and Charybdis, even though they denied him a decent pair of oars. He grasped at any sticks that he could lay his hands upon and paddled the doomed vessel out into the offing.

"Washington had long cherished a desire with the help of the French to dislodge the English from New York." And he intended to try it in '81. Here Pythias and Damon clashed for the first and only time. It ended in Damon's way; and it ended to Pythias's renown. The boldest thing in Morris's career was when he put the cane down to Washington. "Morris of course shrank from the enormous expense of that undertaking." That does not tell it; he maintained that New York was not worth having. He held that if Washington could get in at all, which was very doubtful, the British would immediately drive him out again with their fleet. "It was then determined to march against Cornwallis in Virginia." So his obstinacy, which was never ill-timed, but which was simply terrible when that cane came down, precipitated the most brilliant military movement in history. "When he found the demands upon him for money far exceeded the amount which he possessed (that is when he went to New York to wrestle with Washington) he gave none to anybody but brought it back." The cane was down, you see. Another patriot has left the immortal shibboleth; "Millions for defense, not one dollar for tribute." Morris's idea was "Millions for Yorktown, but not one dollar for New York." "Hence, it was then determined"—a beautifully indefinite proposition to cover a particularly dangerous part of the stone. No money for New York; but "millions of rations" had been sent to Greene in the Carolinas; and, quick as was Washington's march to Philadelphia, when he got there the road-sides were lined for miles with army wagons laden with provisions and other supplies needful in an active campaign. To facilitate rapidity of movement other supplies were waiting at points along the Chesapeake. Morris "laid the train" in a double sense; the avenging fire sped along it and exploded the mine under Cornwallis's feet. Hostilities were ended; though the war dragged on two years longer. He got them temporarily into a safe offing. He got the money it seems by hook or by crook (but never by ways that are crooked.) We are told that he advanced $1,400,000 of his own money to fill those wagons. Our author says that this is probably "apocryphal." "Well, I leave him to fight that out; it is only a question of detail. The short of it is that he got them through; and he held them through with his broken oars and his drift-wood sticks for two years longer—until Independence was definitely secured. When the job became small enough for the others to handle it again he turned it over to them and went back to his neglected and honey-combed business. I have said that in the twenty years of his young manhood he had given a momentum to his business that would keep it going awhile. But ten years is more than "awhile;" he found his own vessel hopelessly out of repair. By superhuman exertions he kept her afloat ten years longer; and then she went to pieces after the manner of the overworked "One Hoss Shay." But in that ten years in which he escaped the prison walls he was enabled to perform three other services for his country. He assisted in making the Constitution which he had been clamoring for for fourteen years; he sat in the first Senate and helped Washington launch his first administration; and he virtually settled the location of the National Capitol. We have seen him financiering under the most trying and distressing circumstances. He was now offered the opportunity to distinguish himself with the finest craft ever launched, and upon the fairest sea. He quietly declined and recommended the brainy young Hamilton. Hamilton straightened matters out on lines laid down by Robert Morris fifteen years before.

The battle of opinion is always on; terrific blows are given and received by those who never forget the amenities. It is unfair warfare to undertake to strike down the opinion by striking down the good man who entertains it. This is worse than persecution; the hero can face the gallows calmly, but he groans under defamation of character. When Epaminondas was asked why the sentence of death should not be passed upon him, he said that it should be passed upon him, for he had deliberately disobeyed a mandate of his country. But he craved that his countrymen would do justice to his memory. He wished it carefully inscribed upon his tomb that he had disobeyed his country in order to save her and in order to bring her lasting prestige and renown, and not through any lower motive. With this assurance he was ready to embrace the block and face posterity. Then did it dawn upon the hearts of his countrymen that there is something higher than legal justice; there is that equity that brings the heart alone to trial. They spared their hero and condoned his noble crime. Morris was never even a constructive criminal; he had not only legal sanction for every act that he performed, but he also had with it the urgent appeal of his countrymen. He obeyed that appeal whenever the emergency was great enough to make obedience a duty. He did become a constructive criminal by becoming poor; but that was a misfortune rather than a deliberate act.

In the heat of passion even good men may make personal attacks which they afterwards sincerely regret. In the strife of factions there are always those who do not scruple to impugn the motives of their adversaries, and to deliberately blacken private character. It is the cowardly method of striking down the opinion by striking down its possessor; it is the carrying out of the atrocious doctrine that "the end justifies the means."

It is dangerous to go groping among the scurrillity of a by-gone time; for one may be caught warming up old venom with which to asperse a pure character no longer able to rise in its own defense. In our history we shall never be all on one side; we shall always have opposing houses; and it is better so. Never will the good men be all in one party; and never will a man's opinion be the key to his private character. Morris could have escaped all obloquy had he stayed at the desk of his counting-house. But he was too brave and high-minded to do that. He accounted the rectitude of his intentions a sufficient safe-guard; and with it he took all chances of annoyance and injury. "The men who have labored to influence public opinion in this direction, however, have always been unpopular." Please bear that in mind, Mr. Sumner, and be careful and charitable when you strike the reckless language of that unpopularity. Please remember how easy it was to screen ones self and what great moral courage it required to face the storm. Washington and Morris had this courage; and the very things for which they were abused are the things for which they are venerated to-day, and for which they will be venerated to the end of time. Yes, the vile things that were said about Washington himself would make a large literature. "They have always had to contend with and overcome the traditional prejudices and the inertia of the popular bodies, while those who floated with the popular tide have enjoyed popularity and ease together." Please remember that you are saying this yourself, and that you are saying it about Robert Morris. It is all that I have contended for; and it is all that is necessary to establish his noble character. I am glad that your book is written; for this is the testimony of an opponent, but I will be glad to see it succeeded by one that comes straight from the heart; and that one we will put into the hands of our children. You have made a discriminating life of this good man necessary; and the man who will prepare it will confer a boon.

In Western New York we have a special interest in Robert Morris. He appears in our annals as the first proprietor of most of the beautiful Genesee country. He is one of us; and it is with clansmen's loyalty that we spring to arms against his defamers. We are not ashamed that our titles all run back to that great man, that worthy gentleman. He lived in Philadelphia; and Philadelphia gives him a "cold, dark corner." He just appeared among us; and we give him the warmest place in our hearts, and will make as manful battle as we can for justice to him. He is the beginning of our history; the centuries of savagery led down to Robert Morris and civilization. We are glad that the epoch was a Titan—that the new era began with a moral and intellectual giant. As well strike down Arminius in Germany as Robert Morris along the banks of the Genesee. They may be able to forget him in Philadelphia; we could not forget him here, if we would; the slightest retrospect of our region compels us to go back to "the time of Robert Morris." But we don't want to forget him; we feel honored in dating our history from a man who twice saved the Revolution from failure, and who did it as much by his "honor," his "credit," and his respectability, as by his imperial intellect and his sublime pertinacity. We feel honored in dating our history from a man who gave the United States its liberty, its independence, its Constitution, and its polity, and who did it without incurring a single stain upon his integrity, without disturbing in the least the quiet simplicity of his character—the trusted friend of Washington. "Morris was the one man to whom Washington unbent." The words of his own step-son—the voice out of his own household —the *ex cathedra* assertion of Morris's personal worth. "Probably because" —be careful, Mr. Sumner; you are on dangerous ground; you are now imputing motives to Washington. I know that you are at the tenderest part of your stone; you have my sympathies; but—forbear.

That is what Washington thought of him. How did the others regard him? "Mr. Otis said that Morris was esteemed next to Washington;" and Mr. Otis appends no "probably" at all. "Was esteemed"——by whom? There is only one interpretation to that sentence; Washington and the implied subject of that passive verb esteemed only good men. We all have our limitations. I could not write a book on music; and I would not try it. Never can a painting of mine grace the gallery wall of a Columbian World's Fair. The Lord has blessed me with powers to admire far beyond my powers to create. "Along the smooth sequestered vale of life" I am content to pursue "the even tenor of my way." I cannot make the rose that blooms for my delight; but I can resent the vandalism that would ruthlessly trample it down. I cannot make the flowers of art; but I can storm with wrath when the destroyer's hand gets among them. But the flower of all creation is a noble human character;

"An honest man's the noblest work of God."

The hand of the iconoclast reaches the height of audacity when it assails a good name. History has no meaning except in the types of men it has produced; a much greater offence than the destruction of Washington's statues, would be an attempt to destroy his identity. The hero worship that consists in admiring a man who displayed the extreme of fortitude in contending for a great principle, is the hero worship that the world needs. The present is inspired to noble deeds by remembrance of the past. Webster knew what chord to touch when with the names of good men north and south he fired the popular heart to the defense of the Union thirty years before it was directly assailed. Men have a prevision of victory when a supreme effort is to be made; when he sat down in cosy comfort that night before his reply to

Hayne, he knew that he had won not only the battle of the forum but also the greater battle of the field. He knew that his words would resound like clarion notes should the question ever come to the stern arbitrament of war; he knew that "Liberty *and* Union, now and forever, one and inseparable!" would call millions of citizens from their vocations to the defense of the Star Spangled Banner. The blaze of that cavernous deep dark eye was the blaze of prophecy. He knew that they would save the Union; for he told them what "it was worth" in terms which they could understand. It was worth just what it cost —the heroic sacrifices of "good men and true." Marathon, Thermopylae, Salamis, Platæa and Bannockburn, are only names to sum up cases of individual heroism. The heroism consisted in baring the breast for a principle. Thousands of more destructive conflicts have passed into oblivion, because they were fought by the victors solely for advantage. But the names mentioned above have furnished a battle cry in every subsequent struggle for the right. How much greater is the force of the appeal when one is called to his duty by the heroism of his own country. The ghostly leaders of Regillus were no empty fiction; the shades of departed worthies do hover above the banners of every new host arrayed in the battle for right. The magician who can evoke them is the real leader of the time.

"One blast upon his bugle horn
Were worth a thousand men."

I have no sympathy with the precisionism that lays its clammy hand of destruction upon the harmless little myths that spring up in popular tradition. Those myths are often an inspiration to youthful minds; and they are quite likely to have at their basis a solid kernel of fact. To destroy them is to take much food from youthful enthusiasm; it is to take from youth the history which it can understand; and it is to mutilate history itself. It is the people's way of telling their own story; and in them the youth sits down at the fireside of his ancestors. Historical evidence proved that there was no Troy, and that Homer had a marvelous imagination. The people said that there was a Troy; and Dr. Schlieman believed them. He admitted that the precisionists had proved their case; but he went over just the same and dug up Troy. It was still questioned whether there had been such persons as Agamemnon and Menelaus; so he went over to the other side and dug up Mycenæ. The Berkleyan philosophers proved that there is no food; but when the dinner time came around they somehow did not exactly relish an empty plate. So the wisest of men sometimes find themselves staggered by the troublesome facts of history. You may explain them away, argue them away, deny their existence; but, like Banquo's ghost they will not down; when you get through they are still there. Common report is a wonderful receptacle of history; and it has its basis in the contact with concrete facts. Who will doubt that this generation has a pretty clear notion of Sheridan? Yet it is quite among the possibilities that some one a hundred years hence may arise and prove that we don't know anything about him at all. I prefer to get my ideas of Socrates from some one who has seen him. A utilitarian philosopher of the nineteenth century, after spending a night with the Sophists, may claim that Xenophon and Plato knew nothing about their master; but I prefer all the same to listen to Xenophon and Plato. There may be a pardonable bias in the minds of these admiring youths faithful to the end, and affectionately painting him for posterity; but it is far less misleading than the bitter prejudices of those bad men whom Socrates had stung to the quick and driven out of the schools. But there is always a consensus of opinion that adjusts the portrait to very correct proportions. And what perfect pictures the people do draw; Hector is Hector, and nobody else; Andromache has her sweet individuality; even Astyanax is not the generic baby. Brutus and Tarquin could be identified on the streets. Bruce and Wallace will never be confounded. And so I take it that remotest ages will see Lincoln just as we see him, not in the light of his photograph, but in the light of his character; and they will see him as we see him, because we have seen him. There is no other law in the matter. Somebody may try on the basis of musty and obsolete documents, on things said in a corner, and so on, to reconstruct his character so as to suit the writer's prepossessions; but the wave of a world's consensus will move right over such an experiment, and engulf it in a prompt oblivion. It is a pretty well established principle that all the world knows more than any man in it; and woe to the man who would reverse the principle. In recognition of this principle it is the settled practice of psychologists to study the content of the terms used by the people as a whole in speaking of any of the mental activities. They find in this study the side-lights which they know must be there. The idea is the aggregate result of millions of shrewd observations; and the analyst finds a golden mine of laboratory work well done. The people live to teach.

You cannot by writing change the altitude of Mont Blanc; you cannot argue away the snowy crown of that "Monarch of mountains," bathed in eternal sunlight; but I deplore the temporary mental confusion which you can produce by the attempt to do so.

In defense of Robert Morris I have called up his life and deeds to speak for him; I have cited the opinions of the highest authorities of his time; I have called into court his neighbors, his friends, his public to speak for him; I have attempted to force his critic to construct the apotheosis of the great hero whom he would belittle. I might have multiplied citations to a voluminous extent, but I have tried to make a few characteristic types do the work of the whole. I will now permit the worthy defendant to speak for himself. The Spartan mother told her son to come back with his shield or on it. A French King sent back to his Capital the dispatch: "All is lost but honor." This was a note of triumph; and his people did not put on sack-cloth and ashes. Our Samson shorn of the locks which he had deliberately scattered right and left in the service of his country, staggers at last to his fall: "I am sensible that I have lost the confidence of the world as to my pecuniary ability, but I believe not as to my honor and integrity."

"It is the duty of every individal to act his part in whatever station his country may call him to in times of difficulty, danger, and distress."

"I think that the individual who declines the service of his country because its councils are not conformable to his ideas makes but a bad subject. A good one will follow if he cannot lead."

"You may be sure I have my full share of trouble on this occasion; but having got my family and books removed to a place of safety, my mind is more at ease, and my time is now given up to the public, although I have many thousand pounds' worth of effects here, without any prospects of saving them."

"Should time be lost in tedious negotiations and succours be withheld, America must sue for peace from her oppressors."

"Our people knew not the hardships and calamities of war when they so boldly dared Britain to arms. Every man was then a bold patriot, felt himself equal to the contest, and seemed to wish for an opportunity of evincing his prowess. But now when we are fairly engaged, when death and ruin stare us in the face, and when nothing but the most intrepid courage can rescue us from contempt and disgrace, sorry am I to say it, many of these who were foremost in noise shrink coward-like from the danger, and are begging pardon without striking a blow."

"Nothing but the most arduous and virtuous conduct in the leaders, seconded by a spirited behaviour in the army, and a patient endurance of hardships by the people in general, can long support the contest."

"No treason either has operated or can operate so great injury to America as must follow from a loss of reputation."

"After serving my country in various public stations for upwards of four years, my routine in Congress was finished, and no sooner was I out than envious and malicious men began to attack my character. But my services were so universally known, and my integrity so clearly proved, I have, thank God, been able to look down with contempt on those that have endeavoured to injure me; and, what is more, I can face the world with that consciousness which rectitude of conduct gives to those who pursue it invariably."

"The various scenes of distress and the extreme difficulties which presented themselves to my view at that time were sufficient to have deterred any man from the acceptance of such an appointment. But, however unequal to the station, the attempt was indispensable."

"This appointment was unsought, unsolicited, and dangerous to accept, as it was evidently contrary to my private interests, and if accepted, must deprive me of those enjoyments, social and domestic, which my time of life required, and to which my circumstances entitled me; and a vigorous execution of the duties must inevitably expose me to the resentment of disappointed and designing men, and to the calumny and detraction of the envious and malicious."

"A full conviction of the necessity that some person should commence the work of reformation in our public affairs, by an attempt to introduce system and economy, and the persuasions that a refusal on my part would probably deter others from attempting this work, so absolutely necessary to the safety of our country."

"Putting myself out of the question, the sole motive is the public good; and this motive, I confess, comes home to my feelings. The contest we are engaged in appeared to me, in the first instance, just and necessary; therefore I took an active part in it. As it became dangerous, I thought it the more glorious, and was stimulated to the greatest exertions in my power when the affairs of America were at the worst."

"I cannot on any consideration consent to violate engagements or depart from those principles of honor which it is my pride to be governed by."

"My necessary commercial connections, notwithstanding the decided sense of Congress, expressed in their resolution of the 20th of March, might, if the business were transacted by myself, give rise to illiberal reflections, equally painful to me and injurious to the public. This reason alone would deserve great attention; but further, I expect that my whole time, study, and attention will be necessarily devoted to the various business of my department."

"If from any other cause I am forced to commit a breach of faith, or even to incur the appearance of it, from that moment my utility ceases."

"In accepting the office bestowed on me, I sacrifice much of my interest, my ease, my domestic enjoyments and internal tranquility. If I know my own heart, I make these sacrifices with a disinterested view to the service of my country."

"I am ready to go still farther, and the United States may command everything I have except my integrity, and the loss of that would effectually disable me from serving them more."

"I must again repeat my serious conviction that the least breach of faith must ruin us forever."

"I am very confident, when they shall see exertions on the one hand and economy on the other, they will be willing to assist us all they consistently can."

"Many who see the right road and approve it continue to follow the wrong road, because it leads to popularity. The love of popularity is our endemial disease, and can only be checked by a change of seasons."

"For your reimbursement you may either take me as a public or a private man; for I pledge myself to repay you with hard money wholly if required, or in part hard and part paper, if you so transact the business. In short, I promise, and you may rely that no consideration whatever shall induce me to make a promise that I do not see my capability to perform, that I will enable you to fulfill your engagements for this supply of flour."

"The various requisitions of Congress to the several States, none of them entirely complied with, create a considerable balance in favor of the United States, and the claiming this balance is delivered over to me as revenue; while on the other hand, the dangerous practice of taking articles for the public service, and giving certificates to the people, has created a very general and a very heavy debt. The amount of this debt is swelled beyond all reasonable bounds, nor can the extent of it be at present estimated. These things need no explanation, but it may be proper to observe that if the certificates were not in my way, there is still an infinite difference between the demand of a balance from the States and an effectual revenue."

"It gives me great pain to learn that there is a pernicious idea prevalent among some of the States that their accounts are not to be adjusted with the continent. Such ideas cannot fail to spread listless languor over all our operations. If once an opinion is admitted that those States who do the least and charge most will derive the greatest benefit and endure the smallest evils, Your Excellency must perceive that shameless inactivity must take the place of that noble emulation which ought to pervade and animate the whole Union."

"It is by being just to individuals, to each other, to the Union, to all; by generous grants of solid revenue, and by adopting energetic methods to collect that revenue, and not by complaining, vauntings, or recriminations, that these States must expect to establish their independence, and rise into power, consequence, and grandeur."

"The faith of the United States is pledged to the public creditors. At every new loan it must be pledged anew, and an appeal is now made to the States individually to support the public faith so solemnly pledged. If they do, it is possible the public credit may be restored; if not, our enemies will draw from thence strong arguments in favor of what they have so often asserted—that we are unworthy of confidence, that our Union is a rope of sand, that the people are weary of Congress, and that the respective States are determined to reject its authority."

"A dangerous supineness pervades the continent; and recommendations of Congress, capable in the year 1775 of arousing all America to action, now lie neglected."

"The precedent of disobedience once established, our Union must soon be at an end, and the authority of Congress reduced to a metaphysical idea."

"Have anticipated the revenue and brought us to the brink of destruction."

"Whatever may be the fate of my administration, I will never be subjected to the reproach of falsehood or insincerity. The public opinion as to the conduct of other princes and states (besides France and Spain) has greatly injured us by relaxing our exertions; but the opinion as to pecuniary aid has been still more pernicious. People have flattered themselves with a visionary idea that nothing more was necessary than for Congress to send a Minister abroad, and that immediately he would obtain as much money as he chose to ask for."

"Have the efforts to borrow in this country been so successful as to ground any hope from abroad? Or is it to be supposed that foreigners will interest themselves more in our prosperity and safety than our own citizens?"

"It is high time to relieve ourselves from the infamy we have already sustained, and to rescue and restore the national credit. This can only be done by solid revenue. Disdaining, therefore, these little timid artifices which, while they postpone the moment of difficulty, only increase the danger and confirm the ruin. I prefer the open declaration to all of what is to be expected, and from whence it is to be drawn."

"When I tell you that I am not much deceived in my expectations, you will readily form a proper conclusion as to the relaxed habits of administration in this country."

"To increase the means of payment by retrenching every other expenditure is my constant object. To increase the means of payment by grants of money, the States alone are competent to."

"We have reason to apprehend a continuance of that shameful negligence which has marked us to a proverb, while all Europe gazed in astonishment at the unparalleled boldness and vastness of our claims, blended with an unparalleled indolence and imbecility of conduct."

"My family, being chiefly at Springetsbury, affords me the opportunity of appropriating my house in town to your use. I believe we can accommodate your aids, etc., with mattresses, but our beds are chiefly in the country, and as what I have cannot possibly be appropriated to a better use, I beg

"Your Excellency will consider and use my house and what it affords as your own."

"While I was in advance, not only my credit, but every shilling of my own money, and all which I could obtain from my friends, to support the important expedition against Yorktown, much offence was taken that I did not minister relief to the officers taken prisoners at Charleston."

"This country by relying too much on paper is in a condition of peculiar disorder and debility. To rescue and restore her is an object equal to my warmest wishes, though probably beyond the strength of my abilities. Success will greatly depend on the pecuniary aid we may obtain from abroad, because money is necessary to introduce economy, while at the same time economy is necessary to obtain money."

"By accepting the office I now hold, I was obliged to neglect my own private affairs. I have made no speculations in consequence of my office, and instead of being enriched, I am poorer this day than I was a year ago."

"I write sir, to apprise you of the public danger, and to tell you I shall endeavor to fulfil engagements which I have entered into already, that I may quit my station like an honest man; but I will make no new engagements, so that the public service must necessarily stand still. What the consequences may be I know not; but the fault is in the States. They have not complied with the requisitions of Congress; they have not enabled me to go on; they have not given me one shilling for the service of the year 1782, excepting only the State of New Jersey, from which I received $5,500 a few days ago, and this is all that has come to my hands out of two millions which were asked for. Now, should the army disband, and should scenes of distress and horror be reiterated and accumulated, I again repeat, that I am guiltless; the fault is in the States. They have been deaf to the calls of Congress, to the clamors of the public creditor, to the just demands of a suffering army, and even to the reproaches of the enemy."

"This language may appear extraordinary, but at a future day, when my transactions shall be laid bare to public view, it will be justified. This language may not consist with the ideas of dignity which some men entertain; but, sir, dignity is in duty and in virtue, not in the sound of swelling expressions. I have borne with delays and disappointments as long as I could, and nothing but hard necessity would have wrung from me the sentiments which I now expressed."

"I find the publications of 'No Receipts' are by no means very pleasing. Men are less ashamed to do wrong than vexed to be told of it."

"The people are undoubtedly able to pay; but they have easily persuaded themselves into a conviction of their own inability, and in a government like ours the belief creates the thing."

"Our enemies hold up to contempt and derision the contrast between resolutions to carry on the war at every expense and the receipts of nothing in some States, and very little in all of them put together."

"The experience of other countries could not satisfy America. We must have it of our own acquiring. We have at length bought it; but the purchase has nearly been our ruin."

"Let us apply to borrow wherever we may, our mouths will always be stopped by the one word 'security.' The States will not give revenue for the purpose, and the United States have nothing to give but a general National promise, of which their enemies loudly charge them with the violation."

"Would be very happy to apologize to the world for doing nothing, with the thin and flimsy pretext that it has been asked to do too much. It is a vain thing to suppose that wars can be carried on by quibbles and puns; and yet laying taxes payable in specific articles amounts to no more, for with a great sound they put little or nothing in the treasury."

"Imagine the situation of a man who is to direct the finances of a country almost without revenue (for such you will perceive this to be), surrounded by creditors whose distresses, while they increase their clamour, render it more difficult to appease them; an army ready to disband or mutiny; a government whose sole authority consists in the power of framing recommendations. Surely it is not necessary to add any coloring to such a piece, and yet truth would justify more than fancy could paint."

"To increase our debts while the prospect of paying them diminishes, does not consist with my ideas of integrity. I must, therefore, quit a situation which become utterly unsupportable."

"Nothing would have induced me to continue in office but a view of the public distresses. These distresses are much greater than can easily be conceived. I am not ignorant that attempts are made to infuse the pernicious idea that foreign aid is easily attainable, and that of the moneys already obtained, a considerable part remains unappropriated."

"The distresses we experience arise from our own misconduct. If the resources of this country were drawn forth, they would be amply sufficient; but this is not the case. Congress had not authority equal to the object, and their influence is greatly lessened by their evident incapacity to do justice. Nothing should induce me in my public character to make such application for money as I am obliged to in my private character. If these notes are not satisfied when they become due, the little credit which remains to this country must fall, and the little authority dependent on it must fall too."

"I might also appeal to the clamors against me for opposing claims I could not properly comply with. Long have I been the object of enmities derived from that origin. I have therefore the right to consider such clamours and such enmities as the confession and the evidence of my care and attention."

"If I had met with that support which, unmerited by my abilities, was due to my zeal for the public service, I believe that I should have continued in office until, all accounts being settled and all debts provided for, I could have left to my successor the pleasing prospect of future wealth, unclouded by any dismal retrospect of past poverty. But all other things out of the question, there is such a disposition among men to traduce and vilify, that no prudent man will risk a fair reputation by holding an office so important as mine."

"It becomes impossible to serve a people who convert everything into a ground for calumny."

"We certainly ought to do more for ourselves before we ask the aid of others."

"It gives me great pleasure to reflect that the situation of public affairs is more prosperous than when that commission issued. The sovereignty and independence of America are acknowledged. May they be firmly established and effectually secured. This can only be done by a just and vigorous government. That these States, therefore, may be soon and long united under such a government is my ardent wish and constant prayer."

"Will deal with me and trust me; not that I expect that they may like me better than now, but they have confidence in me, and for the sake of their own interests and convenience they will deal with me."

"The State is charged in the treasury of the United States with the interest arising on the balances, being the excess of the cost of those supplies beyond the moneys received from the State. And this is done because that excess was partly supplied by the moneys of the United States, and partly by the credit of their officer."

"An union of measures and views between the several States and the Union must prove beneficial to all and to every one of them."

"Congress have appointed Commissioners to examine the receipts and expenditures during my administration. This is a very proper measure, and ought to have been adopted at the time I resigned. I am, however, very glad it is now done, as by this means I shall have an opportunity of stopping the malicious and envious who are fond of insinuating suspicions which they dare not charge. But I shall get the better of all these sons of darkness in the end, and oblige them to acknowledge the services they try to traduce."

"God has blessed me with a disposition of mind that enables me to submit with patient resignation to His dispensations as they regard myself."

"I am daily undergoing the most mortifying and tormenting scenes that you can imagine."

"I am, to be sure, disagreeably situated, but my affairs are retrievable, if I could get the common aid of common times, and I will struggle hard."

"I would fain hope that he does not wish to take advantage of my necessities to obtain my property at less than its worth."

"There is no bearing with these things. I believe I shall go mad. Every day brings forward scenes and troubles almost insupportable, and they seem to be accumulating so that at last they will like a torrent carry everything before them. God help us, for men will not."

"Have patience, and I will pay thee all."

"That painful distress of mind which has become my constant companion."

"Good heavens, what vultures men are in regard to each other!"

"Confidence has furled her banners."

"I am a martyr to the times."

"Advertised, sold, sacrificed, and plundered."

"I am sensible that I have lost the confidence of the world as to my pecuniary abilities, but I believe not as to my honour or integrity."

"I will try to see you before I go to prison."

"Starvation stares me in the face."

"I have not money enough to buy bread for my family."

"I feel like an intruder everywhere: sleeping in other people's beds and sitting in other people's rooms. I am writing on other people's paper, with other people's ink,—the pen is my own; that and the clothes I wear are all I can claim as mine here. If my creditors were wise for their own sakes, they would not keep me idle here, when if I had my liberty, I might work efficiently for their benefit."

"I received your letter yesterday, by which I see the prison scene has made its impression on your mind. You must come every Sunday; and it will grow so familiar that you will think little of it, so long as you keep out on week days."

"The hotel with grated doors."

"I have just heard of an estate of mine worth $100,000 being sold for $800 to pay taxes. 'Such things are done.'"

"For that furniture which was my own is selling by piece-meal, because I cannot raise money to save it."

"If you should find it necessary to write again, be good enough to pay the postage of your letters, for I have not a cent to spare from means of subsistance."

POSTSCRIPT.

The people have responded The Land Office is saved. The following extracts will, no doubt, speak for themselves:

(*Buffalo Commercial.*)

Saturday next, October 13th, will be a great day in our neighboring village of Batavia, Genesee county. May it be the brightest and balmiest Indian summer day of the season. The occasion will be the formal dedication of that historical relic, the old office of the Holland Land Company, to the Holland Purchase Historical Society, and the memory of Robert Morris, the first, and one of the most famous, of our national financiers. Most fittingly, the dedicatory address will be delivered by Morris's successor of to-day, the Hon. John G. Carlisle, Secretary of the Treasury, and the occasion will be graced by the presence of other members of the Government, including Secretaries Gresham and Lamont, and Postmaster-General Bissell.

The Holland Purchase Historical Society, of which Mrs. Dean Richmond is President, recently bought the ancient building, which is of stone, and in an excellent state of preservation; the intention is to convert it into an historic museum, in which will be displayed and preserved the relics of pioneer days in Western New York. In this laudable work the Buffalo Historical Society will no doubt cheerfully lend a helping hand.

The Land Office is the oldest structure in Western New York; it is much more than that, however, as the central historical landmark of this entire region. It was the radiating point for the development of the whole section, including the city of Buffalo and its neighborhood. It brings to mind the trials and achievements of the hardy pioneers, who pushed on through the unbroken wilderness, to their allotted settlements, and in a few years made the desert blossom as the rose. A century ago business was brisk in that old Land Office, and Buffalo was unknown. The operations of the Holland Land Company, were on a large scale, and whatever questions may have arisen as to its methods, the one substantial fact remains that it was the direct agency of opening up Western New York to civilization. In a certain sense every city and town in this region is its monument, though nothing it once owned now remains to perpetuate its memory except the quaint old building at Batavia that was so long its headquarters.

There are many thousands of the descendants of the pioneers who dealt with the Holland Land Company, and that large class will be especially interested in the forthcoming celebration. There are those, too, who will look back to an earlier day, before the advent of the white man, when the beautiful valley of the Genesee, and all the surrounding country, was the home of a long vanished race. All such can well afford to adopt the thought expressed by David Gray in the loveliest poem he ever wrote—"The Last Indian Council on the Genesee." It was written primarily of Glen Iris, but its application is much wider:

> When **Indian Summer** flings her cloak
>   Of brooding azure on the woods,
> The pathos of a vanished folk
>   Shall haunt thy solitudes.
> The blue smoke of their fires, once more,
>   Far o'er the hills shall seem to rise,
> And sunset's golden clouds restore
>   The red man's paradise.
>
> * * * *
>
> Quenched is the fire; the drifting smoke
>   Has vanished in the autumn haze;
> Gone too, O Vale, the simple folk
>   Who loved thee in old days,
> But, for their sakes—their lives serene—
>   Their loves, perchance as sweet as ours—
> Oh, be thy woods for aye more green,
>   And fairer bloom thy flowers!

(*Buffalo Express.*)

While Buffalo has just let pass an anniversary which might appropriately have been celebrated along with the installation of ordinance relics in Lafayette Park, her wideawake little neighbor, Batavia, has laid hold of an opportunity to win credit to the present by recalling the past, and has planned a celebration which already interests the country at large, and which reflects the greatest credit on the citizens and public spirit of Batavia.

The occasion is the dedication of the old land office building of the Holland Purchase as a memorial to Robert Morris, "the great patriot and financier of the Revolution and the first owner of the lands in Western New York." The dedication occurs next Saturday at Batavia. President Cleveland and several members of the Cabinet have accepted invitations to be present; and the principal address of the day will be made by John G. Carlisle, the 31st Secretary of the United States Treasury, of which Robert Morris was the first Secretary. The celebration is also to include a parade, the installation of a memorial tablet and exercises in the park. Besides Secretary Carlisle's address a poem by John H. Yates and devotional participation by Bishop Ryan and Bishop Coxe are announced. The oldest clergyman on the Holland Purchase will also be invited to take a hand in the festivities if he can be discovered. For people who take the slightest interest in historical matters, this celebration offers strong attractions. We trust that the Buffalo Historical Society will be creditably represented.

Odd as it may seem, this humble little office building, now 90 years old, is the first memorial which citizens of America have seen fit to dedicate to the memory of the first Secretary of the United States Treasury, and the man who ruined himself to save the credit of the United States during the Revolution and enabled the Colonies to keep on fighting until they had won their cause. To the student of American history, Robert Morris's career is an exceedingly interesting one. He was a rich Philadelphian when in 1775 he was elected to the Continental Congress. He signed the Declaration of Independence and a year later, when Washington appealed to him for help in raising money to pay the troops, he raised a loan, backing it with his personal notes, and handed over $50,000 in coin for the disheartened army. Other loans— largely negotiated in Holland—followed, and the campaign was prosecuted with new vigor. But for Robert Morris, the French alliance of 1777 probably never would have been formed. In 1780 he was made Superintendent of Finance and invested with well-nigh absolute control of the Treasury and its phantom resources. Of the wonderful manipulations by which he made those resources amount to something, of his reorganization of the system of tax collection so that taxes were really collected, of his establishment of the Bank of America, and of all the devices by which he bolstered up the country's credit and kept the army supplied with the sinews of war, the interested reader may easily find ample accounts, as well as of his downfall, his confinement in a debtors' prison, and ... last days.

It was through his efforts to save his ... that Morris went into vast land speculations. Before he left the Government service he had tied up all of his once great fortune in large tracts in several States. The most valuable of these tracts embraced what are now the western counties of New York. When through lack of capital to enable him to await for the advancing settlers to create a profitable demand for his land, he was finally driven to the wall, his Holland creditors bought from him, through American residents, the tract since known as the Holland Purchase.

(*Rochester Herald.*)

Robert Morris was a great man, and the establishment of this land office at Batavia was a great factor in the development of Western New York, and the fact need not by any means be lost sight of in considering the virtues and useful career of the man, even if the connection is somewhat remote.

Robert Morris deserves to be affectionately remembered by all Americans on account of the conspicuous part which he played in the Revolutionary struggle. He was one of the few wealthy men who served in the Continental Congress. Naturally a conservative, a native of England, and a merchant with large commercial connections with the mother country, he voted in Congress against the Declaration of Independence, but finally affixed his name to the historic document. Curiously enough, the financial prosecution of the war fell upon this converted promoter of independence. As a member of the Ways and Means Committee, he was practically the financial minister of the government from the first and gave it the full benefit of his personal credit. In one year he raised $1,400,000 to assist Washington's army, and in February, 1780, he was put in complete charge of the Treasury, with the title of Superintendent of Finance. It was Morris who organized the Bank of North America, by which expedient the funds were provided for carrying the war to a successful end. He was a member of the first United States Senate from Pennsylvania, and was offered the post of Secretary of the Treasury by Washington, but declined in Hamilton's favor. It was a hard ending to so distinguished a career that he should afterward have lost his private fortune, spent four years in a debtor's prison, and only had a home of his own to die in through the foresight of his wife. According to one biographer Mrs. Morris had an interest in the Holland Land Company bequeathed to her, and as a compensation for signing certain papers to which her signature was indispensable, she obtained a life annuity of $2,000. This appears to have been the sole support of the great financier and his wife from the time of his release from prison in 1802 to his death, at the age of 72, in 1806.

It is seemingly well established, however, that Mrs. Morris' interests were derived from those of her husband, who speculated in Western New York lands before his failure. Perhaps she had not joined with him in some of the numerous deeds that must have passed, and was therefore in a position to enforce her dower rights by securing the annuity mentioned. Mr. Morris began his land investments in this vicinity in 1790 by buying a part of the Phelps and Gorham purchase east of the Genesee, which he sold to English capitalists the next year at a handsome profit. The Holland purchase west of the Genesee was secured by him from the Indians, he having bought all rights of the State of Massachusetts in the tract. This he sold to Holland investors and the establishment of the Holland Land Company's office in the old stone building at Batavia followed. This building is now the property of the Holland Purchase Historical Association, which deserves great credit for preserving this valuable historical monument. Besides Secretary Carlisle, other members of the Cabinet will be present on Saturday, and the exercises will be in every way worthy of the occasion.

(Progressive Batavian.)

Saturday of this week, Oct. 13th, will occur the great event in Batavia's history, the dedication of the Old Holland Land Company's office on West Main street to the memory of Robert Morris, America's first Superintendent of Finance. It is to be a national affair, as many members of President Cleveland's cabinet, with their wives, will be present, and Hon. John G. Carlisle, Secretary of the Treasury, will be the orator of the day.

The members of the cabinet expected are as follows: Hon. John G. Carlisle, Secretary of the Treasury; Hon. Walter Q. Gresham, Secretary of State; Hon. Wilson S. Bissell, Postmaster-General; Hon. Richard Olney, Attorney-General; Hon. Daniel S. Lamont, Secretary of War; Hon. Hilary A. Herbert, Secretary of the Navy; Hon. Hoke Smith, Secretary of the Interior. Hon. R. A. Maxwell, Fourth Assistant Postmaster-General, will accompany the party from Washington over the Lehigh Valley road, arriving in a special car in Batavia at 10 a. m. on Saturday. Carriages will convey the distinguished guests to the Hotel Richmond, and from there to a platform in front of the old land office, where they will review the parade.

Other distinguished men are expected to be present from different parts of the country—senators, judges, ministers, mayors, editors, etc.

The parade will form on the State grounds at the Institution for the Blind, and move at 10 o'clock sharp.

(Batavia Daily News.)

The great day is at hand.

Members of the Cabinet, with the ladies who accompany them, will arrive on the Lehigh Valley road at 10:05 a. m. and be escorted to the Richmond. From there the Cabinet officers and such of the ladies as desire to will be driven to the reviewing stand in front of the Land Office, where the tablet will be unveiled by Secretary Gresham and the Dedication prayer offered by Bishop Ryan.

Luncheon will be served by Teall at the Richmond to all of the invited guests except the Cabinet ladies, who will be entertained at luncheon by Mrs. D. W. Tomlinson, the ladies going thence to the State park, where all of the Cabinet officers also will have seats on the speaker's stand. Exercises at the park will begin at 2 o'clock, opening with selections by the Sixty-fifth Regiment band. "To Thee, O Country," will be sung by the chorus of a hundred voices, and Bishop Coxe will offer prayer. The song of "Zion Awake," by the chorus, will be followed by the reading of the Dedication poem by John H. Yates, the author, after which the chorus will sing "O, Columbia, Columbia Beloved." Secretary Carlisle then will deliver his address, "America" will be sung by the chorus, and the closing prayer and benediction will be said by the Rev. Philos G. Cook of Buffalo, the oldest clergyman in active service on the Holland Purchase.

Batavia today is more gayly decorated than ever before, and fresh decorations are going up all the time. Some displays are of particular beauty.

The Washington party leaves for Batavia at 4:20 p. m. to-day.

A dispatch from General Maxwell this afternoon says the party will consist of Secretary Gresham, Secretary Carlisle and Secretary Lamont, with the ladies; Secretary Herbert and his daughter, Mrs. Micou, Secretary Smith, Postmaster-General Bissell and Mrs. Bissell will come from Buffalo. Attorney-General Olney is not coming. General Maxwell will come with the party from Washington.

WASHINGTON, Oct. 12.—(Associated Press).—There will be a good delegation of distinguished officials from Washington in attendance at Batavia, N. Y., to-morrow on the occasion of the ceremonies in honor of Robert Morris, the great financier of the early days of the Republic. The party will consist of Secretary and Mrs. Carlisle, Secretary and Mrs. Lamont, Secretary and Miss Herbert and Mrs. Micou, Secretary Smith and Fourth Assistant Postmaster General Maxwell.

The Ladies' Auxiliary Reception committee met yesterday afternoon at the residence of the Chairman, Mrs. Adelaide R. Kenney. The purpose of the meeting was to make provisions for entertaining a large number of Buffalo ladies who are expected to be present and who will be invited to make the homes of the ladies their headquarters. The visitors will be apportioned among the following ladies: Mrs. Alice G. Fisher, Mrs. George W. Lay, Mrs. J. F. Hall, Mrs. W. D. Smith, Mrs. Richmond and Mrs. Kenney, Mrs. S. E. North, Mrs. H. S. Hutchins, Mrs. George Bowen, Mrs. F. G. Ferrin, Mrs. William C. Watson, Mrs. Duane Armstrong, and Mrs. Wilber Smith.

The committee in a body will be present at the Hotel Richmond at 10 o'clock to greet the invited guests. The Cabinet ladies will be entertained at lunch by Mrs. D. W. Tomlinson at her residence at 12:30 o'clock and will drive to the Park from there. Mrs. D. W. Tomlinson will be assisted by Mrs. Robert A. Maxwell, Mrs. Frank B. Redfield, Mrs. LeRoy Parker, and Mrs. Trumbull Cary.

The other invited guests will be entertained at lunch served by Teall at the Hotel Richmond. Mrs. George H. Holden, Mrs. H. S. Hutchins, Mrs. Hinman Holden, Mrs. S E. North, Mrs. William C. Watson, Mrs. Joseph F. Hall and Mrs. G. S. Griswold will be the hostesses of this occasion.

The Reception committee hope to be able to arrange for a reception by the ladies from Washington at the Richmond immediately after their return from the State park at the conclusion of the exercises to-morrow afternoon, to give the ladies of Batavia and elsewhere an opportunity to meet the distinguished guests.

The Grand Parade.

The Marshal's General Order No. 2 gives information about the parade, which is expected to move at 10 o'clock.

HEADQUARTERS HOLLAND LAND OFFICE,
DEDICATION DAY,
BATAVIA, Oct. 12, 1894.

General Order No. 2:

1.—Headquarters for Dedication day will be at the corner of State street and Park avenue.

2.—Assistant Marshal and Staff will report at headquarters mounted and uniformed at 8:30 a. m.

3.—The headquarters of the Marshals of divisions will be as follows, viz: Mounted men, First and Fifth divisions at general headquarters; the Second and Third divisions, corner of State and North streets; the Fourth division at the corner of State street and Richmond avenue.

4.—The divisions will form as follows: The mounted men on State street, right resting on Park avenue; the First division on State street, right resting on the left of the mounted men; the Second division on State street, right resting on the left of the First division; the Third division on North street, right resting on State street; the Fourth division on Richmond avenue, right resting on State street; the Fifth division on Park avenue, right resting on State street.

5.—The several divisions will be composed of the following organizations:

Genesee County Mounted Men,

W. L. Colville, Commander.

THE FIRST DIVISION.

G. W. Stanley, Assistant Marshal and Staff.
Sixty-fifth Regiment Band and Drum Corps,
National Guard,
G. A. R. Posts,
Continental Drum Corps,
High School Cadets,
Clerks from Erie County Clerk's Office,
Indian Band,
Indians.

SECOND DIVISION.

Captain Timothy Lynch, Assistant Marshal and Staff,
Select Knight's Band,
C. M. B. A., C. B. L., A. O. H.,
Le Roy Total Abstinence Society,
St. Aloysius Society.

THIRD DIVISION.

Frank Lewis, Assistant Marshal and Staff,
Citizens' Band,
Johnston Harvester Co.,
Wiard Plow Works,
Ott & Fox,
Batavia Wheel Co.,
Wood Working Co.,
Cope Brothers,
L. Uebele.

FOURTH DIVISION.

C. H. Reynolds, Assistant Marshal and Staff,
Le Roy Band,
Le Roy Chemicals,
Bergen Fire Department,
I. O. O. F.,
A. O. U. W.,
Turners,
School Children.

FIFTH DIVISION.

G. H. Wheeler, Assistant Marshal and Staff,
Bergen Band,
Pioneers in Carriages,
Officers in Carriages.

After passing in review the several divisions will proceed as follows and be dismissed:

Mounted men to and down Washington avenue; the First and Second divisions to and down Park avenue; the Third division to Richmond avenue and turn to the left; the Fourth and Fifth divisions to and down Richmond avenue to the right.

By Command of

J. A. LE SEUR,
Marshal.

L. L. CROSBY,
Adjutant.

(*Rochester Democrat and Chronicle.*)

The season's sunset had cast its beams abroad, and painted with rich and ruddy tints the woodland and orchards of Batavia. Round about that historic and quiet hamlet of the mesa lands of New York, the waning season, with seeming prodigality of pigment, had touched the foliage with gold and blue and purple, amber and red.

The surpassing decorations of the fair village, upon the grandest historic occasion of her existence, were the garlands that nature wove in crimson, brown, and green. The wooded land in its blaze of glorious coloring was nature's tribute to the festive day.

Here upon this broad mesa land, with its returning autumnal coloring and spring blossoms, in the days when the century and country were young together and danced to the merry rythm of June breezes and the beating of time to the sturdy pioneers axe; here, upon this broad plateau extending from the placid Genesee on the east to the line of the great lakes upon the west, what more worthy place could have been chosen by the far-seeing old Holland company and its representative than this very spot within the environs of what is now Batavia.

Aye, shades of Hendrick Vollenhoven and Pieter Van Enghen, what far seeing old fellows those few Hollanders were who more than a century ago could look forward with confidence to the time when the chipmunk, hiding behind the flushing leaves of the beech tree, stuffing his chops with the nuts which went to make up his winter's store, to the chirping encouragement of the cat bird, would scurry away to thicker woods before the keen blade of the woodman; and the plateau would bend its fields of golden tasseled corn and ripened grain to the sighing lake winds!

What a financier and prophet, too, indeed, was Robert Morris when he shouldered this burden willingly! What a far sighted genius, too, was Joseph Ellicott!

That their confidence was not misplaced they all lived to know. Round the newly established land office a village grew to fine proportions; the village which yesterday bedecked herself in honor of the Holland Land Office and Robert Morris, an occasion which many of the nation's leading citizens took delight in honoring.

The night of Friday saw Batavia in bright array. Flags were flying, streamers floating upon the air, and gay-colored bunting fluttering in the night wind. The stores, the shops, the churches, the land office itself, the old stone court house, the houses and the buildings and the stands at the State Park were all one blaze of red, white, and blue.

The preparations for the greatest event in her history, the event which was to honor her with the presence of the cabinet officers, the occasion of the dedication of the Holland Land Office to the memory of Robert Morris, had all been made, and the village wore her smile of welcome.

(*Rochester Union and Advertiser.*)

If a former resident of Batavia should drop into town to-day he would not recognize the place, so changed it is in appearance during the past forty-eight hours. The town is taking a day off and is decked in holiday attire. And the streets look very pretty in their robings of red and white and blue.

(Col. Sherman D. Richardson.)

I stand beside the landmark old,
  As bright the setting sun
Turns Tonawanda's tide to gold,
  As if from diamonds spun.
With magic tints of autumn dyes
  The shrub-decked lawn is dressed;
A holy calm on nature lies
  Like heaven's eternal rest.

"REARED ON THE BANKS OF TON-A-WAN-DA'S STREAM."

The ivy climbing to the eves;
  The tree tops towering high;
A canopy of shimmering leaves;
  With patchwork of the sky.
The mossy roof, the gables gray.
  The river winding by;
The azure hilltops leagues away;
  The clouds that on them lie.

The buried years come floating by
  Like phantom-haunted dreams;
Each vision that is hovering nigh
  With sacred memory teems.
The resurrected long ago
  Commingles with the new;
The future throws its living glow
  On each dissolving view.

I see a forest wild inlaid
   With trails by nature's art;
I watch beneath the gloomy shade
   The feathered headdress dart.
The wild beast and the wilder man
   Speed by in eager chase,
Before that culture's evil ban
   Was placed on tint of face.

Here comes the hardy pioneer
   From o'er the ocean wide,
To plant beside the waters clear
   A home by kings denied.
The manhood of a royal line,
   The founders of a race,
That fashioned out a grand design
   That years cannot efface.

I see the structure rude of wood,
   Transformed to lasting stone;
I see the fields where forests stood
   With grain of plenty sown.
And as the shepherds once the star
   Pursued with eager feet,
So pilgrims journeying from afar.
   Now at this Mecca meet.

A change comes o'er the hallowed scene,
   As shifts the mimic stage,
A teeming town and fields of green
   Reveal the present age.
The background and the frame are new
   Long may their beauties last;
But grander is this relic true
   From out the sacred past.

Each stone, to me, is richer than
   If formed from polished gold;
It's outline framed from ancient plan,
   Than if from modern mould.
It tells a story of the past,
   And links the old and new
With possibilities so vast
   In time's sublime review.

Well may the nation gather round
   To dedicate thy walls
With poets' lore and words profound
   From out the college halls.
Their incense cannot be too great,
   Their precious gifts too grand,
Upon this altar true of state
   Set up in freedom's land.

(*Batavia Daily News.*)

Never was any prearranged and anticipated event in Batavia given such prominence as the dedication to-day of the old land office of the Holland capitalists who with their surplus funds little more than a hundred years ago purchased the bulk of the 3,800,000 acres of land in Western New York known and described as the Holland Purchase. The preservation of the

Land Office, with the object of devoting it to the purposes of an historic museum, has been agitated for several years in the *News* and other papers, and the hope has been expressed that the landmark would not be permitted to fall into decay and, crumbling to pieces, be eternally ruined. After the demolition of the arsenal on West Main street, which, though not erected until after the War of 1812, had a cloud of antiquity and a mist of patriotism overhanging it, the Land Office was revered more and more as the years went by until finally the sentiment that it should be saved in memory of the past became so well grounded that plans for its preservation were consummated.

On November 15, 1892, the *News* in its Past and Present column printed the following, the speaker quoted being Andrew T. Miller, teller of the Bank of Batavia:

"One thing that ought to be agitated in Batavia until it takes form and gives promise of consummation is the matter of the preservation of the old Land Office," said a level-headed young business man. "It's a shame to have that old building, about the only landmark Batavia has, go the way of all the earth. It should be purchased by an historical society, which should be formed here and be restored as far as possible to its ancient form. I have taken pains to learn from the records who owns it and I think it could be bought and put into shape for not more than $2,000. I'd like to hear from the readers of the *News* on the subject."

In the middle of July, 1893, were taken the first steps that led to the celebration of to-day. On the 18th of that month the *News* contained an item in which it was said:

A movement that undoubtedly will result in the preservation of the old office in Batavia of the Holland Land company has been inaugurated. William C. Watson, who has interested himself in it, has secured an option on the property for $1,850, and concerted action will be taken soon to organize an historical society, to buy the old landmark and hold it.

On August 1st, following a meeting in the furtherance of the undertaking that now has been practically perfected was held in the office of the Board of Education and a committee was appointed to consider the feasibility of the plan. On September 18th the committee reported in favor of purchasing the Land Office and soliciting subscriptions in amounts ranging from $1 to $10, such limits being fixed in order that the movement might be a popular one. Considerable money was raised in the ensuing two months, and on November 11th a deed was filed conveying the property to Daniel W. Tomlinson as trustee, $850 having been paid in cash on the purchase and a mortgage for the balance having been recorded on the same day. About three months later, on February 5, 1894, the Holland Purchase Historical Society was organized and on March 17th the Land Office was transferred to that association, whose officers are as follows:

President—Mrs. Mary E. Richmond.
Vice President—William C. Watson.
Corresponding Secretary—Arthur E. Clark.
Recording Secretary and Librarian—H. P. Woodward.
Treasurer—L. C. McIntyre.

BOARD OF MANAGERS.

Mrs. Adelaide R. Kenney,
John Kennedy,   G. D. Weaver,
Gad B. Worthington,   F. B. Redfield,
George Bowen,   John H. Ward,
J. J. Washburn,   D. W. Tomlinson.

A committee of arrangements for the dedication of the building was appointed on July 18, 1894, and on August 3d numerous other committees were named. The Hon. Robert A. Maxwell of Batavia, Fourth Assistant Postmaster-General, had from the outset manifested a lively interest in the project, and, soon after the organization of the Historical society, began to interest his friends in the Cabinet in the matter of the forthcoming dedication, with the idea of securing their attendance. Therefore, when Judge Safford E. North, representing the society, visited Washington on August 23d to see Secretary Carlisle, who had virtually promised to deliver the address, and have a date fixed for the dedication, he found the way made easy for him. Secretary Carlisle, however, had concluded then that it would be impossible for him to come, as he was deeply engaged in Tariff matters and apprehended that it was desired to have the dedication soon, but when he learned that it was preferred to have the date fixed for some time ahead he consented to be present and to speak, naming the day. Judge North, in company with General Maxwell, visited other Cabinet officers, several of whom promised to accompany Secretary Carlisle. Arrangements for the dedication were then perfected as speedily as possible.

Those who first proposed the preservation and enlisted in the movement resulting in the dedication to-day had in mind an unostentatious transfer of the Land Office property to a society organized to hold and maintain it. The old structure was considered to have an historic value as the office where sales of land to the early settlers were consummated. It was the office whence deeds of the pioneers' lands were issued and where the original purchasers from the Holland speculators paid their money for their possessions; and these facts attached to it an interest that seemed sufficient to warrant it being held in veneration. Professor John Kennedy, Superintendent of Schools in Batavia, became engrossed in the subject, however, and in a number of admirably written articles, the first appearing in the *News* of July 20, 1893, connected Robert Morris of Revolutionary fame with the old office, through his sale to the Hollanders of the greater part of the territory west of the Genesee river. These articles attracted considerable attention, and when the Land Office finally was secured by the Historical society Professor Kennedy's suggestion that it be dedicated to the memory of Robert Morris and made a National affair, by reason of its consecration to his memory being a tribute to the first financial officer of the Federal Government, was in its main parts favorably acted upon.

The demonstration of to-day is the result. Through the efforts of and friendship for General Maxwell, whose home is in Batavia, members of the Cabinet of the President of the United States take part in the ceremonies, the Secretary of the Treasury delivering the address of the day. Other distinguished men in various walks of life also are present and an affair that promised to be simple in its character has become one of uncommon importance, giving Batavia a distinction that few towns in the United States ever enjoyed. Rarely indeed have so many heads of the great departments of the general Government been assembled together in a town outside of the National Capital, and rarely have so many other men, eminent in public affairs and in ecclesiastical circles, met on the same day to participate more or less conspicuously in the same event.

Batavia extends a cordial welcome to all these guests and to the thousands of spectators who are within its gates. Batavia is proud of their presence and hopes that the impression they may gain of this village, long established but filled with the enterprise and enthusiasm of youth, may be to its credit. Genesee county, the mother of counties, also acknowledges the honor that is inseparable from the advent within her boundaries of so many men of reputation and so many of those who occupy the lands that Morris sold.

(*Buffalo Express.*)

Yesterday's dedication of the Holland Land Office to the memory of Robert Morris was a National affair. While the great financier whose latter days were clouded with embarrassments and saddened by imprisonment for debt had not much to do with the settlement of Western New York, yet, had the efficient committee which planned and so admirably carried out the celebration stopped at lesser lines the ceremonies would have been local, and Western New York would not have been linked with the history of the Nation in so marked a manner.

It was no small undertaking which Batavia's people so successfully carried out yesterday. Planned on broad lines and executed without a hitch, the people of Genesee's county-seat have every reason to feel proud of what they accomplished. The presence of members of the Cabinet lent the affair National importance in addition to its historical interest. And among some of the invited guests were lineal descendants of the great Morris.

(*Batavia Spirit of the Times.*)

Next Saturday, October 13, the people of Batavia will dedicate the old Holland Land Office in this village as a historical relic, it having been purchased by the Holland Purchase Historical Association, which has made provision for its preservation to future generations. They will be assisted by distinguished citizens from other places, and the celebration will include a very elaborate and entertaining programme.'

The principal address of the occasion will be delivered by the Hon. John G. Carlisle, Secretary of the Treasury. Other Cabinet members who are to be present are Postmaster-General Bissell and Secretary of War Lamont. Others are expected.

The programme includes an extensive pageant that will illustrate American history and modern progress. A great choir of several hundred voices will sing at the dedication ceremonies. The railroads offer special rates and ample provision has been made for a large number of visitors. The preparations for the celebration have been going on for months.

On the Sunday evening preceding the Fourth of July, 1893, the Rev. C. A. Johnson, pastor of the First Baptist church, conceived the idea of holding a patriotic Union service in his church. A meeting was held to take steps in the matter and among those present was Mr. Kennedy. The speakers were unanimously in favor of teaching the rising generation the lesson of patriotism. Mr. Kennedy upon being called upon to speak, among other things said that the material landmarks of a Nation's history were of the utmost importance, as they served to awaken vividly the memories of bygone struggles and to stir and call out the sentiment of patriotism. He cited as instances the residence of Washington at Mt. Vernon, Old Faneuil Hall, the "Cradle of Liberty," and the headquarters of Washington at Newburgh and Tappan. Those structures were fortunately secured from private ownership and placed under public protection to be preserved through long years as reminders of the revolutionary struggles. While no one could appreciate those buildings and their associations more than he did himself, yet there was a structure in Batavia, here in our very home, neglected and overlooked and idly passed by, that stirred him even more profoundly than the structures already alluded to—the old Holland Land Office. Continuing on that subject he so impressed his audience with the grandeur of the old building that an interest was awakened that has grown slowly but surely and at last has resulted in accomplishing his object, the saving and restoring of the old building. Mr. Kennedy did not let the matter drop at that point, however, but throughout the year contributed many articles to the newspapers bearing on the subject ; keeping the matter constantly before the public mind until his arguments took effect. Great credit is due him for the energetic way in which he has pushed the work through to a successful ending.

The first sign of interest shown by the public in the saving and restoration of the Holland Land Office was when Upton Post. G. A. R., of Batavia, on the evening of Friday, July 28, 1893, held a special meeting for the purpose of taking action and starting a movement for the preservation of this relic of the Revolution and bygone years. The meeting resulted in the members of that body resolving that an attempt should be made to obtain possession of the structure and if this could be done it could be put in repair and a Historical Society formed to take possession of it. This was the first practical step taken, the result of which has terminated so successfully.

On the evening of Tuesday, August 1, 1893, a fair-sized gathering of Batavia's representative citizens assembled at the rooms of the Board of Education in the Walker Block to take further action. Daniel W. Tomlinson, President of the Bank of Batavia, stated the object of the meeting and called for suggestions. William C. Watson who had shown great interest in the project was called upon and stated that the property in question was owned by R. R. Lawrence. Two years ago, he said, the property had been offered for sale for $1,800; $400 of that sum had been pledged, but the owner having become aware that an attempt was being made to secure the property, raised his price to $2,000 and the scheme dropped through. On motion of Dr. J. W. Le Seur a committee was appointed consisting of W. C. Watson, D. W. Tomlinson, J. H. Ward, John Kennedy, and C. A. Hull to formulate a plan of action and devise means to secure the building. The matter drifted on for over a month, but at last, on the afternoon of September 18, the committee met at Lawyer Watson's office and after considerable discussion it was decided to raise the sum necessary by popular subscription, making the minimum amount $1 and the maximum $10. Preparations were made to circulate the subscription papers. While this was being done an option was secured on the property for $1,850, the option to expire October 20, 1893. The plan of the citizen's committee was to raise the $850, paying that down and giving a mortgage for the balance. The members having charge of the subscription papers pushed matters vigorously, but up to within a week of the expiration of the option only $500 of the $850 had been secured. The balance, however, was secured, and on the morning of November 13, 1893, a deed was filed in the County Clerk's office conveying to Daniel W. Tomlinson the Land Office property, the consideration being $1,850. A mortgage of $1,000 was executed and the balance paid in cash. From that time on the subscriptions have been constantly flowing in, as each one makes the donor a charter member of the Holland Purchase Historical Society.

A meeting was held on Friday, January 12, 1894, to discuss the details preparatory to drawing up articles of association, constitution and by-laws. A draft of a constitution and by-laws was made, and an adjournment taken until Tuesday of the following week. On that day the committee met but transacted no business beyond deciding to appoint Mrs. Dean Richmond President of the Society. On Tuesday evening, February 6th, a meeting was held and incorporation papers were prepared to be sent to Albany. The society it was decided should be known as the Holland Purchase Historical Society. Officers were elected as follows: President, Mrs. Dean Richmond; Vice-President, William C. Watson; Recording Secretary, Herbert P. Woodward; Corresponding Secretary and Librarian, Arthur E. Clark; Treasurer, Levant C. McIntyre; Managers, Gad B. Worthington, the Hon. George Bowen, Frank B. Redfield, John Kennedy, Mrs. Adelaide R. Kenney, John H. Ward, Daniel W. Tomlinson, Julian J. Washburn, and George D. Weaver.

Mrs. Richmond accepted the Presidency upon condition that she should not be called upon to discharge any of the duties of the office. The Hon. R. A. Maxwell was requested to persuade Secretary Carlisle to dedicate the building at some future time. He promised to use his influence in that direction. A few weeks later Mrs. Richmond received a letter from the Secretary stating that he would be pleased to dedicate the building.

About July 17th, Vice-President Watson named a general committee to make arrangements and prepare a programme for the dedication. The committee is as follows: Dr. J. W. Le Seur, chairman; Hon. Safford E. North, Frank S. Wood, Daniel W. Tomlinson, Hinman Holden, Dr. H. J. Burkhardt, Louis B. Lane. J. J. Patterson, E. A. Washburn, A. W. Caney, John H. Yates, John H. Ward, Frank B. Redfield, F. A. Lewis, John McKenzie, A. W. Skelley, Fredd H. Dunham, C. A. Snell, D. D. Lent, C. R. Winslow, A. E. Clark, R. S. Lewis, W. E. Webster, Dr. Ward B. Whitcomb, G. S. Griswold, J. A. Le Seur, John M. Hamilton, A. J. McWain, William C. Watson, J. H. Bradish, J. F. Hall, B. R. Wood, J. C. Barnes, Nelson Bogue, W. D. Sanford, H. T. Miller, C. W. Hough, D. Armstrong, Dr. C. L. Baker, F. E. Richardson, A. D. Scatcherd, M. H. Peck, Jr., C. Pratt, E. A. Dodgson, Delos Dodgson, C. H. Dolbeer, Rev. J. H. Durkee, S. Masse, Rev. Thomas P. Brougham, Arthur Ferris, Rev. C. A. Johnson, Carlos A. Hull, John Dellinger, S. A. Sherwin, W. T. Eagar, H. O. Bostwick, John Glade and J. W. Holmes. The General Committee appointed the following sub-committees: Committee on Ways and Means, Committee on Reception, Ladies' Auxilliary Reception Committee, Programme Committee, Printing Committee, Press Committee, Railroad Committee, Committee on Invitations, Committee on Decorations, Committee on Music and Committee on Flowers. Upon these committees has devolved the work of bringing order out of chaos and making the dedication possible.

(*Buffalo Evening Times.*)

In the latter part of July, 1893, Prof. Kennedy's work began to bear fruit. Members of Upton Post, G. A. R., held a special meeting to devise means whereby the old land office could be preserved to future generations. It was the sentiment of those present that a Historical Society should be formed and that the building should be purchased of its owner, R. R. Lawrence.

On November 13th, 1893, the sum of $850 was paid to Mr. Lawrence, and the property, subject to mortgage, was turned over to D. W. Tomlinson, who was selected to act as trustee for the Association which had been determined upon but had not yet been organized. Less than two weeks later a meeting was held to discuss details and draw up articles of association. A constitution and by-laws were drafted and then those present adjourned for a week. When they met again the following officers were elected: President, Mrs. Dean Richmond; Vice-President, William C. Watson; Recording Secretary; Herbert P. Woodward; Corresponding Secretary and Librarian, Arthur E. Clark; Treasurer, Levant C. McIntyre; Managers, Gad B. Worthington, the Hon. George Bowen, Frank B. Redfield, John Kennedy, Mrs. Adelaide R. Kenney, John H. Ward, Daniel W. Tomlinson, Julian J. Washburn, and George D. Weaver. Mrs. Richmond agreed to accept the place of honor provided she was excused from active participation in the duties of the office. Her request was granted and the burden fell on the shoulders of Mr. Watson. How well he has discharged the onerous duties is shown by the success which attends to-day's celebration.

(*Batavia Spirit of the Times.*)

To the Hon. R. A. Maxwell, Fourth Assistant Postmaster-General, who is an honored resident of this town, Batavia has good cause to extend her thanks, as it may be said that it was through his courtesy and efforts that the attendance of the distinguished visitors, who will be present at the dedication, was obtained. Although Mr. Maxwell is a very busy man, he has still found time from his duties to lend a little assistance to his town, and what he has done is greatly appreciated. The assistance which he rendered the Hon. Safford E. North, who went to Washington in the interests of the general committee of the Holland Land Office, was invaluable. Mr. Maxwell left his work at that time and conducted him to the different offices of the members of the Cabinet; exerting his influence wherever needed cheerfully and gladly. The citizens of Batavia extend to the General their sincere thanks.

(*Rochester Democrat and Chronicle.*)

A Patriot Honored. Batavia dedicates the first memorial to Robert Morris, Financier of the Revolution. The Holland Land Office becomes a national monument. A memorable celebration. Historical address by Secretary of the Treasury Carlisle. Other members of the President's Cabinet in attendance with their families. A great array of distinguished visitors. Imposing parade. The affair was a success in every particular.

(*Rochester Union and Advertiser.*)

In memory of Robert Morris. Dedication of the Old Holland Land Office. The greatest day Batavia has seen. Address of Secretary Carlisle. Members of the Cabinet present. Robert Morris' acts in the Revolutionary war rewarded. At noon Secretary Carlisle unveiled the tablet amid great cheers. The parade. Reception of the Cabinet members.

(*Buffalo Courier.*)

Batavia's day. Robert Morris honored. Streets thronged with twenty thousand people. An interesting parade. Rain drenched the procession, but did not deter it from carrying out the programme mapped out for it. Hosts of distinguished visitors from far and near. Secretary Carlisle's masterly oration. The celebration was decidedly a success and the Land Office was formally dedicated. Many Buffalonians present at the ceremonies.

(*New York Sun.*)

Tribute to Robert Morris. Dedication of the Old Holland Land Office in Batavia. Secretary Carlisle recalls the history of the man to whom he said, the people were indebted more than to any other man in civil station for the successful termination of the Revolutionary war. All that he had he consecrated to his country and never hesitated to use his personal credit to promote success.

(*Batavia Daily News.*)

In memory of Morris. Impressive dedication of the Old Office in Batavia of the Holland Land Company. Honor to the Financier. First tribute in America to the earliest Secretary of the Treasury. His successor orator of the day. Address delivered in the State Park by the Hon. John Griffin Carlisle. Six Cabinet members in town. Other prominent men attracted here by the ceremonies of the occasion. This is a day unparalleled. Streets filled with people and buildings gay with flags and bunting.

(*Rochester Post-Express.*)

This is a notable day for Batavia. Never was such a gathering seen in the village before. Never was the place so gaily decorated and never before was seen in its streets such a parade. As everybody knows the occasion was the dedication of the Holland Purchase Land Office. Business is suspended and all Genesee and neighboring counties are witnessing the interesting celebration. All the members of President Cleveland's cabinet are here except Secretary Morton.

The great feature of the morning was the parade which was the largest and most imposing ever held in Genesee county. Every interest, educational, industrial, religious and civic was represented in the line. The various organizations were loudly cheered. In front of the Land Office the parade was reviewed by the officers of the day and distinguished guests. The tablet erected to the memory of Robert Morris was here unveiled and a prayer of dedication delivered by Rt. Rev. Bishop Stephen Vincent Ryan, of Buffalo. The order of parade as follows:

Advanced guard of mounted men under command of W. L. Colville; aids, George Douglass, L. A. Terry and M. S. Dunlap.

Marshal and Staff.

Marshal, James A. Le Seur; chief of staff, I. D. Southworth; adjutant, L. L. Crosby; orderlies, J. F. Read and Burt Williams; marshal's staff, C. S. Pugsley, A. D. Lawrence, Collis Samis, Asher Davis, Harry Ames, Frank Harris, Will Torrance, Roy Barringer, George Parish, Frank and Will Lusk.

First division—G. W. Stanley, assistant marshal. Aids W. W. Plato, Dwight Dimock, and Walter Chaddock.

Sixty-fifth Regiment Band and Drum Corps,
National Guard,
G. A. R. Posts,
Sons of Veterans,
Continental Drum Corps,
High School Cadets,
Clerks from Erie County Clerk's Office,
Indian Band,
Indians.

Second division—Captain Timothy Lynch, assistant marshal. Aids, James McMannis, John Leonard, William Burnes and P. Buckley.

Select Knight's Band,
C. M. B. A.
C. B. L.
A. O. H.
Le Roy Total Abstinence Society,
St. Aloysius Society.

Third division—F. Lewis, assistant marshal. Aids, Ira Howe, William H. Walker and I. W. White.

Citizens' Band,
Johnston Harvester Company,
Wiard Plow Works,
Ott & Fox,
Batavia Wheel Works,
Wood Working Company,
Cope Brothers,
L. Uebele.

Fourth division—C. H. Reynolds, assistant marshal. Aids, Wolcott Van DeBogart, C. B. Avery, Ed. Moulthrop.
Le Roy Band.
Le Roy Chemicals.
Bergen Fire Department.
I. O. O. F.,
A. O. U. W.,
Turners.
School Children.

Fifth division—G. A. Wheeler, assistant marshal. Aids, R. J. Page, Lewis Johnston, George Constable.
Bergen Band,
Pioneers in Carriages,
Officers in Carriages.

The school boys made a splendid impression, their drilling being really excellent. They received great applause all along the line. The only Rochester organization in line was the Eighth Separate company, Captain H. B. Henderson commanding. They had 50 men in line and made a very creditable appearance.

Many of the displays in the industrial part of the parade were splendidly decorated floats illustrative of the growth of Batavia and its commercial importance. The Johnston Harvester company had an immense display, one covering over a quarter of a mile.

The exercises at the park of the State Institution for the Blind this afternoon were impressive and interesting. Following is the programme:

Selections ....
By the Sixty-Fifth Regiment Band.

Music—To Thee, O Country........................John Eichburg
Chorus.

Prayer...
By Rt. Rev. Arthur Cleveland Coxe, Bishop of Western New York.

Music—Zion, Awake.....................................Costa
Chorus.

Dedication Poem.....................................John H. Yates
Read by the Author.

Music—O Columbia, Columbia Beloved,................Donizetti
From Lucretia Borgia.
Chorus.

Address ....Hon. John G. Carlisle

Music—America ....
Chorus.

Closing prayer and benediction by Rev. Philos G. Cook, the oldest clergyman on the Holland Purchase.

(*Buffalo Courier.*)

Batavia was filled with people yesterday as it had not been even on circus, election, or general training day since the corner-stone of the old Holland Land Company's building was placed. The people came from all directions, save from above and below, and they came in all manner of conveyances known to Genesee county. They came on the first trains in the morning and on the last trains in the afternoon; they came on foot, on horseback, in old-fashioned high-box buggies, in lumber wagons, in two-wheeled carts drawn by seven-foot steers, in band-wagons, and in every sort of conveyance that could be pressed into service. And in spite of the rain they continued to come till the busy little town was busier even than was the revered Robert Morris when he was trying to lift thirteen bankrupt colonies, burdened by a war with the richest nation on earth, from depths beside which the Slough of Despond was but a mud puddle.

(*Buffalo Evening Times.*)

In years to come when the question is asked, "What was the greatest day in the whole of Batavia's history?" the answer, without hesitation and with truth, will be, "October 13, 1894."

If the interrogator has his curiosity aroused to a sufficient degree by this prompt reply to still further pursue the subject and inquire why the date above all others marked an epoch in the life of the village, he will be told that it was the day on which the office of the Holland Land Company was dedicated to the memory of that distinguished patriot, Robert Morris.

Should the stranger be a guest, his hospitable host will suggest that they visit the spot where the historic structure stands. If, as they walk along the busy streets, for by this time Batavia will have attained to the dignity of city-hood, the resident falls into a gentle reverie as a flood of recollections sweeps over his memory, surely he may be pardoned for his momentary lapse of courtesy.

* * * * *

He will tell how the Secretary of the Treasury, John G. Carlisle of Kentucky, prepared and delivered an exhaustive review of Robert Morris's life and career, and how the effect of this discourse was heightened by all the arts of oratory for which this distinguished statesman was justly celebrated. He will tell how various organizations from the surrounding country aided by their presence in making the day a success; how the village was decorated with gay colors, and how thousands upon thousands of visitors poured into Batavia until the old town was a mass of surging humanity.

By this time the old building will have been reached, and as they pass through its portals and enter the rooms in which are displayed and neatly catalogued the various relics of the early century, the Batavian with lowered tones, but unlessened enthusiasm, will tell the salient points connected with the history of each, and thus his guest will in a few minutes absorb and mentally digest a great deal of valuable data.

As they turn away from the dead past to the living present the guest will thank his host for the pains he has taken, and assure him that the remembrance of the pleasure he has experienced from this visit to the old structure will remain with him to the end of his days.

(Rochester ~~~~~ Chronicle.)

In they came from the country and the city; came in pairs and singly, came in carriages and lumber wagons; came on foot and came in palace coaches.

By 10 o'clock the streets were streaming with people, young and old, rich and poor. At the Lehigh station, where Secretary Carlisle and the ladies of the cabinet were expected to arrive, the crowd was densest and the impatience of the visitors grew strongest. From the break of day, too, the hybrid bands and regulars, the hose and fire companies, the cadets and high school boys in festival array, the floats and carriages, the men, boys and children, who were to take part in the parade, joined their discordant music and commands with the murmuring voice of the crowds, and blocked the thoroughfare here and there by their numbers. Boys and countrymen and countrywomen crowded and jostled each other in their eagerness to see and understand each and every new feature, and the crowds swayed. Ten thousand strangers were crowded into the environs of the village, and great was the day.

(Bessie Chandler.)

For years I've stood alone disgraced,
  'Mid the surrouding villas,
And foolish boys with birthday knives,
  Have come and hacked my pillars

And lovers, lingering at me,
  Have hurt me to the marrow
By carving two ill-shaped hearts,
  Pierced by a crooked arrow.

And though I've tried to hold my own
  I could not help but mutter,
When first a chimney'd tumble down,
  And then I'd drop a shutter.

With all the insults I have borne,
  My old blood burns and tingles;
It's hard to proudly rear your head,
  When you have lost your shingles!

But now, all this is past, is gone,
  I wake,—or am I dreaming?
Is this respect, this honor mine,
  Or only empty seeming?

It is no dream, I live again,
  And time's increasing treadle
The wheel of Fortune turns once more,
  And now I've got a medal!

My portrait from a cup shines forth,
  Yet on a spoon looks richer,
It lurks within a pickle dish,
  It gleams upon a pitcher!

They tell my story far and near,
  With many different versions
They hold committees every night,
  They're going to run excursions!

And all the things that once were mine
They're busy relic hunting,
And swept and garnished I shall be,
And all dressed out in bunting.

Far, far away those old days seem,
When I was first erected,
And it is sweet in one's old age
To be once more respected.

So now, brace up, oh peaked roof!
Stand fast, oh oaken portal!
Instead of slipping in the creek,
We're going to be immortal!

(*Batavia Spirit of the Times.*)

Handsome souvenirs of the occasion have been prepared, among them being the medallion. It is of aluminum, a trifle larger than a silver half dollar, and shows on one side a picture of the old Holland Land Office surrounded by the words, "Holland Purchase Land Office, Erected 1804." The following inscription appears on the obverse side. "Dedicated to the memory of Robert Morris, Patriot and Financier of the Revolution, Batavia, New York, Oct. 13, 1894." Handsome souvenir spoons are also on sale. These spoons are made of sterling silver, the handle being convex both back and front, and showing on the front the coat of arms of the State of New York, and the words "New York" down the shank of the handle. The Land Office appears in the bowl in fine hand engraving and etching. In addition to the above a large line of fine souvenir china is on sale, which consists of cups and saucers, bonbon trays, olive trays, cream pitchers, pin and pen trays, comb and brush trays, bread and milk sets, fruit plates, salad bowls, etc. The articles are all of fine Limoges china, finished in white and gold, and each piece has a photograph of the old Land Office underneath the glaze.

(*Buffalo Express.*)

A large delegation of Buffalo people went to Batavia on the morning trains. As the ceremonies themselves were commemorative of an occurrence so ancient in point of time, as time goes in these modern days, it was proper that every Buffalonian should have a lineage as old as possible. So everyone was decorated with a neat orange badge reading: "1804—New Amsterdam —1801."

Buffalo took so prominent a part in the day's proceedings that even the Cabinet officers were wearing these badges before the day was over.

Some of the Buffalonians, however, could do even better than the badges indicated. First there were representatives of the Holland Sons of New York. Every member of this Society can trace his lineage back through the male line to some Hollander who was a resident of the colonies prior to 1675. Members of this Society present were Sheldon T. Viele, Peter P. Burtis, Dr. F. P. Van Denbergh, Robert L. Fryer, J. M. Provoost and Judge A. A. Van Dusen of Mayville.

The Sons of the Revolution were represented by Sheldon T. Viele, C. K.

Remington, W. Y. Warren, E. S. Warren, E. B. Guthrie, C. R. Wilson, George Clinton, T. B. Carpenter, T. C. Welch, Harrison Granger, Dr. J. T. Cooke, Harvey W. Putnam, Walter Devereux, George A. Stringer.

Among the Sons of the American Revolution were Andrew Langdon and John Otto.

The Sons of the Colonial Wars were represented by Dr. Percy Brant and others.

The Historical society delegation was headed by President Andrew Langdon, George S. Hazard, James O. Putnam, W. C. Bryant, H. S. Hill, George Townsend, E. C. Sprague and Dr. Joseph C. Greene.

Various other Buffalo societies and organizations were also represented. Among them was a party of titlesearchers. The presence of these men was very appropriate, for of all residents of Western New York none has more often to go back to the time of Robert Morris. They deal with his deed of all New York west of the Genesee River to the Holland Land Company in their daily business.

Documents of rare historical value were also taken to Batavia from Buffalo. They comprise the original Morris deed and all the papers and correspondence pertaining thereto, which are now the possession of the Buffalo Historical Society, thanks to the efforts of Mr. George S. Hazard, ex-president of the Society, and to the kindness of Maj. Glowacki of Batavia, the last agent of the Holland Land Company. These papers were sealed in a large tin box and placed in charge of a guard of twelve men of the 65th Regiment, commanded by Sergt-Maj. Philcox. On arrival at Batavia they were taken to the Land Company's office and placed in a large glass case. At the end of the day they were resealed and, still under guard, were returned to Buffalo last night.

Seventy-nine officers and men of the 65th Regiment, under command of Capt. A. C. Lewis and Lieuts. L. L. Babcock and Theodore Beecher, and the 65th Regiment Band also went down.

Col. Welch, Quartermaster Putnam, Maj. A. H. Briggs, Capt. Clarence Wilson, Capt. G. Reed Wilson, Capt. Harry Mead and Lieut. William F. Fisher also went down in uniform, but did not parade.

(*Batavia Daily News.*)

Henry I. Glowacki and Leander Mix are now the only residents of Batavia who were employed by the Holland Land company. Mr. Glowacki entered the employ of the original company in 1834 while David E. Evans was the Local Agent. He was 21 years of age and though sixty years have passed he recalls many interesting reminiscences of those days.

Mr. Glowacki was one of the little band of Polish exiles, who landed in New York in the early thirties after having known the miseries of prison life for engaging with his compatriots in the Polish revolution in which the effort was made and failed to throw off the yoke of Russia. Born of parents in the higher walks of life he had received a good education in his native land and when he came to America he had letters of introduction to some of the most influential citizens. Through these letters he became acquainted with many prominent people and in passing through Batavia with a company of distinguished men on the way to Niagara Falls he met David E. Evans, who offered the young patriot a position in the Holland Land Office. Though unable to speak or read English at the time Mr. Glowacki could copy papers and draw maps by following copy, and he made himself useful and soon acquired a knowledge of the English language.

While serving as a clerk he studied law and was admitted to the bar and afterward, when the new owners of the land took possession, he acted as attorney for the Farmers' Loan and Trust company. While he was a clerk in the Land Office the exciting times of the Land Office war transpired and he, Robert W. Lowber, who is a resident of Bald Mountain, Washington county, and to-day is Mr. Glowacki's guest, Leander Mix, and a man named James Backus, then employed by Heman J. Redfield were entrusted with the duty of taking charge of the sleighs in which the records of the Land Office were transported to Rochester for safe keeping in the winter of 1836, when the attack of the disgruntled land owners was anticipated. When the danger from the mob had passed the same persons took the teams and brought the books back from Rochester.

Mr. Mix, whose home is on Mix place, was 79 years old on September 19th last. He is in vigorous mental and bodily health and remembers much that is of interest connected with the pioneer times.

(*Batavia Daily News.*)

The members of the Reception committee who went to the Lehigh Valley depot to greet the members of the Cabinet upon their arrival were D. W. Tomlinson, J. J. Washburn, William C. Watson, Arthur E. Clark and Frank B. Redfield. The Washington special consisting of a locomotive and two sleepers followed the Express train which arrives from the east at 10:05. While the regular train stood at the station the Buffalo train came in on the eastbound track and while the committee were waiting the portly form of Postmaster-General Bissell appeared between the baggage and day coach of the westbound train down at the west end of the platform. The members of the committee immediately recognized him and by the time they reached the car steps Mrs. Bissell had joined her husband. General and Mrs. Bissell stood on the platform for some moments awaiting the coming of the special, which drew in as soon as the regular train pulled out. The first of the Washington party to step off the train was General Maxwell, who looked hearty and well.

It seemed as if the clouds had broken away just to give the distinguished guests a cheery welcome. Secretary-of-War Lamont and Mrs. Lamont followed from the rear car and Secretary-of State and Mrs. Gresham, Secretary-of-the-Treasury and Mrs. Carlisle, Secretary-of-the-Navy Herbert and his daughter Mrs. Micou, Mrs. Thurber, wife of the President's Private Secretary, Secretary-of-the-Interior Hoke Smith, General Frank H. Jones, First Assistant Postmaster-General, and the Hon. Thomas P. Benedict, Public Printer, appeared from the platform between the two cars. It took but a moment to place the distinguished visitors in carriages put at the disposal of the committee by residents and they were all driven at once to the Hotel Richmond.

The Lehigh regular from the east brought Mr. and Mrs. John B. Church of Geneva, and Mr. and Mrs. S. Fisher Morris of Eckman, W. Va., who were driven immediately to the Richmond in Mrs. Dean Richmond's carriage. General Peter C. Doyle of Buffalo and General Northern Superintendent Beach of the Lehigh Valley arrived on the eastbound train.

When the hotel was reached an enormous crowd pressed about the ladies' entrance and some difficulty was experienced in keeping a passage way opened, but in a short time all the distinguished visitors were disembarked and went to their quarters in the hotel.

The members of the Ladies' Reception committee who greeted the Cabinet ladies were Mrs. Robert A. Maxwell, Mrs. D. W. Tomlinson, Mrs. Trumbull Cary, Mrs. F. B. Redfield, Mrs. Dr. Hutchins, Mrs. George Bowen, Mrs. S. E. North and Mrs. W. C. Watson. The Cabinet ladies were introduced by Mrs. Maxwell.

At 4:30 o'clock this afternoon all the Cabinet officers and their wives will hold a public reception in the parlors of the Hotel Richmond to which all are invited.

The Cabinet party, with the exception of Postmaster-General and Mrs. Bissell, who will depart tonight for Washington, will leave Batavia over the Lehigh Valley road at about 8 p. m., for Niagara Falls, where they will spend Sunday, leaving to-morrow evening on their return to Washington. Quarters for the guests have been engaged at the Cataract House by ex-Collector O. W. Cutler.

(Buffalo Express.)

The parade was largely Batavia's, too, and here, as elsewhere, Batavia did itself proud.

Led by the marshal, James A. Le Seur, the procession started south on State street towards Washington avenue and continued east on Washington avenue to Vine street, south on Vine street to East Main and west on Main to the Land Office on West Main street. First came the Genesee county mounted men with W. L. Colville as commander. The 65th Regiment Band headed the militia, the Eighth Separate Company of Rochester having the right of line inasmuch as its commander, Capt. Henderson, is the senior captain in the State service. Next followed the 65th detachment, the G. A. R. posts, including delegations from Attica, Le Roy, Bergen, Corfu, Akron and Johnsonburg, the Sons of Veterans, Continental Drum Corps, High School Cadets, followed by the Indian band bedecked in war paint and feathers, which one old settler seemed to regard with a feeling akin to awe as he recalled the days when the Indians were but partly initiated into the society of the Pale Face. This division was commanded by Capt. G. W. Stanley, who was on Gen. Sheridan's staff during the war.

The second division also made a good showing. It was headed by Capt. T. Lynch and staff. First came the Select Knights' Band, followed by the Catholic Mutual Benefit Association, the Catholic Benevolent Legion, the Ancient Order of Hibernians, all of Batavia, assisted by visiting societies; the Le Roy Catholic Total Abstinence Society, and the St. Aloysius Society of St. Joseph's church, assisted by a band of orphans from Rochester.

The third division was headed by Frank Lewis, assistant marshal and staff. For this division the Citizens' Band rendered the music. This was the division of industrial displays and was viewed with keen interest. The Johnston Harvester Company's display occupied about half a mile. It came first and was followed by that of the Wiard Plow Company, Ott & Fox, the Batavia

Wheel Company, the Wood Working Company, Cope Brothers and L. Uebele.

The fourth division was commanded by C. H. Reynolds, assistant marshal and staff. The Le Roy Band furnished the music and was followed by the Le Roy Chemicals, the Bergen Fire Department, the Independent Order of Odd Fellows, the Ancient Order of United Workmen, the Turners, and the school children.

The fifth division was led by G. H. Wheeler, assistant marshal and staff. The music for this division was rendered by the Bergen Band and was followed by a line of pioneers in carriages and officers in carriages.

The industrial display attracted the most attention. The Johnston Harvester Company made a fine display. First came a pair of oxen hitched to one of the primitive reapers and binders, and this was followed by the most modern and magnificent pieces of mechanism turned out of this enormous factory. There were about fifteen machines and various sizes of each kind. On a large platform wagon, covered with straw, were about a dozen Batavia young ladies attired in the garb of the pioneer days, 100 years ago. This was followed by the sugar cane cultivator, in which Hoke Smith was interested.

(*Rochester Democrat and Chronicle.*)

The display which passed through Batavia's principal thoroughfare as between two solid columns of red, white and blue, received from the Washington party unstinted praise. Under the difficulties with which they had to contend, it was a magnificent display and the originators of the various novelties deserve great credit for their enterprise.

(*Rochester Democrat and Chronicle.*)

The State park presented an appearance similar to none which has ever been witnessed within the confines of Batavia's borders. For a time all seemed chaos and confusion, but when the command was given to march, things immediately assumed an appearance of order, and the parade, led by the marshal, James A. Le Seur, started south on State street towards Washington avenue, and continued east on Washington avenue to Vine street, south on Vine street to East Main and west on Main to the Land office on West Main street, followed by a mass of humanity, which had great difficulty in passing through a compact jumble of humanity, who preferred to stand while the parade passed.

(*Rochester Democrat and Chronicle.*)

The decorations at the State park, at the Land Office, and all along the streets of the embryo city, were of the most elaborate description.

At the Land Office the decorations were in keeping with the other displays in the village. The small stone structure which served the Holland Company for its offices was one blaze of color, with the pillars and cornices sheathed in the national ensign. Above the gable peak which shades the porch was perched an eagle above a national shield with quiver and arrows astant.

At the State park the decorations in bunting and flags were in abundant evidence. The speakers' stand was draped in red, white and blue. The grand stand and press box were also covered with streaming bunting and the national colors.

(*Rochester Union and Advertiser.*)

The procession was over an hour passing the reviewing stand.

(*Batavia Daily News*)

Assistant Marshal Frank Lewis and staff headed the division and were followed by two men in Continental uniform bearing aloft a streamer on which was inscribed: "The Continental Light Battery of the Johnston Harvester Company." The Citizens' band came next and then followed the magnificent display of machinery manufactured by the Johnston company, the display being over a quarter of a mile in length. The advance guard consisted of three pioneer farmers on foot, who bore in their hands a scythe, a hay rake and a grain cradle, all labeled "1804." They were followed by a rude ox cart constructed from pieces of small timber with the bark left on and drawn by a yoke of oxen. On this cart was one of the first mowers made by the company in 1854. It had but one wheel and a rigid cutting bar, and the wood and iron work showed the effects of time.

The present period, 1894, came next being represented by one of the company's "Continental" mowers, with all the up-to-date improvements. It was drawn by three blanketed ponies, two abreast and one ahead. The parts of this machine were painted in red, white and blue and decorated with bunting, as were all of the machines in the display. Its driver wore a Continental uniform and so did nearly all of the drivers. A "Continental" reaper, with four rakes, drawn by a pair of horses, whose driver was dressed in Turkish costume, was next in order, and that was followed by three mowing machines with a 5, 6 and 7 foot cut, each drawn by two horses. Then came the "King of Reapers," with five rakes drawn by two horses, whose driver wore the dress of a Russian peasant.

A beautiful float, 14 feet long and eight feet wide, drawn by four horses whose driver was "Uncle Sam" followed. It was gayly decorated with the national colors and on it were nine young ladies. One of them was attired to represent the Goddess of Liberty and the balance wore the costumes and bore the flags of the foreign countries in which the company sells many machines; England, France, Germany, Russia, Turkey, Argentine Republic, Spain, and Denmark.

Next came a cotton cultivator, drawn by a pair of mules with a colored driver, and that was followed by a wheel corn cultivator and a sugar-beet harvester, each drawn by two horses, and a beet cultivator with eight spiders, drawn by one horse. A seven-foot-cut twine binder, with gaily decorated high reel with a double star on its outer end, was drawn by three horses abreast. The "Bonnie," a new harvester and binder which has just been put on the market by the company, and which has a six-foot cut and is only 5½ feet high, came next, being drawn by two light carriage horses, whose blankets bore the date "1894." On the bundle carrier were sheaves of grain. This was followed by a "Continental" pulverizer and a new diamond frame Vineyard harrow, each being on trucks and drawn by two horses.

Next came a curiosity in the shape of machinery in this section. It was a monster header, used for cutting only the heads from grain, a machine made for the South American trade and called in that country "La Espigadora." It cuts a swath 12 feet wide and was in operation. It was pushed, instead of drawn, by four white horses, with two drivers and a steerer.

The last feature of the display was a monster float sixteen feet wide and thirty feet long, drawn by eight well matched horses. From the outer edge of the float to the ground bunting was draped and a heavy nickel railing surrounded it with steps leading up from the ground on either side. From the railing on one side the words "The Johnston Harvester Company" in gilt letters were suspended, and on the other "Batavia, N. Y., U. S. A." At each corner was a silk banner bearing the name of the company, and three American flags were displayed. In the center of the float, on a revolving pedestal, were four frames containing medals received by the company. Grouped about were two moulders at work, a blacksmith and his helper at a forge, a carpenter at his bench, a machinist working a drill and another at a vise, a painter at work, a box maker making packing crates, a finisher and a packer boxing parts, and an expert testing a binder tire. From elevated seats George and Martha Washington in miniature watched the workmen.

The Wiard Plow company's display excited much admiration. First was a float of novel construction. It was 12 feet high in the center and was stepped down on either side. On the summit were grouped plows, weeders and corn planters, and on the steps on each side were beautifully finished plows. The float was covered and decorated with white cloth and bunting and was covered with a peculiarly shaped canopy formed of many-colored fabrics. It was drawn by four horses wearing blankets on which were inscribed the words: "The Wiard Plow Company, Established 1856." The float was followed by a Wiard wheel rake, gayly decorated and drawn by one horse.

Ott & Fox, blacksmiths, were in line with a novel display. On a large float decorated with bunting and drawn by two horses, was a forge and anvil and blacksmiths were at work making horseshoes.

Next came two floats representing the Batavia Wheel company's industry. The first, which was drawn by four horses, was ten feet wide and twenty-four feet long. It was surrounded above the floor with a decorated railing and below was trimmed with evergreens. At the front end of the float was a revolving wheel, thirteen feet high, trimmed with flags and bunting, and four men were at work on it—one at a forge, another welding tire and the remaining two doing handwork on wheels. The second float, which was handsomely decorated and drawn by two horses, had on it a pyramid of beautifully finished wheels.

The Batavia and New York Wood Working Company's display was very appropriate and attracted much attention. It was a float about twelve feet long with bunting on the sides, wood rosettes in the center and bunting-decorated wheels. Six posts were erected from the sides of the float and various colored shavings were festooned between them. It was drawn by two horses wearing brass-mounted harness which was also decorated with shavings. On the float were half a dozen cabinet-makers, wearing aprons and caps, and making picture frames for cabinet-sized pictures, which were distributed to the crowd, together with butter pats, cups and saucers and rolling pins turned from wood.

O. G. & W. E. Cope, pump manufacturers, were the next in line with a good-sized float, nicely trimmed. It was drawn by four horses. At the forward end was a complete display of the wood pumps made by the firm, in the center were the iron force-pumps for which they are agents, one of them being in operation, and in the rear were an old oak pump constructed in 1794 by an ancestor of the firm, an old well crotch and "the old oaken bucket."

W. C. Underhill, clothier, was out with his advertising wagon drawn by a yoke of oxen. On top of the wagon was a mechanical figure which created much amusement. J. B. Fonda and A. E. Brown also had advertising wagons in line.

Batavia Union School.

(*Batavia Spirit of the Times.*)

The project began to drag and seemed in some danger of falling through, when the class of '94 of the Batavia High School took hold of the matter, and by raising $300 made the purchase of the building possible.

(*Rochester Post Express.*)

The school boys made a splendid impression, their drilling being really excellent. They received great applause all along the line.

(*Rochester Union and Advertiser.*)

The High School Cadets made a fine showing. They are considered the best drilled company of boys in the State.

(*Buffalo Express.*)

The High School Cadets were up long before daylight and donned their neat blue-and-white Continental uniforms. The veterans brushed their blue uniforms and polished their badges. The women folks got breakfast out of the way bright and early. Then the last touches were given to the house decorations. If there was a building in the entire town which did not have its trappings of red, white and blue, it must have been somewhere out of sight. Batavia was decorated as it had never been before. American flags and bunting was everywhere. Every house was hung with them. Every part was wrapped with them. Every man, woman and child wore from one to a dozen badges and a proud smile. For wasn't Batavia to become famous from this day forth in the annals of the land? Certainly. The members of the various committees were everywhere. They had much to do, and did it all well.

People from the surrounding towns poured into Batavia early. The first big delegation by train was that from Buffalo. The famous old Continental Drum Corps and the High School Cadets met the guard of the Morris deed and escorted it to the Land Office.

(*Buffalo Courier.*)

The High School Cadets marched to the quickening music of the Continental Drum Corps. They are a fine-looking company of 60 young students who were commanded by Captain William Homelius. The boys wore natty and showy Continental knee breeches of white, dark blue coats, trimmed with white, with straps and black hats. The Corps gave ample evidence all along the route of march of the efficiency of its drill and executed well numerous movements which elicited round after round of applause.

(*Batavia Daily News.*)

The Continental Drum Corps, ten men, and the High School Cadets, numbering sixty, came last in the division. Dean Hickox was captain of the Cadets and William Hooker, Lieutenant.

The celebrated Continental Fife and Drum corps attracted lots of attention. Of the ten members who are present six are over seventy years of age, the oldest being Snare Drummer Edwin Rowley, a veteran of the Black Hack war. Three of the drums used saw service in the Revolutionary war. The corps was reorganized from the old 184th Regiment drum corps, which disbanded in 1841, and six of the members of the old corps are members of the present organization. The leader and Drum Major is George W. Carr of Buffalo, aged 60 years. The musicians were costumed in Continental uniforms.

Behind the corps marched sixty excellently drilled High School Cadets, looking very handsome in their bright Continental uniforms.

(N. A. Woodward.)

I can see him now—as I saw him then,
When I was a lad—and my years but ten.
Though the years have sped and my beard is gray
I can see him now as I did that day;
That aged miller—whose locks thin and white,
Were fanned by a breeze that was cool and light,
At eventide of a summer's day,
When the old grist mill had ceased to play,
And the over-shot wheel no longer rolled round,
With a splash of water, and rumbling sound;
When the King of day with a shining vest,
Behind the green hill retiring to rest,
Cast a golden gleam o'er the sky's deep blue,
As he bade the world an evening adieu,
Then he came forth from that old brown mill,
That stood by the race that ran down the hill ;
With his ruddy cheeks and his look serene,
His full round chest and his martial mien.
Though his garb was white with flour and dust,
He looked like a man a nation could trust.
The music he loved and had from a boy,
Was the shrill toned fife—his solace and joy,
And he played it still ; and at close of day,
When the old mill ceased its jarring play,
Its whirring around with a rumbling sound,
While many a grist for neighbors was ground.
In "Seventy-six" with his fife in hand,
Then a lad—he joined the patriot band,
Who periled their lives that this might be,
From thenceforth called "The Land of the Free."
Though then too young to take up arms,
He sought a place mid war's alarms.
The thicker the bullets around him flew,
The louder his shrill toned fife he blew,
And its piercing tones gave the patriots cheer,
For the fifer showed no signs of fear ;
And that fife was heard on the left and right,
Wherever occurred the thickest fight.
That war was a long and weary one ;
But it ceased at last, when freedom was won;
And the lad, a youth, unharmed went home,
But clung to that fife—where'er he might roam,
In the war with England which next occurred,
That warlike fife at the front was heard,
He marched at the head of a martial band,
That played for the men who fought for the land,
Warlike and stirring were the tunes he played,
When battalions stood in battle arrayed;
Sad and mournful were the notes for the dead,
When a comrade's tears for the slain were shed.

He went through the war with never a wound
Became a miller—and many grists ground;
Yet, still played the fife, and at close of day,
In front of the mill, would stand and play.
I can see him now as I saw him then,
When I was a lad and my years but ten;
Though the years have sped and my beard is gray,
I can see him now as I did that day;
That aged fifer with locks thin and white
Blown back by a breeze that was cool and light,
And the tune he played was a dirge for the brave,
It was called, he said: "Napoleon's Grave;"
So mournful the notes, that they touched my heart;
And he played them too, with such magic art,
That I saw before me a great man dead,
Who had lately stood at a nation's head;
A soldier of fortune who had won renown,
A coffined hero, who late wore a crown,
Who fought great battles, his last battle o'er,
And monarchs shall dread his frown nevermore
An august warrior—so mighty and brave,
About to be laid in the cold, damp grave,
And I saw them place the turf o'er his head,
As they laid him to rest in his lonely bed,
On a rocky isle—where the sobbing surge,
And the wind's sad wail, are his only dirge.

* * * * *

The musical notes of that tuneful fife,
Oft heard by the brave, in the battle strife,
No longer are heard in front of the mill,
For that mill is gone,—it hath passed away—
The tooth of time hath wrought its decay;
The grists at the mill, no longer are tolled,
By that robust miller—so brave and bold;
At four score and ten, the good man died.
They laid him to rest—his fife by his side,
For he loved it still, with his latest breath,
And they parted them not, in sable death.
A plain marble slab now marks the place,
A worthier monument ought to grace.

(*Buffalo Express.*)

The party from Washington was expected over the Lehigh Valley shortly after 10 o'clock. It was near 11 o'clock before Messrs A. E. Clark, F. B. Redfield, D. W. Tomlinson and J. J. Washburn of the Reception Committee were enabled to put on their best smile and shake the hands of the distinguished Government officers and raise their hats to the ladies. The party was speedily driven to the Hotel Richmond, where they greeted a number of friends. Postmaster General Bissell and wife were there to receive them. In the party were Secretary and Mrs. Gresham, Secretary and Mrs. Carlisle, Secretary and Mrs. Lamont, Secretary Herbert and Mrs. Micou, Secretary Smith and the wife of Private-Secretary Thurber ; Gen. Jones, First Assistant Postmaster-General ; Robert A. Maxwell, Fourth Assistant Postmaster General, and Public-Printer Benedict. State-Treasurer and Mrs. Colvin were also present.

Among noteworthy guests of the day were Fisher Morris and wife of

West Virginia, Robert Morris of Pottsville, Pa., and Mr. and Mrs. John B. Church of Geneva. Their interest was more direct and personal than that of any other persons present, for they are lineal descendants of Robert Morris, and they thus were able to participate in ceremonies attendant upon the erection of the first and only monument to the memory of their famous ancestor.

Politics were barred on this trip. Great pains had been taken to make this fact known. The man who said, "Well, how's politics?" would have seen the Secretary addressed vanish into thin air. Even Secretaries Bissell and Smith, big as they are, could have done the trick. This rule is to be

strictly adhered to until the party gets back to Washington. It won't even talk politics at Niagara Falls to-day.

At the Central and Erie depots the distinguished guests were welcomed by the following official committee: The Hon. John M. McKenzie, Dr. H. J. Burkhart, J. H. Bradish, C. H. Dolbeer, A. D. Scatchard, F. S. Wood, the Rev. A. M. Sherman, the Rev. Thomas Cardus and Dr. W. B. Whitcomb.

All distinguished visitors immediately on their arrival were driven to the Richmond Hotel, where they were welcomed by the following special Reception committee: The Hon. George Bowen, the Hon. Edward C. Walker, the Hon. H. F. Tarbox, D. Armstrong, J. H. Ward, John Thomas, W. D. Sanford, George W. Lay, C. W. Hough, Byron E. Huntley, E. W. Atwater, George Wiard, Holden T. Miller, John F. Ryan, B. R. Wood, John M. Seacord, Myron H. Peck, Jr., Dr. W. T. Bolton and Andrew T. Miller.

(*Batavia Spirit of The Times.*)

The following resolution was adopted: "Resolved, that every community in Western New York be requested to raise the American flag at 12 o'clock sharp, in recognition and honor of the great event, as it is estimated that the parade will be completed by that time, and that the unveiling of the tablet will take place at that moment.

(*Rochester Union and Advertiser.*)

It was at high noon. Whistles screeched, guns boomed, and flags dipped. The drums of many bands rolled a long reveille and the trumpets shrilled a mighty fanfare. The long procession of men stood with uncovered heads. Horses, looking gay in gorgeous trappings, pawed the ground nervously and champed their bits impatiently. And above this impressive scene from horizon to horizon line hung a dark, forbidding sky of wind swept gray. The big hands of the clock in the red church tower clasped and pointed to the hour. It was high noon. And at that moment, amidst this impressive demonstration, Secretary Gresham touched the button and the veil that shrouded the large white tablet in the Holland Land Office parted and fell at the feet of the Cabinet officers grouped about with uncovered heads.

Then in fitting, eloquent, almost burning words, the Rt. Rev. Stephen Vincent Ryan, Bishop of Buffalo, delivered the dedicatory prayer.

There was a long silence until the last words of the Bishop had trembled away, and then the bands all broke into melodies, and men cheered and women waved their handkerchiefs, small boys jumped about and yelled, whistles screeched. It was a great moment. And just for a moment the sun pierced the tissue of leaden clouds and smiled on the white tablet dedicated to the memory of Robert Morris.

Here, in a little village in Western New York the people have, after many long years, honored the name of a great man. In striking contrast is the neglected weed grown grave in an obscure corner of a Philadelphia cemetery, where is confined the dust of the man who did as much as any man to win the war of the Revolution.

(*Rochester Democrat and Chronicle.*)

The marble tablet, which now proclaims to the world that Robert Morris is not to be forgotten by his country is set in the Land Office wall directly above the front entrance. It is two feet wide and four feet long, and has the following inscription upon it in large letters :

ERECTED 18—.
DEDICATED 1894.
TO THE MEMORY OF
ROBERT MORRIS.

(*Buffalo Express.*)

The tablet on the Land Office Building was still to be unveiled before the morning's exercises came to an end. Great crowds thronged down to West Main street. The building was first opened yesterday as a museum, and already contains a number of valuable historical relics, prominent among which are the great iron doors which once swung to and fro on the vaults of the Holland Land Company. Of course, the next interesting feature of the display was the papers brought from Buffalo by the Historical

Society. Crowds had thronged the building during the morning, but when the hour for the unveiling of the tablet arrived, the building was cleared. The clouds broke away at this time, and it promised to be fair for the remainder of the day.

The ceremonies were very brief here. No speeches were made. Mr. J. W. Le Seur introduced Secretary Gresham as the one to unveil the tablet over the entrance. As Judge Gresham pulled the strings attached to the two small American flags which hung over the tablet, the sun came out and flooded it with golden light. The tablet is about two feet square, and bears this inscription:

ERECTED ———.
DEDICATED 1894.
TO THE MEMORY OF
ROBERT MORRIS.

It had been supposed that the building was erected in 1804, but on search it was found that no trustworthy record was in existence, and so the date of erection is left blank.

(*Buffalo Courier.*)

When the last of the procession had passed in review the Cabinet officials, including Secretaries Gresham, Carlisle, Smith, Lamont, and Bissell took places upon the platform before the Land Office and with them the Rt. Rev. Bishop S. V. Ryan and Chancellor Sheahan of the diocese of Buffalo, Chairman of General Committee Dr. J. W. Le Seur, County Judge North, and other distinguished personages. Dr. Le Seur introduced Bishop Ryan, who offered the dedicatory prayer. The venerable and beloved clergyman braved weather that would have caused a much younger and hardier man to shrink, and his expression of thanks for the past, appreciation for the present, and hopes for the future was in every way what the occasion required. Secretary of State Gresham entered the Land Office and pulled the cord that drew from before the tablet over the door the American flag which draped it. The 65th Regiment Band played, and that part of the programme was completed.

(*Batavia Daily News.*)

By 11:20 o'clock, when the head of the procession passed the Land Office, fully 2,000 people had assembled in the vicinity of that building. The distinguished guests reached the reviewing stand in front of the building at 11:30, being brought in carriages from the Richmond.

Exactly at 11:40 o'clock Chairman Le Seur of the General Committee announced the opening of the unveiling exercises and the Sixty-fifth Regiment Band rendered a selection. Secretary Gresham then stepped to the entrance to the Land Office and pulled aside the flags which concealed the tablet over the doorway, which announced that the building was dedicated to the memory of Robert Morris.

Bishop Ryan of Buffalo was then introduced by Chairman Le Seur. When the venerable prelate stepped to the center of the platform the sun appeared and shone brighter. In his invocation the Bishop referred to the early struggles of the infant nation for freedom and referred to Robert Morris as one whose patriotism and generosity did so much in furthering the righteous cause which he espoused. He prayed that the blessing of the Deity might fall upon the monument dedicated to-day, upon the nation, and upon all those in authority.

After the prayer the exercises were brought to a close with a second selection by the band.

The distinguished guests then entered and inspected the interior of the Land Office, passing between ranks of Sixty-fifth Regiment soldiers, and afterwards returned to the Richmond.

(John H. Yates.)

DEDICATION POEM.

When to the banks of Jordan's rolling tide
   The hosts of God from far off Egypt came—
With cloudy pillar their long march to guide,
   Past Sinai's awful mount of smoke and flame.

They found no passage the dark waters o'er,
   No way to cross the overflowing stream,
And Israel's warriors stood upon the shore
   But could not reach the Canaan of their dream.

Then Joshua, their leader, strong and true,
   Lifted his voice and soul to God in prayer,
While angel hands the billows backward threw,
   And made a passage for God's people there.

The ark of God moved on at his command,
   And forward moved the host o'er Jordan's bed ;
Their feet as dry as when, through burning sand,
   Their weary way the cloudy pillar led.

Then reared they high a monument of stones,
   To tell to generations yet unborn
How he, the King of Kings, on throne of thrones,
   Held back the waters on that glorious morn.

In after years, when sunny youth inquired
   " What mean these stones ? " the gray haired fathers told
The story that again their bosoms fire'd,
   The story of deliv'rances of old.

Before us stands this monument of ours,
   That hath these many years the storms withstood ;
Reared 'mid the perfumes of the forest flowers,
   In shadows cast by monarchs of the wood.

Reared on the banks of Ton-a-wan-da's stream,
   Which, fed by living springs and rippling rills,
Winds down the vale as gentle as a dream,
   From the blue domes of the Wyoming hills.

Reared at the junction of two Indian trails,
   Where chieftains met to seal some white man's doom ;
While war cries mingled with the night wind's wails
   And council fires lit up the forest's gloom.

To-day, when sunny youth of us inquires
  "What mean these stones?" we stop with pride to tell
Of wonders wrought by high Ambition's fires,
  And honest toil, o'er every hill and dell.

As sea shells sing forever of the sea,
  Though borne inland a thousand miles away,
So do these walls give forth to you and me
  The sounds and songs of our forefathers' day.

I hear the echo of the woodman's stroke
  Resounding through the aisles of forest gray ;
The crash of giant elm and sturdy oak,
  As they for towns and fertile fields make way.

I hear the stage horn's blast at close of day,
  The wheels that ramble o'er the rugged road,
While feeding deer affrighted speed away,
  To tangled thickets of their wild abode.

I hear the postman as he hastens here
  From forest op'nings, where the blue smoke curled,
O'er winding pathways, desolate and drear,
  Where now are beaten highways of the world.

The breaking twigs in thicket dense I hear,
  Where stealthy panther creeps upon his prey ;
The victim's struggle and his cries of fear,
  Which fainter grow, and die, at last, away.

I hear the whirring of the spinning wheel,
  The crackling of the logs on fireplace bright,
The scythe stone grinding on the blade of steel,
  The owl complaining through the lonely night.

I hear the merriments of olden times,
　The apple-parings and the husking bees ;
The laughter ringing out like merry chimes
　From rustic haunts beneath the forest trees.

"What mean these stones?" They tell of honest men,
　Who lived in years now flown away,
Who toiled for us with hammer, plow, and pen,
　From rosy morn until the evening gray.

Their grandest castles, builded in the air,
　When they at noon sought rest in shady dell,
Were not, though fancy painted, half so fair
　As these in which their children's children dwell.

We now enjoy the fruitage of their toil,
　From where the Genesee's bright water's flow,
To where Niag'ra's billows in turmoil
　Plunge o'er the precipice to depths below.

All honor to those noble men who laid
　The firm foundation of our wealth and pride !
They rest to-day beneath the maple's shade,
　All undisturbed by traffic's surging tide.

O, could they wake from slumber of the tomb,
　What changes would they note beneath these skies !
A wilderness transformed to Eden bloom,
　With wonders everywhere to greet their eyes.

What though their forms have crumbled into dust,
　Their deeds shall shine resplendent as the sun ;
What though their plowshares are consumed by rust,
　The work they wrought will never be undone.

All honor to that man who forward came
　In "times that tried men's souls," long years ago,
And gave his wealth and pledged his spotless name,
　To drive forever from our shores the foe.

The memory of Morris long shall stand,
　With honor crowned beneath these sunny skies ;
The sons and daughters of our favored land
　Will not forget his love and sacrifice.

'Twas he who wakened from their wild repose
　These hills and valleys, stretching far away,
That now unfold their beauty like the rose
　That gives its dew drops to the kiss of Day.

When armies faltered for the lack of bread,
　When bugles ceased to call and drums to beat,
He came with patriot heart and hasty tread,
　And laid his millions at his country's feet.

Freedom's immortal Declaration bears
　The name of Morris on its sacred page ;
With changing years his record brighter wears,
　While granite crumbles at the touch of Age.

Then dedicate this structure to his name,
　While music sweet floats out upon the air
These walls shall to the world speak forth his fame,
　And these fair valleys shall be still more fair.

　　　　*　　*　　*　　*　　*　　*

As sea shells sing forever of the sea,
　Bear them away from ocean where thou wilt,
So shall ye sing, O walls, through years to be,
　Of great success on firm foundation built.

The storms and tempests of the rolling years
  Have beat thy granite walls by night and day,
Yet thou hast stood, amid man's hopes and tears,
  To see the hands that made thee mould away.

Thou shalt remain to bid this land rejoice,
  Till these fair youths who gaze upon thee now
Shall speak thy praises with a trembling voice,
  When hoary hairs adorn each wrinkled brow.

The waves of progress which have swept away
  Thy brother landmarks, built of wood or stone,
Broke at thy feet and vanished into spray,
  And left thee, gray old monarch, here—alone.

" A thing of beauty " thou hast always stood,
  " A thing of beauty " thou shalt ever stand,
At first the glory of the lonely wood,
  But now the glory of the teeming land.

Sing on O walls, though years their changes bring,
  Sing on while all the bells of progress chime,
Sing of the past, of future glory sing,
  While thy quaint form defies the march of time."

(*Rochester Democrat and Chronicle.*)

The cabinet officers entered the Old Land Office on a tour of inspection. While within, the descendants of Robert Morris were presented to them. Their names are Fisher Morris of Virginia, a great grandson of the famous financier; Mrs. John B. Church, a great granddaughter; and Robert Morris, a great, great grandson, who hails from Pottsville, Pa. There were many ancient historical curiosities on exhibition in the old building, which were closely scrutenized by the members of the distinguished party. Each of the cabinet officers then signed the book and became charter members of the Holland Purchase Historical Society. A guard of soldiers was then placed outside the building.

(*Batavia Daily News.*)

Thousands of people visited the Land Office and inspected the many interesting relics exhibited there. As far as is known only one theft occurred there. A very old linen pillow case is missing.

Mr. and Mrs. Leander Mix were at the office during a portion of the day and entertained visitors with many interesting reminiscences of pioneer days.

At one time the crowd in the room on the east side of the hall was so great that the floor sunk about four inches.

(*Batavia Daily News.*)

Mrs. George W. Lay has presented to the Holland Purchase Historical Society a fine half life-size portrait of Red Jacket, from Wakeman's studio. J. C. Youngs has presented a corn mash, bread bowl and pappose holder made by Seneca Indians ; Thomas Cary of Buffalo a family tree of the Cary and Brisbane families ; Mrs. Royce of Batavia a spinning wheel, and F. B. Redfield and William Seaver four old fire buckets which belonged to H. J. Redfield and Seaver & Son.

(*Rochester Union and Advertiser.*)

The present structure is located just west of the Walnut street bridge on West Main street, which spans the Tonawanda creek, and faces the north. At the rear only a few yards back is the creek. The building itself has a frontage of about 46 feet and in depth is about 35 feet, the height being in proportion. The lot extends back to the creek. The structure is a two-story edifice, well lighted by large windows in the front, rear and sides. In the front is a quaint wooden porch. The floor of the porch is laid with flagging. The builders evidently intended that the structure should stand the storms of many years, building it of stone in the most substantial manner. As you enter the front door you find yourself in a roomy hall which divides the rooms, four in number, two on each side. The apartments are commodious and airy. The rooms above are practically the same, all well lighted as those below. All of the apartments are well supplied with closets for storing papers. In the rear room on the first floor on the west side can be seen the old vault with its iron doors locking with a key, which was used as a storing place in case of fire and robbery, of many valuable papers. It is only when the dusty garret is reached that the individual realizes the sturdy strength of the old building. There can be seen the massive oaken beams which were hewn out and remain to-day without a sign of decay to show that they were not just placed in position. The building stands to-day practically the same as it did years ago when first erected, time having caused but few changes, and as I will undoubtedly stand for years to come a monument to the skill of its builders. Of recent date a force of carpenters, painters and masons have been at work restoring it to its original state. A new roof has been put on, and the building thoroughly overhauled and repaired. A cement walk has been laid at the front, and the building now presents an entirely different aspect from what it did several months ago. The Holland Purchase Historical Society proposes to use it as a museum, storing historical relics connected with the Holland Purchase within its walls. The office was discontinued in 1837.

(*Batavia Daily News.*)

Lunch was served in the corridors of the Hotel Richmond at 1 o'clock. Among the distinguished guests who sat at the tables were Robert Morris of Johnsonburg, Pa., a great-grandson of Robert Morris, S. Fisher Morris of Eckman, W. Va., also a great-grandson of the distinguished patriot, and Mrs. Morris, who is a descendant of the family of George Washington ; Mr. and Mrs. John B. Church of Geneva, Mrs. Church being a descendant of Robert Morris; the Hon. Walter Q. Gresham, Secretary of State ; the Hon. John G-

Carlisle, Secretary of the Treasury; the Hon. Daniel S. Lamont, Secretary of War, th Hon. Wilson S. Bissell, Postmaster General, the Hon. Hilary A. Herbert, Secretary of the Navy; the Hon. Hoke Smith, Secretary of the Interior; First Assistant-Postmaster-General Jones, Public-Printer Benedict and the other invited guests as follows: The Hon. William Pool, editor of the Niagara Falls *Courier*; H. A. Dudley, editor of the Warsaw *New Yorker*; the Hon. A. G. Dow and his daughter, Mrs. Jackson, of Randolph; Mr. and Mrs. Charles M. Dow of Jamestown; William C. Bryant, John Otto and Miss Otto, descendants of Jacob S. Otto, second local agent of the Holland Company; Mrs. Ellen Stone, Mrs. M. A. Chase, Dr. Joseph C. Green, Mrs. Green and Miss Green, Thomas Cary and Miss Love of Buffalo, ex-Senator James H. Loomis of Attica, and many others.

Members of the Reception Committee who were present were D. W. Tomlinson, J. H. Bradish, J. H. Ward, M. H. Peck, Jr., Arthur E. Clark, Andrew T. Miller, J. J. Washburn, C. W. Hough, John M. McKenzie, and the following ladies of the Auxiliary Reception Committee: Mrs. George H.

HOTEL RICHMOND.

Holden, Mrs. W. C. Watson, Mrs. Hinman Holden, Mrs. Joseph F. Hall and Mrs. G. S. Griswold.

Dinner will be served by the same caterer at the same place at 5 p. m., 54 covers having been laid. The menu will be as follows:

Blue Points
Cream of Asparagus Soup.   Salmon, Hollandaise Sauce
                         Parisian Potatoes
                   Fillet of Mignon, with Mushrooms
                           Potato au Gratin.
                   Baked Cauliflower, with Cream Sauce
                           Maraschino Punch.
Roast Partridge, Madeira Sauce.   Lettuce, French Dressing.
                         Crackers and Cheese.
Fancy Ice Cream.   Assorted Cakes.
         Fruit.   Coffee

The tables are set in the form of a T on the Main street side of the hotel, and potted plants are prettily banked at the north end of the corridor. The rooms occupied by distinguished guests are also decorated with cut flowers and potted plants.

(*Buffalo Express.*)

Not the least pleasant side of the day was the various social courtesies extended. Shortly after 12 o'clock all the Cabinet officers were entertained at lunch served in the Hotel Richmond. The tables were spread in the parlors of the hotel and were handsomely decorated. The members of the reception and General Committees sat down. In the meantime the ladies of the Washington party were driven to the home of Mrs. D. W. Tomlinson, where they were graciously received by the hostess, who was assisted by Mrs. Robert A. Maxwell, wife of the Fourth Assistant Postmaster General. Luncheon was served here and then the ladies were driven to the State Park.

Another pleasant social event was the reception given the visiting newspaper men. The handsome rooms of the Alert Hose Company on Main street were set apart as press headquarters, and there a Committee headed by Postmaster Hall did everything possible to make them comfortable. The visiting G. A. R. posts were well cared for at the rooms of the local post, where the wives of the Batavia G. A. R. men furnished refreshments. The visiting soldiers were quartered at the Court house, where they were made at home.

(*Rochester Democrat and Chronicle.*)

Luncheon was ready for the Cabinet party when the members returned from the Land Office. The lunch was served in the corridors at the Richmond at 1 o'clock. There were many distinguished guests who partook of luncheon with the nation's officials. Among them were Robert Morris, of Pottsville, Pa.; S. Fisher Morris, of Eckman, West Virginia; and Mrs. Morris, who is a descendent of the family of George Washington; Mr. and Mrs. John B. Church, of Geneva; the Hon. William Pool, editor of the Niagara Falls Courier; H. A. Dudley, editor of the Western New Yorker, of Warsaw; the Hon. A. G. Dow and daughter, Mr. and Mrs. Chas. M. Dow, of Jamestown; William C. Brant, John Otto and Miss Otto, descendants of Jacob S. Otto, the second agent of the Holland Land Company; Mrs. Ellen Stone, Mrs. M. A. Chase, Dr. Joseph C. Greene, Mrs. Greene and Miss Greene. Thomas Cary and Miss Love of Buffalo; ex-Senator James H. Loomis, of Attica, and thirty or forty others. The following members of the reception committee were also present D. W. Tomlinson, Myron H. Peck, Jr., J. H. Bradish, J. H. Ward, A. E. Clark, A. T. Miller, J. J. Washburn, C. W. Hough, Hon. John M. McKenzie, and the following ladies, members of the reception committee: Mrs. William C. Watson, Mrs. Joseph F. Hall, Mrs. G. S. Griswold, Mrs. Hinman Holden and Mrs. George H. Holden.

(*Buffalo Express.*)

No better place could be imagined for a gathering like that of the afternoon than the beautiful State Park, the grounds surrounding the State Institution for the Blind. Here, on the broad and spacious lawn fronting the Institution, the speaker's platform had been erected. Two o'clock was the hour set for the main exercises of the day. By some mistake the sun was shining brightly, and people took heart and flocked to the park until there were 10,000 of them there. And 10,000 people are a good many in a town the size of Batavia. The young and the old, the fat and the lean, the townsman and the farmer—all were there. The executive officers of the land were to be there, and it isn't every day in the week that the populace has the opportunity to do honor to its servants. So everybody turned out. The gentlemen of the Washington party were entertained at lunch at the Hotel Richmond and the ladies at the home of Mrs. D. W. Tomlinson, so it was not until a quarter of 3 o'clock that the exercises began. At 2.20 the ladies drove up and everybody applauded. Then, headed by the 65th Regiment Band and the men of that command, the Cabinet officers and members of the various committees arrived. They, too, were applauded.

And the clouds were gathering.

One of the interesting features of this time was the presentation of old

NEW YORK STATE INSTITUTION FOR THE BLIND.

Leander Mix, whose picture is printed in this paper, to the Cabinet officers. Mr. Mix was one of the early agents for the Holland Land Company.

A selection, played by the 65th Regiment Band in superb style, opened the exercises. A chorus of 100 voices, under the direction of Prof. Crane, sang "My Country 'Tis of Thee" admirably.

And a few rain drops fell.

Evidently the weather man had been fooling everybody. But it was too late now to repent. The exercises must go on, rain or no rain. Prayer was offered by the Rt. Rev. A. Cleveland Coxe, Bishop of Western New York.

The reading of the dedication poem written by Prof. John H. Yates which is printed in full in the *Express*, was omitted, as were several musical selections.

Dr. J. W. Le Seur hastened to introduce Secretary Carlisle. He said:

Our honored guests and fellow citizens—The possibilities of yesterday have become the certainties of to-day. We meet to do justice to one who loved his country and counted no sacrifice too great to save her honor. It is especially gratifying to this society, and to every patriotic citizen that, amid the multiplied responsibilities of his official station, the worthy successor of the immortal Morris consents to pay tribute to his high character and noble services. I have the distinguished honor and special pleasure of introducing to you the orator of the day, the Secretary of the Treasury of our United States, the Hon. John Griffin Carlisle.

Secretary Carlisle put on a bold front and took off his high hat and his overcoat. He had been talking too long in public to mind a little thing like rainwater. He speaks easily, slowly, strongly, and impressively.

(*Batavia Daily News.*)

The singing of the chorus of a hundred voices was much enjoyed and showed careful training on the part of Professor E. F. Crane and ready reception of instruction on the part of the participants. Their selections were appreciatively received.

The chorus was made up as follows:

Sopranos—Mrs. E. K. Calkins, Mrs. I. E. Mecorney, Mrs. W. R. Durfee, Mrs. Fred H. Fargo, Mrs. P. Welch, Mrs. Charles Scott, Mrs. Sarah Peck, Mrs. C. B. Peck, Mrs. Bessie Carpenter, Mrs. Kate Crosby, Mrs. Lounsbury, Mrs. B. H. Bean, Mrs. Preston Case, Mrs. George Crofoot, Mrs. Lord, and Misses Ella Hirsch, Ida Kellar, Miriam Kellar, Emily Carr, Mary A. Lewis, E. Alice Smith, Edna King, Bessie Kellar, Emily Hartshorn, Gracia Morse, Minnie Ingersol, Frankie Ingersol, Cornelia Brownell, Rachael McNab, Mertie McNab, Lizzie Shepard, Ada Mockford, E. Maud Baker, Edith M. Knapp, Mertie Knapp, Grace Perkins, Lillian Hatch, Jessie Wallace, Cora J. Gardner, Alice Parmelee, Ora Rapp, Mary Poultridge, Mary Maltby, Ruth Benjamin, H. A. Langdon, Adelle Clark, Eva Milward, E. F. Wood, Nellie Day.

Altos—Mrs. W. C. Gardiner, Mrs. E. E. Leavenworth, Mrs. F. A. Lewis, Misses Clara Mills, Lottie Rogers, Mary Milward, Helen M. Iveson, Cora W. Palmer, Gertrude Cardus, Bertha L. Johnson, Agnes C. Rimmer, Hattie Hartshorn, Jean Brownell, Louise H. Morse, Nellie McNair, Blanche Lewis, Fannie Stanley.

Bassos—Henry Chiswell, Matthew Robinson, William Mills, E. H. Perry, William C. Gardiner, C. A. Snell, the Rev. Thomas Cardus, Lucius A. Parmelee, John C. Squires, Fred H. Fargo, E. E. Leavenworth, George W. Pratt, Myron A. Pratt, Myron A. Williams, W. H. Kearns, John Skehan, Harry C. Norton, Thomas Trick, Wilbur Trick.

Tenors—J. T. Whitcomb, Frank E. Howe, Clarence Meserve, George Mower, A. H. Plock, S. P. Stephens, E. I. Nott, Edward Gamble, Charles B. Peck, F. C. Chadwick, F. A. Lewis.

(*Progressive Batavian.*)

The platform was packed and there was a crowd of from 5,000 to 10,000 awaiting the speaker and distinguished guests when they arrived on the ground. The exercises opened with a selection by the 65th Regiment Band. The chorus of 100 voices followed with "Zion Awake." Chairman Le Seur then announced prayer by Rt. Rev. Bishop Coxe, who made these prefatory remarks:

"By a coincidence truly noteworthy, we have heard this week of the death of the last chieftain of the Iroquois; of General Parker, who shared the blood of Red Jacket, and who nobly united in himself the citizenship and soldiership of this Republic and that of the ancient race to whom these pleasant lands and lakes originally belonged. The last of the Senecas has just expired, and we are here to celebrate the life and character of him who is the true founder and father of Western New York, rearing a new society upon the graves of the Iroquois. I shall therefore make no apology for uniting in the memorial prayers which I have been called to offer some reference to the older race of whom the "Indian Summer" will annually remind us, and our children's children after us, while these autumn leaves falling around us may well recall the red men of the forest, whose blood seems to crimson the turf under our feet in the hues of scattered foliage which strews the ground. Let us pray."

The prayer which followed was very feeling and appropriate.

(*Buffalo Courier.*)

At 2.30 p. m. the State Park began to show signs of life and an hour later the meeting was called to order. When this had been dismissed the public formalities were over, save for the semi-private reception to the members of the Cabinet held at the Hotel Richmond at 4.30 p. m.

The crowd began to disperse about five o'clock, the Buffalo militia taking a special train for home at that hour. From then on the departures were many and frequent. The Cabinet party departed at eight o'clock over the Lehigh and went to Niagara Falls, where they will remain until this evening before retracing its steps to Washington.

Ample accommodations were provided for all, and the people of Batavia did themselves proud in providing for their guests. Mrs. Tomlinson of East Main street entertained the ladies of the Cabinet party at luncheon, and the ladies of St. James Episcopal Church saw to it that the Buffalo and Rochester soldiers did not lack for food.

Of all the entertainers Alert Hose Company No. 1 was at least the peer. This organization, desirous of adding its mite to the general time of rejoicing, took upon itself the tax of entertaining the representatives of the press. The parlors on West Main street were open from early morning till late at night, and food and drink and smoke were pressed upon every one entitled to enter the portals. The press of Western New York extends its thanks for many courtesies received from Alert Hose Company No. 1 of Batavia.

The decorations in general were good. Almost every place of business in the city was trimmed with flags, streamers, and bunting, and even the headstalls of the horses on the streets bore the National flag. Souvenir badges were as many as the dead leaves blown from the trees, and the person without at least one badge was the exception. All in all it was a great day, not greater than the occasion deserved, but still it was the greatest day Batavia ever saw.

(Buffalo Courier.)

The exercises at the park were scheduled to begin at 2 p. m. A large stand had been erected seating about 300 persons. About noon the rainstorm cleared and the sunshine somewhat drove away the gloomy aspect of the celebration. It had been decided, in case the rainfall continued, to hold the exercises in the Opera House. A crowd of about 7,000 persons assembled in the Park, and there were many seats vacant, hundreds of people preferring to stand. It was nearly 3 o'clock when the distin-

ON THE LINE OF MARCH—EAST MAIN ST.—IN FRONT OF THE TOMLINSON RESIDENCE.

guished guests and their ladies arrived at the Park escorted by the company of the 65th Regiment. As each Secretary was recognized by the people he was applauded enthusiastically. To the orator of the day was given a very warm welcome, and that to Postmaster-General Bissell was most cordial. Representatives were on the stand from the various societies, including a large number of the best known and most representative citizens of Buffalo and Western New York.

Among those who were introduced to the secretaries and the Postmaster-General was Leander Mix, an aged citizen of Batavia, who formerly was an agent for the Holland Land Company.

The assemblage was called to order by Chairman Le Seur of the General Committee who, after a selection by the 65th Regiment Band, and the singing by a chorus of Eichberg's "To Thee, O Country," introduced the Right Rev. A. Cleveland Coxe, who offered an appropriate prayer. The chorus sang, "Zion, Awake!"

Secretary Carlisle was then introduced. A demonstrative and heartily cordial welcome was given to him as he stepped to the front of the platform. He had spoken about five minutes when rain began to fall. The rainfall rapidly grew heavier and umbrellas went up. The Secretary had delivered about half of his oration when the storm became so severe that he was forced to cut off his address abruptly and the crowd dispersed.

(Rochester Democrat and Chronicle.)

At the State Park at 2:30 o'clock in the afternoon a concourse of people which is variously estimated all the way from 10,000 to 15,000, awaited patiently the arrival of the Washington party. Soon the procession, headed by the Sixty-fifth Regiment band of Buffalo, proceeded up Ellicott avenue and the honored guests and their wives and daughters, accompanied by the reception committee, proceeded to the platform, upon which were already seated fully 500 people, including about one hundred representatives of the press.

The ladies of the Washington party were assigned seats near the speakers stand. As each cabinet officer appeared upon the speakers' platform, he was greeted with applause. After the excellent selections had been rendered by the Sixty-fifth Regiment band, the chorus of 100 voices sang "To Thee, O Country."

Chairman Le Seur then introduced the Right Rev. Arthur Cleveland Coxe, Episcopal Bishop of Western New York, who offered prayer. The prayer lasted about ten minutes, at the conclusion of which "Zion, Awake!" was sung by the chorus.

The reading of the poem and further music, which was on the programme, had to be dispensed with, as all realized even then that a mistake had been made in not reversing the programme in order that Mr. Carlisle might get through with his speech before the rain again drove the people to shelter. It was evident to all that the ominous clouds which came rolling up rapidly from the west meant mischief, nor was this a mistaken impression. It was about 3 o'clock when Chairman J. W. Le Seur stepped to the front of the speakers' stand.

(New York Sun.)

Tribute to Robert Morris. Dedication of the old Holland Land Office in Batavia. Secretary Carlisle recalls the History of the man to whom, he said, the people were indebted more than to any other man in civil station for the successful termination of the Revolutionary war. All that he had he consecrated to his country and never hesitated to use his personal credit to promote its success. The history of the Holland patriot.

The morning of the day set apart for the dedication of the Old Holland Office building broke dark and threatening, but the gloomy outlook did not prevent the assembling of the largest gathering this village has ever witnessed. The normal population of 9,000 was by the influx of visitors from various sections of Genesee, Wyoming, Livingston, Niagara, Erie, and Orleans counties swelled to twice that number. Every train that came rolling in over the half dozen railroads that pass through or have their terminus here brought filled coaches. Among the delegations was a band of Tuscarora Indians, 100 in number, dressed in native costume.

Promptly on time the Lehigh train, bearing the members of the Cabinet and others from Washington, rolled into the depot. The distinguished visitors were welcomed by a reception committee and escorted to the Richmond Hotel. The party was made up of Secretary Gresham, Secretary and Mrs. Carlisle, Secretary and Mrs. Lamont, Secretary Herbert and daughter, Secretary Smith, Assistant Postmaster-General Jones, and Fourth Assistant Postmaster-General Maxwell. Postmaster-General and Mrs. Bissell arrived from Buffalo on a morning train, and joined the party at the hotel, where a reception was held.

Following the reception the distinguished visitors were driven to a stand in front of the Land Office, from which they reviewed a parade of civic and military organizations. Then the unveiling of the tablet took place, followed by a prayer by Bishop Ryan. The tablet is of marble, 2 by 4 feet in size, and contains the inscription:

ERECTED 18—
DEDICATED 1894
TO THE MEMORY OF
ROBERT MORRIS.

The exact year is left blank because it is found impossible to determine in what year the building was completed. At the conclusion of the ceremony of unveiling the tablet the visitors were entertained at luncheon, the ladies by Mrs. D. W. Tomlinson at her residence, and the gentlemen at the Hotel Richmond. After luncheon the ladies were driven to the State Park, where, with the Cabinet officers, they occupied seats on the stand.

The weather had cleared, and the sun was shining brightly. The exercises at this point began promptly at 2 o'clock with selections by the Sixty-fifth Regiment band of Buffalo. "To thee, O Country" was then sung by a chorus of one hundred voices, and Bishop Coxe followed with prayer. The song of "Zion Awake" was next sung, and was followed by the reading of the dedication poem by John H. Yates, the author. The chorus sang "O, Columbia, Columbia, Beloved." Secretary Carlisle then delivered his address. He said:

(Honorable John G. Carlisle.)

Robert Morris, or, as he was sometimes called, Robert Morris, Jr., was for many years one of the conspicuous figures in the galaxy of great men whose statesmanship and courage achieved the independence of the American colonies, and to him more than to any other man in a civil station, the people were indebted for the successful termination of the Revolutionary war.

It is characteristic of the martial race to which we belong to appreciate to the fullest extent, and frequently to overestimate, the services of the successful soldier, while simple justice is not always done to the quiet statesman and financier, without whose co-operation and support the armies of the greatest commander could neither make a movement nor fight a battle. The most ordinary military operations are more dramatic, and therefore more attractive to the common mind, than the patient and laborious achievements of the civilian, but they cannot be conducted without money or credit, and the man who contributes these essential elements to the aggressive force of a nation has at least as strong a claim to the admiration and gratitude of

HON. JOHN G. CARLISLE

his countrymen as the man who plans campaigns and directs the movements of armies and fleets. So long as the people of the United States hold in grateful remembrance the names and deeds of Washington and his brave associates in arms, they ought not to forget the services of the merchant-financier who, at a most critical period in their history, substantially created and sustained the credit without which the most heroic efforts of these patriotic soldiers would have been unavailing; and yet, although a century has elapsed since Robert Morris finished his public work and retired to private life, and nearly ninety years have passed since his death, there is no public memorial to attest the people's appreciation of his great services, and very few even know the place of his burial. Nearly seventy years ago his earliest biographer concluded a sketch of his life in these words :

"The memory of a man of such distinguished utility cannot be lost ; and while the recollection of his multiplied services are deeply engraven on the tablet of our hearts, let us hope that the day is not distant when some public monument, recording the most momentous occurrences of his life, and characteristic of national feeling and gratitude, may mark the spot where rest the remains of Robert Morris."

Monuments of bronze and marble have been erected in every part of the land to perpetuate the fame of the men who were associated with him during the war and afterwards, so that even their forms and faces are almost as familiar to us as the forms and faces of our nearest friends, but this hope of his early biographer has not been realized. In nearly every park and public place in our great centers of population there stands the figure of some hero or statesman of the revolutionary period, and in nearly every household there hangs a picture commemorative of the person or the services of some prominent actor in the troublous times which preceded the establishment of our independence ; but neither the figure nor the portrait of Robert Morris is among them.

It is alike creditable to the patriotism and the liberality of the citizens of Western New York that they have organized the first public association and inaugurated the first practical movement for the purpose of paying a long-deferred tribute to the memory of a man who, notwithstanding all the malignant accusations made against him while in the public service, has left a record in which the critical researches of a hundred years have failed to discover a trace of dishonor or any lack of unselfish devotion to the true interests of his countrymen. I esteem it a great privilege to be with you in person upon this occasion and to have my name connected with yours in this patriotic movement ; and especially do I consider it a great honor to be invited to say something concerning the life and services of the first Secretary of the Treasury, or, as he was then called, the Superintendent of Finance. While the proprieties and, in fact, the necessities of the occasion forbid elaboration of statement, or even a simple recital of all the public acts of Robert Morris, it will still be possible, I hope, without trespassing too long upon your patience, to present at least such an account of their character and value as will fully justify this spontaneous effort on your part to honor his memory, not only as an able and patriotic public official at a time of great peril and distress, but as a private citizen, personally associated in his latter years with the local history and early development of this and the adjacent country.

Robert Morris was born at Liverpool, England, on the 31st day of January, 1734, new style, and, according to a statement in his father's will, came to America in the year 1748. His father, also named Robert, was a native of the same place, and is said to have been originally a nail maker, but afterwards became a merchant. Precisely when he came to America is not known, but at the age of 30 he became a resident of Talbot county, Maryland, on the eastern shore of Chesapeake bay, where he continued to reside until 1750, when he was accidentally killed by the discharge of a cannon, which was fired in his honor as he was leaving a ship on which he had gone to attend a social entertainment. In this will, which is dated April 17, 1749, after making some bequests to other persons, the testator says:

"I give all my lands and tenements whatsoever whereof I shall die siezed in possession, reversion or remainder, to a youth now living with my friend, Robert Greenway, in Philadelphia, known there by the name of Robert Morris, Jr., who arrived at Philadelphia from Liverpool some time in the year 1718; and to him the said Robert Morris, Jr., now living with Mr. Robert Greenway, merchant, at Philadelphia, I give and bequeath all the lands and tenements I shall die possessed of forever; and I likewise give

IN FRONT OF THE SPEAKER'S STAND.

to the said Robert Morris, Jr., all the rest and residue of my goods, chattels, merchandise, apparel and personal estate whatsoever."

At the time of his father's death Robert Morris was about 16 years old, and was employed in the mercantile house of the Willings, who were at that time perhaps the largest merchants in Philadelphia. He remained with them until 1754, when he and Thomas Willing, a young member of the family, formed a partnership, which continued without interruption for nearly forty years. Although an Englishman by birth, he promptly identified himself with the friends of the colonies in the controversy between them and his mother country, and in 1765, ten years before the battle of Lexington he signed the non-important agreement and was a member of the committee of citizens which waited upon the collector of the stamp tax to compel him to vacate his office, which he did after considering the matter for two or three days. In 1766 he was warden of the port of Philadelphia, and in 1775, when the quarrel between the colonies and Great Britain had almost reached the point where reconciliation upon any reasonable terms was impossible, he was appointed on the council of safety for the state of Pennsylvania. In October of the same year he was elected a member of the provincial assembly under the old charter, and in November the assembly appointed him one of the delegates to the Continental Congress. The next year, 1776, he was again elected to the assembly under the new Constitution of the State, the old charter and the old assembly having been abolished by a mass meeting and a revolutionary committee. On the 20th day of July, 1776, he was again chosen as a delegate to the Continental Congress, although he was known to be opposed to the Declaration of Independence and had voted against it, believing with many other good and patriotic men of that period that the opportunity for reconciliation upon terms which would preserve the liberties of the people had not yet entirely passed, and that an effort to effect an adjustment ought to be made before engaging in a war which was certain to entail great hardship, and which was not certain to be successful. In a letter written on the day of his second appointment to the Continental Congress, he defined his position upon this subject, and, in vindication of his patriotism and fidelity to the cause of his country, I think a very brief extract from it ought to be read. He said,

"I have uniformly voted against and opposed the Declaration of Independence, because in my poor opinion it was an improper time, and will neither promote the interests nor redound to the honor of America; for it has caused division when we wanted union, and will be ascribed to very different principles than those which ought to give rise to such an important measure. I did expect my conduct on this great question would have procured my dismission from the great council, but find myself disappointed, for the convention has thought proper to return me in the new delegation; and although my interests and inclination prompt me to decline the service, yet I cannot depart from one point, which first induced me to enter the public line. I mean an opinion that it is the duty of every individual to act his part in whatsoever station his country may call him to in times of difficulty, danger and distress. Whilst I think this a duty, I must submit, although the councils of America have taken a different course from my judgment and wishes. I think that the individual who declines the service of his country because its councils are not conformable to his ideas makes a bad subject. A good one will follow if he cannot lead."

In February or March, 1777, he was for the third time appointed a delegate to the Continental Congress. An attempt even to enumerate the various services rendered by him during his terms as a member of that body would compel me to omit many other important matters connected with his subsequent career, or extend this address to an unreasonable length. It is sufficient to say that from the beginning he was placed upon some of the most important committees, and was almost constantly called upon to assist in the conduct of financial affairs, not only by his advice and counsel, but by the use of his name and personal credit.

At that time there was no treasury department, nor any national executive organization of any kind. Early in 1779 the Continental Congress had appointed a standing committee, of which James Duane was chairman, to superintend the finances; but its functions were not well defined, and its duties, so far as it had any, were loosely and negligently discharged. By September, 1778, financial affairs had fallen into such a condition of confusion and disorder that Congress established five separate bureaus to assist in the management of the Treasury; but these bureaus quarreled with each other, and in 1779 an ordinance was passed establishing what was designated as a Board of Treasury, consisting of three commissioners, not members of Congress, any three of whom had power to transact business. By the spring of 1780, however, it became evident that the entire financial system must be reorganized upon a more substantial basis, and that there must be such practical management as would secure order in the public accounts

NEAR THE SPEAKER'S STAND.

and some degree of economy in the public service, or the war would prove a disastrous failure and the colonies relapse into a more hopeless condition of dependency than ever existed before. Almost every financial expedient that the ingenuity of man could devise, except regular and effective taxation, had been resorted to for nearly six years to raise money or procure credit for the prosecution of war, and at last the very verge of national bankruptcy had been reached, and it was evidently impossible to proceed a step farther in the same direction without a total collapse of the entire financial system, involving, of course, an abandonment of the struggle. The country was smothered to death under a mass of worthless paper currency far more disastrous to the own material and industrial interests of the people than all the spoilations and devastations committed by the invading enemy. The most discreditable chapters of our history are those which record the repeated and ineffectual efforts of the Continental Congress and the Superintendent of Finance, after he was chosen, to induce the States to raise their respective quotas of money necessary to carry on a war for the establishment of their own independence. The prevailing idea among the people seems to be that, inasmuch as the war was being prosecuted in opposition to the claim of Great Britain to impose taxes upon them, it would be illogical and inconsistent to impose taxes upon themselves. They preferred to rely upon continental notes, issued in anticipation of receipts which never came in, and upon bills of credit emitted by the States, which persistently refused to provide funds for their redemption. The several colonies had been in the habit, long before the Revolution, of issuing their own notes to circulate as money, and, therefore, the Continental Congress very naturally resorted to the same expedient, and the first notes, amounting to about three million dollars, were issued as early as 1775. These notes began to depreciate almost immediately, and before the close of the year 1776 many men were subjected to mob violence, to social and political ostracism and to imprisonment by the civil and military authorities for refusing to receive them in payment of debts, or in exchange for commodities. By 1779 depreciation had gone to such an extent that it was no longer safe to buy and sell in the ordinary way, while transactions conducted upon credit were ruinous to the party who rendered services or parted with his property. Barter was the only safe trade, and it is recorded that at one time it was substantially the only kind of trade carried on in the city of Boston. Prices went up so that a pair of shoes cost $100, and flour sold at prices ranging from $300 to $500 per hundred weight. The price of sugar reached $600 per hundred weight; coffee was $4 per pound, and wheat $75 per bushel, and the cost of most articles of necessity rose in the same proportion. General Washington said that a wagon load of money would scarcely buy a wagon load of provisions. But the currency in which payments were made was depreciating with such rapidity that the merchant who sold even at these exorbitant prices was constantly losing money. The injurious effect of a depreciating currency upon the trade of the country is illustrated in the case of a writer of that period, who says that he purchased a hogshead of sugar and sold it at a large profit, but the currency in which he was paid would buy only a tierce. He then sold the tierce at a large profit, but when he used the proceeds of this sale in making another purchase he got only a barrel. R. H. Lee wrote to Thomas Jefferson that the depreciation of money had nearly transferred his whole estate to his tenants, and that the rent of 4,000 acres of land would not pay for twenty bushels of corn, the rent, of course, being payable in money and having been fixed before the depreciation began.

Conventions were held in many parts of the country to establish scales of prices at which commodities should be bought and sold, and several States enacted penal laws upon the subject. Many merchants and others were punished by imprisonment and by exposure in the pillory for violations of these statutes and necessarily much ill-feeling was engendered among the people. The whole commercial fabric was in imminent danger of destruction on account of the superabundance of so-called money, and the government itself, which possessed unlimited power to issue it, was compelled to retrace its steps or be crushed under the weight of its own paper. I cannot undertake to describe the state of public and private demoralization which this condition of the currency produced. Extravagance, speculation, fraud and selfishness prevailed everywhere to an extent never known in this country before or since. It was the harvest-time of the dishonest public official, the unscrupulous debtor and the unfaithful trustee of private estates. The widow and orphan and the poor and dependent classes in all the walks of life were, as they always have been and always will be, the principal sufferers from every fluctuation in the exchangeable value of the currency. The rich and powerful can generally take care of their own pecuniary interests, no matter what kind of currency may be in use, but the poor, who are compelled to labor for the necessaries of life and to receive whatever is offered them in compensation, and the ignorant, who are always exposed to the seductive devices of the spec-

THE BACKGROUND OF THE SPEAKER'S STAND—AWAY TO THE "BLUE DOMES OF WYOMING'S HILLS."

ulator and the swindler, constitute the classes upon which the evil effects of a vitiated currency invariably fall with the heaviest weight.

At this time continental notes had been issued to the amount of $160,000,000, or about $53 per capita, and the depreciation was 30 to 1, that is $1 in specie was equal to $30 in the paper currency. By July, 1780, it was 64.12 to 1, and early in the next year the whole miserable system broke completely down, and Congress, with only one dissenting vote, resolved that all debts then due from the United States, which had been liquidated according to their value, and all debts which had been, or should thereafter be made payable in specie, should be actually paid in specie, or its equivalent, at the current rate of exchange between specie and other currency. The total issue of Continental notes up to that date, as nearly as can be ascertained, was about $242,000,000, or $80 per capita. But, besides this, the various States had issued large amounts in bills of credit, and there were outstanding large amounts of loan office certificates and quartermasters' and commissaries' certificates, which greatly aggravated the financial situation. It is said that in 1788 a single Spanish dollar would legally discharge a debt of $2,400 in the State of Virginia. The resolution of Congress was absolutely necessary in order to save even the semblance of public credit, and, although the Continental notes continued for a short time to circulate in some parts of the country, especially in the South, they passed for merely a fraction of their nominal value. It was evident to every one at all acquainted with public affairs that the finances of the country must at once be placed in more competent hands and conducted with more vigor and economy than had heretofore characterized their management, or that the war for independence would be brought to a speedy termination by the complete subjugation of the colonies. The opinion was quite prevalent, both in America and Europe, that the struggle could be maintained but a little while longer, and even General Washington had almost abandoned all hope of success. George the III and his ministers relied for success more upon the depressed financial condition of the United States than upon the aggressive operations of their army and navy. This was the condition of affairs when Congress, on the 20th day of February, 1781, unanimously chose Robert Morris to be Superintendent of Finance. His great ability and credit as a merchant, his intimate acquaintance with public matters generally, and especially his familiarity with the financial operations which had reduced the government to such a deplorable state of poverty and helplessness, constituted qualifications for this laborious and responsible position possessed by no other man in the country. The selection at once revived the hopes of the despondent, stimulated the courage of the wavering, and confirmed the faith of the friends of liberty in every part of the world. But he did not accept at once. He knew the magnitude of the task he was expected to perform, and he knew it could not be accomplished unless he was afforded opportunities and invested with powers commensurate with the nature of the duties imposed upon him. He therefore wrote a letter to the President of Congress, in which he made the acceptance of the office dependent upon two conditions, first, that he should not be required to abandon his commercial pursuits or dissolve his existing connections with certain mercantile establishments, and secondly, that he should have the absolute power to appoint and remove all officials serving under him. Upon this point he was very emphatic. He said:

"I also think it indispensably necessary that the appointment of all officers who are to act in my office under the same roof or in immediate connection with me should be made by myself, Congress first agreeing that such secretaries, clerks, or officers so to be appointed are necessary, and fixing the salaries of each. I conceive that it would be impossible to execute the duties of this office with effect unless the absolute power of dismissing from office or employment all persons whatever that are concerned in the official expenditures of public moneys be committed to the Superintendent of Finance, for unless this power can be exercised without control, I have little hope of efficacy in the business of reformation, which is probably the most essential part of the duty."

Congress having, after some hesitation, conformed to the wishes of Morris in respect to these two matters, he accepted the office on the 14th day of May, 1781, but he did not enter fully upon the discharge of his duties until October following. In June, 1781, before he had taken charge of his office, he secured the repeal of the embargo law, believing, to use his own language, that " commerce should be perfectly free and property sacredly secured to the owner." He applied himself with zeal and determination to the difficult task imposed upon him, and the result of his labors soon began to be felt in all the affairs of the government at home and abroad, and in all the business transactions of the people. The extent and variety of the powers vested in him, and the number and character of the various kinds of business transacted by him on the public account, have no parallel in the history of any other financial officer in the world. He was, in fact, the autocrat of finances.

SPEAKER'S STAND FROM THE TOWER OF THE INSTITUTION FOR THE BLIND

He engaged in a great number of mercantile enterprises on account of the government, buying and selling goods here and in other countries, and using the proceeds in the public service. Congress had declared that the obligations of the government should be paid in specie, or its equivalent, but the government had no specie and no visible means of procuring it. It is true that considerable specie, or hard money as it was then called, had been brought into the country and disbursed by the British and French armies, but it had not reached the treasury. The worthless paper currency was now rapidly disappearing from the circulation, and Morris took measures to obtain a supply of specie from Havana and other places, which he accomplished to a very considerable extent by buying and selling goods. In a short time the people began to realize the benefits of that inflexible law of trade and finance under which sound money in sufficient quantities to transact all the business of the country will always make its appearance to take the place of unsound money, if the latter can be got out of circulation. It was not long until specie was circulating in all the channels of trade, and from that time to the close of the Revolutionary war all the business of the government was conducted upon a specie basis. There was then no American dollar nor American coin of any denomination. The principal coin in use was the Spanish dollar, the Seville piece of eight, and the Mexican piece of eight, each of which was rated at 4 shillings 6 pence sterling, and the pillar piece, which was rated at 4 shillings, 6 pence, 3 farthings. But the actual unit of account in America was an imaginary dollar, supposed to contain 24½ grains of fine gold. There was, in fact, no such coin, and never has been, but this quantity of fine gold was apparently, by common consent, recognized as the standard by which the value of the various kinds of currency in circulation was measured, and by which exchange was regulated.

It would be going too far to assert that Morris ever succeeded in establishing the finances of the government upon an entirely firm and satisfactory basis, for it must be conceded that many of his plans failed, principally, however, on account of delinquencies on the part of Congress and the States. Besides, the mistakes committed before he entered upon his office were of such a character, and the injurious consequences so affected the whole system, that it required much time and labor to repair them ; and hence it was that financial questions involving taxation, currency, expenditures and methods of administration continued to perplex the statesmanship and embarrass the civil and military operations of the government throughout the whole period of the war ; and, in fact, they continued to vex the people for a long time afterwards. When Morris took office he was confronted by a financial and political situation which never before or since confronted the chief officer of this or any other government in the world. The Continental Congress possessed unlimited power to issue currency, but no power whatever to raise money by taxation for its redemption. It had unlimited power to make requisitions upon the States, but no power whatever to compel the States to comply with them. It had unlimited power to contract debts, but no power whatever to pay them. It had unlimited power to provide for the organization of an army and navy, but no power whatever to support them. The whole executive and legislative power, so far as it existed at all, was reposed in the Congress. There was no judiciary to interpret its acts, nor any executive to enforce them. Its resolutions and statutes were little more than mere appeals to the patriotism or generosity of the people, and, however reluctant we may be to admit it, the annals of that period show that they were generally made in vain. Taking all things into consideration, the years 1779 and 1780 were, perhaps, the darkest years of the war. It is not my purpose to speak of military operations, although they necessarily had great influence upon the financial situation. As in all other wars, victories improved the public credit and defeats impaired it ; but, independently of these influ-

COMING FROM THE TRAINS—CADETS ESCORTING AN ARRIVING DELEGATION.

ences, the impotency of the central authority and the apathy of the States were of themselves sufficient to render the task of the financier as onerous and apparently as hopeless as that imposed by the Egyptians upon the Children of Israel.

Although the treaty of alliance with France had been concluded in 1778, and very considerable pecuniary assistance had been received from that government, it was evident to Morris, as it was to every other intelligent supporter of the revolution, that the people must rely chiefly upon their own resources for a successful prosecution of the war ; and he labored assiduously from the beginning to the close of his administration to convince his countrymen that their interest and duty alike demanded the prompt payment of all taxes imposed upon them, in order that the public credit might be preserved and the public service maintained. His communications to Congress upon this subject, his numerous appeals to the governors and legislatures of the States, and his correspondence with his contemporaries show how thoroughly he appreciated the necessities of the situation, how sensitive he was concerning the honor and credit of the country, and how deeply he was offended and humiliated by the failure of the States to furnish money and supplies required for the public service. Notwithstanding all his arguments and appeals, however, the States refused to contribute their full quotas, and, according to his own statement, there was received into the treasury during the first five months of the year 1782 only the insignificant sum of $5,500, which, as he said at the time, was about one-fourth of what was necessary to meet the expenditures of a single day. The total amount received into the treasury from taxes during the whole of Morris's administration, that is, from February 20, 1781, to November 1. 1784, a period of about three years and eight months was $2,025,099, although the average annual expenditures during the war, exclusive of the sums expended directly by the several states, was about $16,000,000. In April, 1781, the specie value of the public debt was a little over $24,000,000, and, as it was represented by various forms of obligations and bore different rates of interest, Congress resolved to fund it, if the creditors would consent ; but, as usual, nothing resulted from this resolution.

Morris at once directed his attention to the establishment of a national bank as an auxiliary or aid to the government in the conduct of its financial affairs, and, after much opposition, he succeeded in securing a charter for the Bank of North America, with a capital of $400,000, to be located at Philadelphia. It was the first bank in America that redeemed its notes in specie on presentation, and it undoubtedly afforded great assistance to the government by granting loans from time to time and by effecting exchanges on the public account. For a little while the notes of the bank were at a discount, but they soon rose to par, and never afterwards depreciated.

One of the methods adopted by Congress to induce the States to comply with the requisitions upon them, was to allow them to purchase and furnish supplies for the use of the army, for which quartermasters and commissaries issued certificates. This system of specific supplies, as it was called, afforded almost unlimited opportunities for collusion and fraud, and was, from the very nature of the transactions involved and the difficulties of preserving and transporting the supplies, wasteful and extravagant in the high-

est degree. After a hard struggle, in which, fortunately, he had the support
of General Washington, Morris succeeded in abolishing this system and
procuring supplies by contract, which, to use his own language, was "an immense saving." About the same time he made an ineffectual effort to dis-
continue the practice of issuing loan office certificates, and to procure moneys
from France to purchase and cancel all that were outstanding. The unsat-
isfactory condition of the accounts between the government and the several
States was a source of constant annoyance and embarrassment in the administration of his office and a great deal of his time and labor were devoted to the investigation of this subject with a view of securing settlements
in order that it might be certainly known what each State had actually furnished and how much each was in arrears. Whenever requisitions were

HEAD OF THE PARADE CAUGHT IN A STORM.

made almost every State claimed that it had already furnished more than its
just quota, as compared with other States, and thus each made the same ex-
cuse for not furnishing more. While the first and most pressing duty of the
financier was to provide, so far as he could, by securing taxation and by
loans and otherwise, for the current expenditures of the government, he appears to have had continually in view two other great objects—the settlements of the accounts with the States and the funding of the public debt
neither of which was accomplished. All that any one man could do was
done, and his failures must be attributed to obstacles which it was impossible
to overcome in the existing state of public affairs and public opinion. After
the adoption of the federal constitution, and an effective government had

been established, the entire national debt was funded, the State debts being also assumed by the United States, and in due time the obligations were fully paid and the honor and credit of the country vindicated.

During the first year of his administration Morris caused to be prepared and submitted to Congress a plan for the establishment of a uniform coinage throughout the United States. This paper, while it undoubtedly embodied the views of Robert Morris, was actually prepared by Gouveneur Morris, whose name deserves most honorable mention in every history of the financial operations of that period on account of the able and faithful services which he rendered to the chief financial officer in nearly all his labors. Weights and measures were the same everywhere, but the currency was in a state of almost inextricable confusion, and there were nearly as many methods of computing the value of the money in circulation as there were States in the Confederacy. For instance, 4 shillings in New Hampshire were equal in value to 21 shillings and 8 pence in South Carolina, and the Spanish dollar, which, as already stated, was the principal coin in use, was worth in Georgia 5 shillings, in New York and North Carolina 8 shillings, in Virginia and the four eastern States 6 shillings, and in all the other States, except South Carolina, 7 shillings, 6 pence, and in South Carolina 32 shillings, 6 pence. The most important object to be attained, therefore, was the establishment of a uniform standard by which to estimate the value of all the different kinds of foreign coin in circulation, and Morris, after a brief discussion of the subject, in which he showed a thorough acquaintance with all its details, reached the conclusion that the most convenient unit of value would be one-fourth of a grain of fine silver, which would be the fourteen-hundred-and-fortieth part of a dollar, as that would agree without a fraction with all the different values of a dollar in the several States, except South Carolina. He did not insist that there should be an actual coin of the denomination stated, but simply that the fourteenth-hundred-and-fortieth part of a dollar should be the legal unit of value and account, and that the decimal ratio should be adopted. The next year after this communication was written, Congress took up the subject, and, after discussion, referred it to a committee of which Mr. Jefferson was a member. The report of the committee, which was written by Jefferson, agreed substantially with Morris' recommendations, except to the unit of value, which was said to be "too minute for ordinary use, too laborious for computation either by the head or in figures." The dollar itself was recommended as the unit, and the decimal system suggested by Morris was approved. Congress agreed to this report, and the accounts of expenditures show that some steps were taken towards the establishment of a mint; in fact, a few coins, "pattern pieces," as they were called, were actually struck, but there is no evidence that any of them went into circulation. Thus, the fundamental principles of our present method of account and monetary unit were first presented and explained in the midst of a great war by a man who was hourly engrossed with the drudgery of an office which, even in the most ordinary times, leaves but little opportunity for scientific or historical investigation; but he possessed a practical knowledge of commercial and financial affairs which was worth far more than the most deliberate conclusions of the mere theorist and which enabled him to detect, almost at a glance, the weak points in the existing system. Honesty, economy, and official responsibility characterized the conduct of his administration to an extent wholly unknown to the previous financial operations of the government, and yet it sometimes happened that the exigencies of the public service compelled him to resort to expedients which would not meet with public favor in ordinary times. It must be remembered, however, that he was substantially in his own person the treasury of the United States, and that there were frequent occasions when the preservation of the national credit and the maintenance of the public service, civil and military, depended almost entirely upon his individual capacity to raise money. Many of his operations had to be conducted with the utmost secrecy in order to be successful, while others had to be carried on by unusual and circuitous methods, which afforded his enemies plausible pretexts for intimates of distrust, but no charge of malfeasance in office, or improp-

RICHMOND AVENUE—WHERE THE PARADE STARTED AND ENDED.

er use of his opportunities, was ever sustained after impartial investigation. All that he had was consecrated to the cause of his country, and he never hesitated to use his means and credit to promote its success. His individual notes were issued for the public benefit to the amount of $750,000, and they circulated at par when the notes of the government itself were at a heavy discount. The Yorktown campaign, the most momentous movement of the war, resulting in the surrender of Cornwallis and practically terminating the struggle, could not have been inaugurated or prosecuted if Morris had not, by his personal operations and the liberal use of his own credit, procured money to pay the soldiers and provide transportation and subsistence. When peace had been declared, an unpaid and discontented army still remained to be provided for. It was said at the time that it could neither be kept together nor disbanded with safety; but Morris again came promptly to the relief of the country. He succeeded in raising a sufficient amount of specie to pay for one month's service, and gave his own notes for three months' pay, due in six months, and then the world renowned soldiers of the American revolution quietly dispersed and returned to their homes, leaving the infant republic to begin its career unembarrassed by any fear or threat of internal discord.

The services of Morris in securing loans abroad, and in raising money on bills drawn upon our envoys in France and Holland, were of inestimable value to the country and could not have been so effectively rendered by any other man in America. At that time communication between this country and Europe was necessarily slow and precarious, even if not interfered with by the enemy, but British privateers and vessels of war were patrolling the seas in every direction, and consequently the transmission of goods, money or bills of exchange was hazardous in the highest degree. Under these circumstances, in order to raise money to meet pressing emergencies, he was frequently required to give his personal guarantee for the payment of the bills, and this he never refused to do.

Notwithstanding the prospect of an early peace after the surrender at Yorktown, Morris continued to labor diligently for retrenchment in expenditures and for a strict application of business principles in public matters, and it was universally agreed that his policy in respect to these subjects contributed very largely to the increase of confidence at home and the improvement of the national credit abroad. The instances in which he discontinued useless expenditures by dispensing with the services of unnecessary officials, by simplifying the methods of collecting and disbursing the public funds, by changing the manner of procuring supplies and by a close personal supervision of details are too numerous to be mentioned here, especially as this address is already too much extended. His determination to practice the strictest economy is shown by the fact that the estimate of expenditures for the year 1784, excluding the payment of previous claims and interest on the public debt, was only $457,525.33, about one-half of the amount of the present daily receipts of the treasury.

Provisional articles of peace were agreed upon at Paris on the 30th of November, 1782, but they were not proclaimed by the Continental Congress until April 11, 1783. In the meantime, an armistice, providing for a cessation of hostilities, was concluded, on the 20th of January, 1783; and finally, a definite treaty of peace was entered into, on the 3d of September, 1783, and proclaimed January 14, 1784. The war was now over; the freedom, sovereignty and independence of each State had been solemnly acknowledged by Great Britain, and the young republic was everywhere recognized as a distinct and independent nation.

Morris had long desired to relinquish his office, and in fact had once tendered his resignation, but was induced by Congress to reconsider his determination and remain. On the first day of November, 1784, his resignation was again tendered and was accepted.

He had found the treasury bankrupt, the national credit prostrated, the army naked, hungry and mutinous, the people discontented, the currency worthless, trade paralyzed and the struggle for independence daily growing more feeble and hopeless. He left not a full treasury, it is true, but a national credit higher among capitalists abroad than that of some of the oldest nations of Europe, and he left a happy and triumphant people, with a sound currency and prosperous trade, abundant resources and a free government. Surely he had a right to claim exemption from further official service, but his time for rest had not yet come. In 1785, at the solicitation of his fellow citizens, he became a member of the Pennsylvania legislature, and in 1787 he was elected a delegate to the great convention which framed the present constitution of the United States. When that instrument had been ratified by the States, he and William Maclay were chosen the first Senators from Pennsylvania. Morris drew the long term, and served six years, or until 1795, when he retired finally from public life, and thereafter his entire time was devoted

THE RICHMOND RESIDENCE.

to his private affairs, which had become seriously involved. He had engaged in many large and hazardous speculative enterprises, to which he had not given the attention which their character and importance demanded, and the consequence was that he found himself in his old age, after a long and honorable career, during which his personal credit had never been impaired, embarrassed with debts, harrassed by lawsuits, and ultimately seized and thrown into prison. I will not dwell long upon this part of his life, for it is by no means a pleasant theme. When the federal capital had been located on the Potomac, Morris and James Greenleaf purchased from the commissioners six thousand lots in the prospective city of Washington, at the price of $480,000, and it is said they purchased as many more from other persons. He also

quired an interest in the Virginia Yazoo Company, and owned by himself, or in conjunction with others, large tracts of land in Pennsylvania, North Carolina, South Carolina, Georgia, Kentucky and New York. His several purchases included many million acres of wild lands, and each transaction appeared to subject him to additional complications in his affairs.

By a contract, or treaty, entered into at Hartford on the 16th day of December, 1786, between commissioners of the State of New York and the State of Massachusetts, the conflicting claims of the two States to certain territory west of a line drawn northwardly from the eighty-second milestone on the boundary of Pennsylvania to Lake Ontario, except a strip one mile wide the length of the Niagara river on its east side, were adjusted, Massachusetts ceding to New York full sovereignity and jurisdiction over the land, and New York yielding to Massachusetts the pre-emption or proprietary right. The tract thus described was supposed to contain about six million acres. In 1788 the State of Massachusetts sold all the land to Phelps and Gorham, but they failed to pay the whole purchase money and in March, 1791, reconveyed about 3,750,000 acres to the State. On the 12th day of March, 1791, the State sold to Samuel Ogden, who was acting for Robert Morris, all the land, excepting one million acres, or thereabouts, which Phelps and Gorham had paid for and retained. This purchase embraced all Western New York west of a line which corresponds, substantially, I believe, with the Genesee river, or, in other words, nearly all that part of the State west of Rochester. In 1792 and 1793 Morris sold 3,400,000 acres of this tract to the Holland Land Company, but the conveyances were at first made to other parties, probably on account of the alienage of the Hollanders. Afterwards, however, conveyances were made directly to the individuals composing the company, of which Wilhelm Willink, through whom one of the public loans in Holland had been negotiated while Morris was Superintendent of the Finances, appears to have been the president. After this purchase a colony of Germans, consisting of seventy families, was formed at Hamburg and sent over to settle on the land. They were furnished with tools and put to work to construct a road from Northumberland to Genesee, but, having come mainly from cities, they were unaccustomed to such labor and the settlement finally broke up in a riot. After this, an office was opened by the company and the land was sold and conveyed in parcels to suit purchasers until 1839, when its affairs were closed. In 1802 its office was removed to Batavia, and in 1804 the building which you are here today to dedicate to the memory of Robert Morris, was erected, and for more than a third of a century the titles to the homes of the people who now inhabit the counties of Erie, Chautauqua, Cattaraugus and Niagara, except the Indian reservations, and nearly all the counties of Orleans, Genesee, Wyoming and Allegheny were prepared and executed within its walls. Thus it is that nearly every home in the western part of the beautiful valley which suggested the Indian name of the river that flows through it, is connected with the name of Robert Morris, and, though all others may neglect his memory, and even forget the name of the great financier of the revolution, his fame will live on in this historic region as long as the people love the land on which their children were born and in which their fathers sleep.

Morris' pecuniary affairs grew rapidly worse from day to day, and finally his creditors became so importunate that he was compelled to remain constantly in his home to avoid them. They watched his house, even at night, and lighted fires on his premises in order that he might be intercepted if he attempted to escape. One of them, a Frenchman, went so far as to threaten to shoot him if he made his appearance at the window. In January or February, 1798, he was committed to a debtors prison, where he remained for more than three years and a half. It was his habit, while confined, to walk around the prison yard fifty times each day and drop a pebble at the completion of each circuit in order to keep the count. During the hardest of his misfortunes he never became despondent or uttered a complaint, except to express his profound regret that he was unable to discharge his honest obligations. He never referred to the great service he had rendered his country, or appealed to the sympathy or charity of the public, but silently submitted to

ON THE LINE OF MARCH—COURT HOUSE PARK IN THE ANGLE OF THE INDIAN TRAILS

unjust accusations, to prolonged imprisonment and to the indifference and ingratitude of his countrymen with the heroic fortitude of a great and noble mind.

No period of his long and honorable career better illustrates the stalwart and independent character of the man than those closing years of his life. He had stood on the very pinnacle of fame and listened to the enthusiastic plaudits of his emancipated countrymen and had received even the forced homage of their defeated antagonists. He had been the confidential adviser and trusted agent of the government when a serious mistake would have been fatal to its existence, and had proved his statesmanship and patriotism by the wisdom of his counsels and the cheerful sacrifice of his personal interests. He had been the bosom friend of Washington and nearly all of the great Americans whose names have come down to us from the last half of the eighteenth century and had been the peer of the greatest among them. He had lived in luxury and had at his command all that wealth and political influence and official station could procure; but now he was broken in fortune, imprisoned for debt, denounced as a reckless speculator, separated from his old personal friends and ungenerously neglected by the government and the people he had served so long and so well. But he endured it all without a murmur, and after his release from prison went uncomplainingly to his dismantled home, and by the practice of close economy managed to live in a tolerably comfortable condition, for which he was mainly indebted to the Holland Land Company, which paid to Mrs. Morris as long as she lived an annuity of $1,500.

Morris died on the 8th day of May, 1806, in the seventy third year of his age, and was buried in a little churchyard on Second street in Philadelphia, where his remains now rest, with no monument over them except an ordinary stone slab. The great country which he helped to rescue from the domination of its oppressors has grown rich and powerful under the constitution he helped to frame; the three million people whose liberties he helped to establish, have multiplied until they largely outnumber the population of the mother land; the thirteen feeble States on the shores of the Atlantic, which he helped to unite under a compact of perpetual peace and mutual protection, have become the progenitors of a mighty sisterhood of prosperous commonwealths, whose confines are limited only by their western seas; and still, no obelisk rises to tell the story of his great services, his unselfish patriotism, his honorable life, and its melancholy close.

It may be, however, that hereafter, somewhere in this broad land of ours, which he sacrificed so much to make free and prosperous, there will be gathered beneath the dome of an American pantheon the remains of all our honored dead, and if so, the obscure grave at Philadelphia will give up its tenant, and the mausoleum of Robert Morris will become a consecrated shrine where generations of freemen will uncover their heads in honor of his memory as long as the republic endures.

(*Batavia Daily News.*)

The Cabinet members, during their public reception on the ground floor of the Richmond from about 4:30 until 5:30 o'clock, shook hands with over 1,500 men, women and children. When it was learned that such an event was to take place the main corridors of the hotel were immediately filled with a surging mass of people and the officers had great difficulty in keeping even a semblance of order. The crush was something terrible during almost the entire hour and it was a wonder that some people were not injured.

Secretary Carlisle was introduced by J. Holley Bradish, Secretary Gresham by Judge North, Secretary Lamont by Arthur E. Clark, General Bissell by A. D. Scatcherd, Secretary Herbert by A. T Miller and Secretary Smith by Fredd H. Dunham.

While the Cabinet members were receiving on the ground floor of the

Richmond their ladies held a public reception for ladies on the first day. They were introduced by D. W. Tomlinson, M. H. Peck, Jr., and L. L. Washburn.

The members of the Cabinet, accompanied by General Maxwell and Judge North, called upon Mrs. Dean Richmond and Mrs. Kenney after the public reception.

About fifty people sat down to the dinner served by Teall of Rochester at the Richmond at 6:30 o'clock. The Cabinet members and their ladies occupied seats at a table placed at one side of the main table and the members of the Morris family at a table on the opposite side. The dinner was all that could be desired, and the floral decorations, arranged by Mrs. Hinman Holden's committee, were very fine.

THE JUNCTION OF THE INDIAN TRAILS.

Postmaster-General and Mrs. Bissell left Batavia at 7 p. m. on the Lehigh Valley road for Geneva, Mrs. Bissell's home. The General joined the Washington party there last night and proceeded to the capital.

Secretary and Mrs. Lamont left at 7:20 P. M. on the Central for Buffalo.

It was 8:15 P. M. when the Cabinet members who had not already departed, and their ladies, First Assistant Postmaster-General Jones, Public Printer Benedict and General Maxwell left the Richmond in carriages and were conveyed to the Central depot. There were several hundred people at the depot and the distinguished Washingtonians were thoroughly inspected until 7:45 o'clock, when they left on their special train for Niagara Falls over the Central's Tonawanda branch. They were accompanied by D. W.

Tomlinson, who returned to Batavia last night, coming back with the party, which passed through here about 9 o'clock.

In addition to the two palace cars occupied by the guests the private car of Superintendent Beach of the Lehigh Valley was on the train.

The run to Niagara Falls was made in an hour and a half, including quite a lengthy stop at Tonawanda. The party registered at the Cataract House and the gentlemen at once walked to Prospect Point, where a fine view of the falls was obtained, the moon having come out.

Yesterday every point of interest in the vicinity of the Falls was visited, such a complete tour being made that Secretary Carlisle remarked that he was sure that if there was anything that they hadn't seen it must have been concealed in advance. Mrs. Micou, Secretary Herbert's daughter, and Secretary Smith had never visited the cataract before and several of the other members of the party had caught only flying glimpses of it.

Secretary and Mrs. Lamont arrived in Buffalo yesterday morning and joined the party, but yesterday afternoon the Secretary received word that his mother was sick and left at once for her home at McGrawville. Mrs. Lamont returned to Washington with the party.

Secretary and Mrs. Gresham left the Falls last night for Chicago.

(*Buffalo Express.*)

The Batavians are making no mistake in emphasizing the relation of Robert Morris, a truly great man, with the development of our region. There has been organized the Holland Purchase Historical Society, which has acquired title to the property, and will preserve it and make it an historical museum. It is appropriate that Secretary Carlisle, who now presides over the Department which was first directed by Robert Morris, should make the dedicatory address. The historical celebration at Batavia on October 13th has aroused a widespread interest, and should prove stimulative to other places which have buildings of historic interest worthy of preservation.

(*Rochester Union and Advertiser.*)

To day the people of Batavia dedicate the old Holland Land Office, the historical relic of that village. It has been purchased by the Holland Purchase Historical Association, and the old landmark will thus be preserved for the future generations.

The preservation of the Holland Land Office is worthy of all praise. In these days there are but few relics of the memorable past left in New York State. The New England States are the most prolific in these dumb witnesses of the past. The pioneers of the west are not commemorated in many ways. The Holland Land Office is one of the very few relics left.

(*Rochester Herald.*)

Saturday will be a red letter day in the history of Batavia and Genesee County. The old office of the Holland Land Company is to be dedicated as a historical museum and a memorial address on the public services of Robert Morris is to be delivered by Hon. John G. Carlisle, Secretary of the Treasury. Of late years Mr. Carlisle has seldom been heard on other than political subjects, and an oration of permanent value may be expected from one who is so careful a student of American history and so eloquent a public speaker. Secretary Carlisle will gain special inspiration from the fact that he is called upon to eulogize one of the most distinguished of his predecessors in the important task of managing the National finances.

(Rochester Post Express.)

On October 13th the old stone building at Batavia which was used as an office by the Holland Land Company is to be "dedicated as a memorial to Robert Morris, the great patriot and financier of the Revolution, and the first owner of the lands in Western New York." The dedicatory exercises will

THE BRISBANE CURVE FROM TONAWANDA BRIDGE

be under the management of the Holland Purchase Historical Society, which was organized about a year ago to buy the old land office, save it from destruction, and change it into a museum wherein relics of pioneer days and documents of historical interest may be preserved. The *Post Express* was one of the first newspapers to commend the purposes of the Holland Purchase Historical Society. It is engaged in a good work, and we hope it may have a prosperous and useful career.

(Harper's Weekly.)

It is given to few men to save their country twice.

* * * * * * * *

The close of the war found Mr. Morris a ruined man. But notwithstanding the shameful ingratitude which left him to disappear in oblivion and distress, he unconsciously built his own monument, and that out of his misfortune.

* * * * * * * * * *

Now this venerable building has become the first, and lamentably the only, monument to the memory of a unique patriot—a man who involved himself in financial ruin and went to a debtor's prison that his country might live.

(*Warsaw New Yorker.*)

The dedication of the Holland Land Office at Batavia last Saturday was a success. The weather was not just what could be desired, but the program was carried out in the fullest detail. It was certainly a very creditable affair, and the attendance showed great interest in the purpose of the celebration. The forenoon was occupied in the dedicatory services and the procession was full of interesting events. Secretary Carlisle's address was a fine tribute to the name and fame of Robert Morris. The attendance of several members of the Cabinet and the use of Robert Morris' name nationalized the affair.

(*Philadelphia Inquirer.*)

It is not creditable to the bankers and financial men of Philadelphia that Secretary Carlisle could say with truth what he said in his address on Saturday at the dedication at Batavia, New York, of a memorial to Robert Morris, that although next to Washington, Morris had done more than any other American to establish the political liberties of his country, nowhere in the United States is there a statue of him. It would seem to be the duty of the Philadelphia financiers to care for the fame of the great Philadelphia financier of the Revolution, and it is to be hoped that Mr. Carlisle's remarks will spur them into the removal of what is in the nature of a reproach upon themselves.

(*Batavia Daily News.*)

Land-Office day has passed into history as the greatest day that Batavia ever had, and a great day it was, indeed. Everybody had a good time, from the Cabinet officers down to the humblest citizen of the Holland Purchase who came to town, and all this in the face of the disheartening fact that the weather was beastly. The gentlemen from Washington, speaking for themselves and the ladies who accompanied them, assured General Maxwell and President Tomlinson of the Bank of Batavia, who accompanied the party to Niagara Falls, that they all had passed the day pleasantly and they added that they were never better cared for or more happily entertained anywhere. They were lavish in praise of the arrangements that were so intelligently made and so successfully carried out.

(*Batavia Daily News.*)

Land-Office day has come and gone, and it is due to the not very large number who had in charge the arrangement of the details of the demonstration to say that it was unequivocally a grand success. Preparations were made so carefully and so completely that the wretched weather that was calculated to make nearly impossible the carrying out of the programme was thwarted in its calamitous intents almost at every point, and the thousands of visitors, appreciating the fact that Batavia could not be held accountable for the vagaries of the elements, went home with nothing but words of praise on their lips. It was a magnificent observance of an event that is to be historical, and every member of every committee who actively contributed to its grand consummation is entitled to the greatest credit.

Batavians generally did themselves proud on the occasion, and all must enjoy a feeling of satisfaction that the affair, so important as it was and of such magnitude, passed off so smoothly under weather conditions that of themselves were discouraging.

THE TONAWANDA BRIDGE—LAND OFFICE IN THE DISTANCE.

(*New York Sun.*)

But for Robert Morris and his credit the French alliance of that year would never have been formed. For we must not suppose that France sprang to our aid on impulse. Nations do not do that sort of thing. We may be sure that France looked well to our finances and chance of success before she took the risk of sharing our defeat. And except for the personal responsibility assumed for Congress by Mr. Morris, our finances were all on paper. There was Continental paper money promising to pay on demand, and still other paper money, issued as drafts by individual States on the colonial Treasury, for States loans that in turn were only on paper. And here was a man who stood so high in the confidence of men and nations that his private credit redeemed all.

Mr. Morris's hand showed itself not only in the vigorous policy of his department, but in the rigid economy of its administration. Hundreds of superfluous office-holders, parasites who were sucking their little selves full of the nation's life blood, were summarily dismissed. We find that upon one occasion the Quartermaster-General of the army came to him with a requisition to buy a hundred tons of hay for a certain brigade, and that Mr. Morris, after inquiries as to the size of the brigade, promptly cut down the amount of hay to twelve tons; and that proved to be more than a sufficient supply.

During these years Mr. Morris's private assistance to the army was never relaxed. His ships were constantly running the blockade with supplies from Europe purchased in his name. He would send a cargo of his own commodities to France, the ship would return to America laden with military goods, and, running into the first available harbor, distribute the goods directly to the army. The extent of Mr. Morris's losses by this unbusinesslike but convenient procedure will never be known. FRANK C. DRAKE.

(*Rochester Democrat and Chronicle.*)

The Celebration at Batavia yesterday became an event of national significance because the occasion had been seized to do public honor, for the first time, to the memory of Robert Morris, the patriot, to whom as much as any other one man America owes its freedom, who gave all his substance freely to his country, and whom his country left to die in poverty and forgot with all convenient speed.

The direct occasion of the commemoration that crowded Batavia with visitors yesterday was the preservation of a famous local landmark and historical relic, the old land office, by the Holland Purchase Historical Society. The substantial stone building, dating from 1813, which in its early days had been the business headquarters of the whole region, was diverted from its original purpose in 1839, when the Holland Land Company ceased to exist, and since then has passed through many hands and known evil days. The building was falling into decay, and would soon have been torn down, had not a number of patriotic citizens determined to save it. They formed a historical society, acquired title to the building, and will make it a historical museum, the shrine and conservator of the history and tradition of the region. It was decided to publicly dedicate it to its new uses, and out of this decision grew the celebration of yesterday, which made Batavia a center of national interest.

It was a happy thought that suggested linking the name and memory of a man to whom the country had owed much and rendered nothing, with the local celebration. Robert Morris had been the original white owner of all the land which passed from him to the Holland Land Company, and might have remained its owner but for the fact that he had made himself a bankrupt as a result of his services to his country. There may be other places on whom the duty of honoring his memory rested more particularly than on Batavia; indeed, there was no American city or village or hamlet on which this duty did not rest. But they had all with one accord neglected it, and it is peculiarly to Batavia's honor that, first of all American communities, it paid honor to this great and neglected patriot. It was this feature of the celebration that brought the members of the present national cabinet to Batavia to take part in the celebration, that made it particularly appropriate that the present Secretary of the Treasury of the United States should deliver the address at the dedication of a monument to the memory of the Secretary of the Treasury of the United Colonies.

For the old Holland Land Office will stand as this nation's first monument to one of its foremost founders, somewhat mitigating a long-standing disgrace. He asked for bread and, after many years, we have given him, at least, a stone. Whittier's " Prisoner for Debt " applies, in every line, to Robert Morris, who spent more than one Independence Day in a debtor's prison, and remembering that, no American could read it without a tingle of shame.

Batavia has earned general thanks for the spirit of patriotism that

ACROSS THE STREET FROM THE LAND OFFICE.

prompted yesterday's observance as well as general "congratulations upon the success of the occasion.

> Look on him !—through his dungeon grate
> Feebly and cold, the morning light
> Comes stealing around him, dim and late,
> As if it loathed the sight,
> Reclining on his strawy bed,
> His hand upholds his drooping head,—
> His bloodless cheek is seamed and hard,
> Unshorn his gray, neglected beard ;
> And o'er his bony fingers flow
> His long, dishevelled locks of snow.

No grateful fire before him glows,
  And yet the winter's breath is chill;
And o'er his half clad person goes
  The frequent ague thrill!
Silent, save ever and anon,
A sound, half murmur and half groan,
Forces apart the painful grip
Of the old sufferer's bearded lip;
O sad and crushing is the fate
Of old age chained and desolate!

Just God! why lies that old man there?
  A murderer shares his prison bed,
Whose eyeballs, through his horrid hair,
  Gleam on him, fierce and red;
And the rude oath and heartless jeer
Fall ever on his loathing ear,
And, or in wakefulness or sleep,
Nerve, flesh, and pulses thrill and creep
Whene'er that ruffian's tossing limb,
Crimson with murder, touches him!

What has the gray haired prisoner done?
  Has murder stained his hands with gore?
Not so; his crime's a fouler one;
  GOD MADE THE OLD MAN POOR!
For this he shares a felon's cell,
The fittest earthly type of hell!
For this, the boon for which he poured
His young blood on the invader's sword,
And counted light the fearful cost,—
His blood gained liberty is lost!

And so, for such a place of rest,
  Old prisoner, dropped thy blood as rain
On Concord's field, and Bunker's crest,
  And Saratoga's plain.
Look forth, thou man of many scars,
Through thy dim dungeon's iron bars;
It must be joy, in sooth, to see
Yon monument upreared to thee,—
Piled granite and a prison cell,—
The land repays thy service well!

Go, ring the bells and fire the guns,
  And fling the starry banner out;
Shout "Freedom!" till your lisping ones
  Give back their cradle-shout:
Let boastful eloquence declaim
Of honor, liberty, and fame;
Still let the poet's strain be heard,
With glory for each second word,
And everything with breath agree
To praise "our glorious liberty!"

But when the patriot cannon jars
  That prison's cold and gloomy wall,
And through its grates the stripes and stars
  Rise on the wind, and fall,—
Think ye that prisoner's aged ear
Rejoices in the general cheer?
Think ye his dim and failing eye
Is kindled at your pageantry?
Sorrowing of soul, and chained of limb,
What is your carnival to him?

Down with the law that binds him thus
  Unworthy freemen, let it find
No refuge from the withering curse
  Of God and human kind!
Open the prison's living tomb,
And usher from its brooding gloom
The victims of your savage code
  To the free sun and air of God;
No longer dare as crime to brand
The chastening of the Almighty's hand. —[Whittier.

ON THE LINE OF MARCH—THE TURN JUST WEST OF THE LAND OFFICE.

(N. L. Woodwards)

What careth the world for a man when dead,
When his breath is gone—his spirit hath fled?
 *   *   *   *   *
Though noble and grand was the work of his hand,
Performed for his own or a foreign land ;
Though his fame spread wide, and his name be great,
From ruling a realm or forming a state—
What careth the crowd for his senseless clay?
The lion is dead—he hath had his day.
So they hasten to lay his corpse away
From the sight of men—and the world is gay.

(*Philadelphia Inquirer.*)

Notwithstanding his wretched existence at this time, it is recorded that in his intercourse with people he never lost the buoyant, sanguine disposition which had made him what he had been and perhaps, alas, what he was.

Friends came to the prison on his invitation to dine with him; they found the same magnetic host who had built the first private conservatory in America to adjoin the dining room of his now vanished mansion, serving with genial face the poor fare of the prison.

Upon his release from prison Mr. Morris and his wife took up their residence in a cheap part of Philadelphia. Here the great financier lived the few years remaining to him.

It would be curious to know if the old man ever strolled into that part of the city where were buildings that he used to own and banks that he used to be president of, and men who once toadied to him. Probably he did, and probably it never occurred to his soaring nature that he was a pathetic figure.

Mr. Morris died May 8, 1806, and was buried in a cemetery that then was soft with grass and bright with sunshine, but now is paved with brick and hemmed in with buildings. Some of the graves still have blue sky and sunshine left them, but Robert Morris' resting place has been robbed even of that by the encroaching city.

The memorial to him at Batavia came about as follows: We have said that he had sought to save his credit by land speculation; indeed, all that remained of his great fortune was tied up in large tracts of territory in Pennsylvania, Louisiana, Maryland and New York. The most valuable of these tracts was in the last named State, where he owned all the land west of the Genesee river. It will be remembered that much of the money he borrowed for the colonies came from Holland. When, through lack of capital to enable him to wait for the advancing settlers to create a profitable demand for his land, he was finally driven to the wall, his Holland creditors and others organized the Holland Land Company. To them he transferred his tract in New York. In 1824 this company erected a substantial stone building at Batavia for the transaction of their business. This building, within whose walls has been transferred the original title to every piece of ground in Western New York, is the memorial dedicated to-day to Robert Morris, and with shame be it said, it is the only monument his countrymen have thus far granted to his memory.

Washington's lofty monument is red with the setting sun after the electric lights are lit in the streets; Lincoln's name has not yet died out of the newspapers; Grant will sleep in a marble palace by the lovely Hudson; but Morris——. FRANK C. DRAKE.

(Dr. Henry Morris.)

Seldom in my life have I experienced as much pleasure as was given me by the receipt of your invitation to be present this morning, as a descendent of Robert Morris, the financier of the Revolution, whose memory you have just honored by the dedication to him of the old historic building which stands before us. In honoring the memory of Robert Morris, I feel that we also honor ourselves by perpetuating the memory of one of the noblest patriots, one of the purest men in his domestic life, and one of the most fearless when his duty called him that this or any other country has ever produced.

Born in England in 1734, he was brought to America by his father, at the early age of 13 years.

On the death of his father at the age of 37 years, by the premature discharge of a cannon fired in his honor, the wadding of which struck him on the breast. Robert Morris entered upon his business career, in which he was so eminently successful that, at the outbreak of the Revolutionary War, he was regarded as the richest man in America, and the firm of Morris & Willing was known over the whole mercantile world for its success, probity, and honor.

Married to the daughter of Col. Thomas White of Maryland, and the sister of William White, one of the first Bishops of the Protestant Episcopal Church in America, he had a numerous family of sons and daughters, who in their turn left children behind them, so that two generations ago it seemed as if he were destined to be the ancestor of a long line who would perpetuate his honored name.

At present, however, the sole male representatives bearing the family

ON THE LINE OF MARCH—ELLICOTT AVENUE, IN FRONT OF THE MAXWELL RESIDENCE.

name are myself and son, descended from his eldest son, Robert; and my cousins, Messrs. Gouverneur and Fisher Morris, with their sons, descended from his son Henry Morris.

Being prominent in the colony of Pennsylvania, Robert Morris was naturally selected to represent her as one of the delegates to the Continental Congress, which was held in Carpenter's Hall in Philadelphia in 1775.

The feeling of the Colonists during the early years of the Revolutionary War was a curious one. They regarded England as their mother-country and were not fighting for separation from her, for independence, but against the unjust taxation, the tyranny and oppression of the dominant political party then in power in England as represented by the cabinet of George III, led by the Prime Minister, Lord North.

When, therefore, the question of a separation from the mother-country, as set forth in our glorious Declaration of Independence, was first mooted, it was received by many with feelings of doubt as to its advisability, by others with doubt as to its expediency at that particular time.

Among the latter was probably Robert Morris. He knew there was a strong and rapidly growing party in England under the leadership of Fox and Burke who were favorable to the colonies and who might be antagonized by an expressed desire on the part of the latter to separate themselves once and forever from the rule of the mother-country; and believing that this action on the part of the colonists would tend to unite the English more firmly against them and thus prolong the war—a war which was carried on in his own country, at his very door—he, it is said, opposed this separation.

Was he influenced by personal fear in his opposition?

Not at all, for no sooner had Congress decided to adopt the Declaration of Independence than in a bold, clear, firm hand, he placed his signature upon the document which insures liberty and equality to all. In consequence of this act, he, as well as the other members of Congress who had signed the Declaration, were adjudged guilty of high treason by the British Government, and had they been taken they would have been hanged with but scant time for grace.

Then came the dark days of the Revolution when Philadelphia was in the hands of the British and when the country was too poor to supply the troops with food or clothing; when jealousy arose among the different colonies and when all the colonies were jealous of the authority of the Continental Congress, when the currency of the country had depreciated, and when the farmers would no longer furnish provisions to Washington's starving army at Valley Forge.

You all know the history of that time; how that noblest and purest of men, General George Washington, among the uncertainties of war, with a defeated army shivering in their winter quarters while the British held high revel in the cities, almost in despair applied to his friend Morris, as his last resort, and Morris responded. Giving all his available means, and pledging his personal credit and his honor, he raised the needed money to clothe and feed the army, he saved the country, and he ruined himself.

Why should I take up your time, telling you what every school boy knows, how he raised money time after time for the army, how he was appointed by Congress Superintendent of Finance, a name borrowed from a French office under the Bourbons, and which was afterwards changed to that of Secretary of the Treasury, the position at present so worthily filled by our great American Financier, the Hon. John G. Carlisle, and how finally after the war was over and the finances of the country were beginning to assume a better shape, owing to his exertions and the better feeling of security which began to prevail among all classes of Americans, he refused reappointment to the office he had so long held, and the duties of which he had so faithfully and efficiently discharged, pleading to the repeated solicitations of General Washington, that his private affairs needed his closest supervision and attention, and suggested as the name of the most fitting man for the place, that of your illustrious fellow statesman, Alexander Hamilton.

Robert Morris then retired from public life, and finding his private fortune much diminished, partly owing to his own neglect during the period of his public life, but more especially owing to the (for that time) vast sums which he loaned the Government and which they were unable to repay, and believing in the great future of the country whose welfare he had done so much to promote, he entered into vast schemes for colonization and land speculation with a view to developing the country as well as to retrieve his fortune. Unfortunately for him he was half a century too soon to realize on his vast purchases, and being, as he afterwards said, accustomed during his public life to handling millions of Dollars as others did thousands, he ran in debt and was finally cast into the debtors prison, for what in these days would seem a paltry sum indeed.

Here he remained until Congress, recognizing the debt the country owed

ON THE LINE OF MARCH—HEAD OF ELLICOTT AVENUE.

him, and unable to repay him the money he had loaned, passed the Bankruptcy act, it is said, especially for his benefit.

Of this act he hastened to avail himself, and resigned to assignees all his vast landed estates, but so little was thought of the value of unsettled land at that time that nothing was ever done toward settling his estate, and when the court dissolved his bankruptcy and released his estate in 1827, it was found that but little remained for creditors or descendants. After his release from the Debtor's Prison, Robert Morris, broken in health and spirits, resided until his death, which occurred in 1806, with his daughter, Mrs. Nixon, in Philadelphia, making a request, as I have been informed, on his death bed, that his descendants should never claim from the United States the money he had so freely given. Viewed from a worldly point and in view of his ultimate want of success, the private life of Robert Morris was a failure; but can we deem it a failure when we see what he accomplished in his public capacity, and study the example of pure and unselfish patriotism which he set us?

Patriotism dependent upon interested motives is not uncommon, but here was a man sacrificing great wealth, freely and cheerfully, for the benefit of the country which he loved, at the time when that country was in most pressing need, and when by many the ultimate success of the cause for which he sacrificed himself seemed hopeless.

In this brief sketch I have purposely said nothing about the connection between Robert Morris and your county, because I know this will be dealt with by abler and more eloquent speakers.

I have endeavored merely to call your attention to the great example he set, not only to us but to all future generations, an example which deserves more imitators, that of unselfish and fearless patriotism.

(Contributed.)

ROBERT MORRIS.

Bright star of the bright galaxy that gleamed
Through the long night of danger and of war,
Thy setting was of sadness, while afar
The sunrise shone upon a land redeemed,
On fetters riven, and a fair flag streamed
Into a sky where it shall float as free
As the fond air, through ages yet to be,
Master or man? Whichever thou art deemed,
Thy Nation knows thy nobleness of heart,
Thy sacrifice. The olive bearing dove,
The covenant of progress, peace and art
Came at thy call. While burn the stars above,
While floats that flag, who shall forsay thy part,
Humility, humanity, and love.

(*Mary Morris White Church.*)

Thank you very much for the papers. I am much indebted to you for all the trouble you have taken. Indeed, the whole Morris family will always feel grateful to you and Batavia for the honor shown the memory of our patriot ancestor. To be the first to do tardy justice is something to be proud of, and will always be remembered. The base ingratitude shown him during his final years, shows more clearly now than it probably did then, as our manners and customs are so different, but justice, thanks to Batavia, is at last being done to all that he was in our struggle for Independence.

Too much cannot be said in praise of the patriotism of Batavia, and the name of your town is now known broadcast over the country.

We were sorry not to see you and say good-bye. Also express our appreciation of all the delightful hospitality shown us on Saturday. It will always remain a charming memory.

(*John B. Church.*)

The Revolution gave me my wife. When I first saw Mary White I made bold to introduce myself, which I did in the following terms. " I think I have a right to know you—my great-grandfather bought the provisions for the Revolutionary army, and your great-grandfather found the money to buy them with. My great-grandfather bought from your great-grandfather the land on which I was born and reared—I think our histories touch." That my wife and I are here to-day to witness the dedication of the first monument to her illustrious ancestor, will show how well I fared in my suit. Her gratification is great, but I doubt whether it can much exceed my own.

The death of Hon. Philip Church, at the ripe age of 83, after a residence of 56 years in our midst—the pioneer and patriarch of the county—has awakened in our community the most lively interest, and drawn forth its deepest sympathies. Judge Church but seldom entered the political arena. His

A SIDE GLIMPSE FROM THE LINE OF MARCH—TRACY PLACE.

tastes, his habits, and his avocations, as a large landed proprietor, directed his talents and his energies into other, but not less useful, nor less important channels.

The threads of his life have been of a mingled texture—the epoch in which his years were numbered was one of the most eventful in history. Born to wealth and educated amid refinement and luxury—associated in youth with the prominent and leading spirits of the age in both hemispheres, we find him ere the flush of boyhood had scarcely faded, breasting with self-sacrificing spirit the hardships of the wilderness and developing through a long series of years, with successful energy, the resources of our rugged land till the wilderness had literally blossomed.

The subject of this memoir was born April 14, 1778; his father, John B.

Church, under the assumed name of *Carter*, acted as commissary to the French army during the American Revolution, and afterwards resuming his own name, married Angelica, eldest daughter of Gen. Philip Schuyler.

In 1781, while yet an infant, and during the visit of his mother at the residence of Gen. Schuyler, near Albany, the celebrated attempt was made to capture the General by a detachment of officers and soldiers of the British army; the infant was then asleep in the cradle; his mother rushed into the hall, seized the child in her arms and, while retreating, a wound was inflicted on his forehead, the scar of which he often exhibited as the first and only wound he received in the wars.

His father, in 1783, left this country with his family, and after spending about eighteen months in Paris, fixed his residence in England; in 1797 he was elected member of Parliament, and represented the Borough of Wendover in the House of Commons. His son Phillip, at the proper age, entered Eton, where he pursued his studies for six consecutive years. Eton has ever been the favorite school of the nobility and gentry, and here our subject form ed intimacies with many who afterwards became prominent in English history. During vacations, when he visited his father's house, in London, he met some of the prominent statesmen of the day. On one occasion he met the Prince of Wales, afterwards George IV. The Prince of Wales was always friendly, but George III could never forget the part he had taken during the Revolution; and as the King rode by "Down Place," the country-seat of John B. Church, he would sneeringly point to it as the residence of the "*American Commissary*." Phillip, as the eldest son of a member, was entitled to attend the Parliamentary debates, and enjoyed the rare and enviable privilege of hearing Fox, Burke, Sheridan, and the younger Pitt, a glowing galaxy of orators the most brilliant that ever convened at any one period in the world's history. After leaving Eton, he entered the Middle Temple, and commenced the study of law. About this time he received from the author himself a presentation copy of Walker's Dictionary, still preserved in the family.

The father of the deceased removed with his family from England in the year 1797, and resumed his residence in the city of New York. At this time he ranked as one of the richest residents in the country. He embarked in business, became one of the largest underwriters of the time, leaving his heirs claims against the French Government for spoliation, the payment of which was assumed by the U. S. Government at the purchase from France of Louisiana. These claims, with the interest added, would now amount to an enormous sum. Our Government has never paid a dollar towards them.

In 1799 he visited Canandaigua to attend the sale, under foreclosure, of a tract of land, being part of Morris' Reserve, situated in the then county of Ontario (now Allegany), comprising 100,000 acres. Hamilton was the mortgagee in trust for John B. Church. At the sale, Philip bid in the property and took a deed in his own name, dated May 6, 1800. But the property was actually purchased in joint account with his father. This property has been the theatre of his labors, from the commencement of the present century up to the close of his career.

Soon after this he completed his law studies, was admitted to the bar, but practiced his profession only a short time, and his landed estate was then the subject of absorbing interest.

In July, 1801, he left the city on an exploring expedition, providing himself at Geneva with camp equipage and provisions, and on his route procured the services of Maj. Moses Van Campen and Evart Van Winkle, surveyors, John Gibson, John Lewis and Stephen Price. They all met by appointment at Almond, the *nearest settlement*, eighteen miles from the tract. They made an active and thorough exploration, encountering fatigue, hardships, and privations. Capt. Church, to whom forest-life then opened a new and startling chapter, dwelt upon an incident that evidently made a strong impression. One day he had cut his foot, and was confined to camp; the rest of the party had been out exploring all day, had got bewildered, and Capt. Church heard their shouts afar off while searching for the camp, but they were proceeding in the wrong direction, and, as their voices died away in the distance,

AN ARCHITECTURAL LANDMARK NEAR THE JUNCTION OF THE INDIAN TRAILS. "THE AMERICAN HEROIC AGE DID ITS FIGHTING IN GREEK, AND BUILT WITH ITS EYE ON THE PARTHENON." A PRECURSOR OF THE COURT OF HONOR.

and as the silent, sombre shades of evening were spreading over the profound forest, he described the sensation of loneliness as being almost intolerable. Morning, however, at length arrived, and the lost party returned. The exploration was soon after completed; not, however, till their provisions were nearly exhausted, when they dispersed for their several destinations. Capt. Church determined to visit Niagara before his return. Accordingly, selecting Maj. Van Campen, they two started together by an Indian trail westward, their companions parting from them for their homes in an opposite direction. Major Van Campen was a remarkably athletic man, with a vigorous constitution and indomitable spirit, celebrated for his daring feats in Indian warfare, and for his skilled forest strategy. His life has been written by one of his descendants. The Major, from this time forward, became an important co-adjutor to Captain Church, and continued in his service more or less for the remainder of his life. He moved his family to Angelica soon after the village was founded, and continued his residence there to within a few years of the termination of his life.

After a tramp of three days through the forest, the last forty-eight hours without food, they reached the village of New Amsterdam, now Buffalo, with torn garments, empty purses, and almost famished. They visited the Falls, returned to Buffalo, and there they resumed their pedestrian trip by the "white man's trail," shoeless, moneyless, but with renewed physical power, and full of youth and vigor, for the village of Bath, about 100 miles distant. They passed through Batavia, where the Holland Land Company had just built their office. In this neighborhood Captain Church borrowed money from a Mr. Stoddard, and with replenished finances, well-shod, and comfortably if not fashionably clad, they proceeded cheerily on their winding way." At Geneseo they visited Mr. Wadsworth, a New York friend of Captain Church, and finally reached Bath in safety.

After his return to New York he set himself earnestly at work to commence the settlement of his lands; and, in 1802, sent his surveyor, Evart Van Winkle, to select the site of the village which was accordingly done, and Captain Church named the place "Angelica," after his mother. He also visited the country in person that year, and selected his farm and future residence on the banks of the Genesee. In this selection he manifested shrewdness and sound judgment. Were the selection to be made now, with all the advantages of an open country spread out before him, he could not in any particular have improved upon the selection then made. The 2,000 acres set aside is the finest land in the whole tract, and the situation of the house is incomparably the finest in the whole country. The wonder is that he should so readily have made such a strikingly favorable selection in the unterminable woods, when the sight was so circumscribed and when he could only form his judgment from a knowledge of the general conformation of the country, obtained by personal explorations. This place he named Belvidere.

On the 4th of February, 1805, Capt. Church married Anna Matilda, eldest daughter of Gen. Walter Stewart, of Philadelphia. The succeeding June the youthful pair started for the home prepared for them in the wilderness. "The White House" was ready for their reception. They reached it by riding from Bath to Belvidere, forty-four miles, on horseback, most of the distance by a bridle-path cut through the woods.

Gen. Stewart, Mrs. Church's father, had died in 1796 : he acted a prominent part through the revolutionary war ; was at the battles of Monmouth, Stony Point, and Yorktown. In Trumbull's painting of the surrender of Cornwallis, now hanging in the rotunda, at Washington, Gen. Stewart was represented among the other officers. He was an intimate and familiar friend of Washington. The family have a miniature of Washington, presented to Mrs. Gen. Stewart, accompanied by the following note written by himself :

WEDNESDAY, 16th March, 1796.
Not for the representation or the value, but because it is the production of a fair lady, the President, takes the liberty of presenting the enclosed with his best regards to Mrs. Stewart, praying her acceptance of it.

Capt. Church lived in the "White House" until 1810, when the stone mansion now standing on the banks of the Genesee was ready for their reception. Soon they were established in their new residence.—*Angelica Reporter.*

(*President Cleveland.*)

EXECUTIVE MANSION, WASHINGTON, Oct. 4, 1894.

MY DEAR SIR:—The President directs me to acknowledge the receipt of the invitation of the Holland Purchase Historical Society to attend the

A NATURAL TRIUMPHAL ARCH BELTING THE LINES OF MARCH—IN FRONT OF THE GLOWACKI AND NORTH RESIDENCES.

exercises of dedication of the old Land Office at Batavia as a memorial to Robert Morris. It would give the President great pleasure to be present on that occasion and thus to express his appreciation of the distinguished services of the eminent patriot and financier whose work you will commemorate, but his engagements are such that he regrets that it will be impossible for him to accept this courteous invitation. Very truly yours,

HENRY T. THURBER, Private Secretary.

To Chairman Committee on Invitations, Batavia, N. Y.

(William Kirkpatrick.)

We send with this the Onondaga Centennial Medal, and beg that it may find a place in your collection. The medal commemorated the erection of the County of Onondaga and the Military Tract, which was given to the soldiers of the Revolution of the State of New York. Each private received six hundred acres, and officers according to their rank.

(Hon. Levi P. Morton.)

I beg leave to acknowledge the courtesy of the invitation to be present at the dedication of the old Land Office of the Holland Purchase on the 13th inst. The occasion will be a notable one, embracing as it will so much that is of interest in the development of Western New York. I also recall the patriotic services of the great financier of the Revolution.

I sincerely regret that pressure of my engagements will prevent my attendance and the acceptance of the hospitality of the Holland Purchase Historical Association.

(Hon. James O. Putnam.)

I have the honor to acknowledge receipt of your kind invitation to attend upon the Robert Morris memorial exercises on the 13th inst. Grateful for the courtesy of the Committee, I have pleasure in accepting it. Will the Committee be pleased to accept my congratulations on the wonderful, even national, response to their original memorial thought.

(Governor Flower.)

Governor Flower presents his compliments to the Holland Purchase Historical Society, and regrets exceedingly his inability to be present at the dedication of the old Land Office at Batavia on October 13th, 1894, as a memorial to Robert Morris.

(Gouverneur Morris.)

I beg leave to acknowledge the receipt of your invitation to attend the dedication of the Holland Land Office memorial to Robert Morris on the 13th inst. It is with feelings of great regret that I am unable to be present at the celebration attending this mark of honor to my great-grandfather, but I hope that my son, Robert Morris (9th), who will be present, may be a worthy representative of the family. With thanks for the honor.

(Robert Morris.)

I take great pleasure in accepting your invitation to be present at the dedicatory exercises in honor of the patriot, Robert Morris, and will be in Batavia on the day named.

(Mrs. Robert Morris.)

Mrs. Robert Morris appreciates the compliment and respect offered to the memory of Robert Morris, and thanking you for your polite invitation, regrets exceedingly that it is impossible for her to be present at that time.

— 131 —

(*Dr. Henry Morris.*)

Dr. Henry Morris appreciates the honor of and accepts with pleasure the invitation of the Holland Purchase Historical Society to be present at Batavia as its guest on the 13th of October, the occasion of the dedication of the Old Land Office of the Holland Purchase as a memorial to his great-grandfather, Robert Morris of the Revolution.

(*Buffalo Courier.*)

When the Holland Land Company was first organized the following members controlled the organization: Wilhelm Willink, Jan Willink, Nicholas Van Staphorst, Jacob Van Staphorst, Nicholas Hubbard, Peter Van Eeghen, Christian Van Eeghen, Isaac Ten Cate, Hendrick Vallenhoven,

ON THE LINE OF MARCH—CAUSE AND EFFECT—THE ORIGIN OF THE GOTHIC ARCHITECTURE
—"THE GROVES WERE GOD'S FIRST TEMPLES."

Christian Coster (a widow), Jan Stadnitski, and Rutger J. Schimmelpennick. These were the first members of the Company. The first general agent of the Holland Land Company was Theophilus Cazenove. But little is known of his history. When the Land Company made its first purchases in the interior of this State soon after the year 1790 he had arrived in this country and was engaged to act as their agent. Cazenove returned to Europe in 1799, where he resided in London, and at a later period in Paris. Following him as general agent came Paul Busti, who was a native of Milan, Italy. He was born on October 17, 1749. He faithfully performed the duties of agent for 24 years. He died July 23, 1824. Mr. Busti was succeeded in office by John J. VanderKemp, who was a native of Leyden, Holland. His parents emigrated to the United States in 1788. The first local agent at Batavia was Joseph Ellicott. His agency ended in October, 1821. The corps of assistants under him were as follows: Peter Huidekoper and James Milner, clerks; Walter M. Seymour, cashier, and Ebenezer Mix, contractor. Jacob S. Otto succeeded Ellicott. He came from Philadelphia, and his agency extended from 1821 until the time of his death, 1826. The same assistants were under him. David E. Evans came in next. His agency continued until 1837, at which time the business interests of the Company had nearly reached their termination. The Company then sold out to Le Roy Redfield and others, and Heman J. Redfield was appointed agent. The services of Homer Kimberly, H. I. Glowacki, Robert W. Lowber, Leander Mix, and John Lowber were secured, and the business was placed under their management. Later on this Company sold out to the Farmers' Loan and Trust Company of New York City. D. D. Williamson, president of the Trust Company, filled the position of agent, and was assisted by Julius A. Smith, Homer Kimberly and Leander Mix, who acted as traveling agent, and later on was succeeded by David E. E. Mix. Ebenezer Mix was in the employ of the Company for over 20 years and Leander for 13.

(*Batavia Spirit of the Times.*)

At the close of the Revolutionary war the unsurveyed lands in Western New York belonged to the State of Massachusetts subject to the Indian title. In 1791 the great patriot, Robert Morris of Philadelphia, who had done so much for the cause of the Revolution, bought from Massachusetts nearly all the land lying west of the Genesee river. This great Morris tract became the County of Genesee. The word *Genesee* means in the Indian language "The Beautiful Valley." The name is peculiarly appropriate; for a finer region than the original county of Genesee is not to be found in the world. Its fertility is inexhaustible, and it is now a region of teeming prosperity.

Morris made a treaty with the Indians in which they consented to give up their title to all the land except a few reservations of moderate size. Portions of those reservations are still held and occupied by the Indians. The one in the town of Alabama, in the present County of Genesee, was the residence of the famous Red Jacket, the Chief of the Six Nations.

Morris had been very wealthy, but he had been so reduced by his losses in the Revolution that he was compelled to part with his land. He sold the greater portion of it in 1792 to a company of Hollanders, and the tract thus sold became known and famous as the "Holland Purchase." Morris sank into poverty, and occupied for years a debtor's prison. But he will ever rank with the purest and ablest patriots of the nation, and his name gives a sacred interest to the region that was once in his possession.

The Hollanders employed Joseph Ellicott, an eminent surveyor, to survey their lands and manage the sale of them. Mr. Ellicott continued in the position of agent for the Holland Land Company 21 years, and won great distinction by his remarkable executive ability. He was identified with all the enterprises of Western New York, including the construction of the Erie Canal, in which he took a great interest.

He established his land office at Batavia in 1802 on the line of the Indian trail from the Canadas to Southern New York, and in the line of the immigration that was then moving westward.

The Indians had a council ground within a few rods of the land office. The trail (now Ellicott street in Batavia) became known as the "Big Tree Road," on account of its passing by an enormous tree near Geneseo. The other road (now Main street in Batavia) became the main thoroughfare from Albany to Niagara Falls and Buffalo.

The first land office was a wooden building, but it was replaced early in this century by the present substantial stone structure. Every settler on the Holland Purchase made many visits to this famous structure while paying for his beautiful home in the "Pleasant Valley."

The building is therefore an object of household tradition in six counties. But it was the headquarters of the entire region in every respect. All enterprises were discussed and determined upon at Batavia. Mr. Ellicott,

JOSEPH ELLICOTT.

as a sort of grand seignior, was expected to receive and entertain distinguished visitors, and to be the leading spirit of the Purchase in all matters of common interest. He discharged all his functions so well that his name is remembered throughout the Purchase with admiration.

Mr. Ellicott was succeeded in 1821 by Jacob S. Otto, who held the office of agent until his death in 1826. David E. Evans then became agent, and continued in the office until 1836. In 1836 Heman J. Redfield and Jacob Le Roy bought the interests of the Holland Company in Genesee, Niagara, Erie and Wyoming counties. In 1839 Peter J. Van Hall of Amsterdam, Holland, came as the last agent of the Holland Company and closed out their interests entirely in 1839.

In 1839 Redfield and Pringle took charge of the Land Office and retained it until shortly before the accounts with the settlers were closed. Julius

H. Smith succeeded Redfield and Pringle, and in the final settlement of matters the Land Office passed into his hands. It was sold by him to William G. Bryan, and has since passed through the hands of several other purchasers. A movement is now on foot to procure and preserve this famous building as a landmark of the history of a great region in a great country.

Other names associated with the Land Office are those of Ebenezer Mix, the remarkable mathematician who had charge of all calculations and records of distances and bounds, Ebenezer Cary, the appraiser, and James Brisbane, the commissary of provisions.

Supplies were brought by way of the Hudson and Mohawk rivers to Rome, thence by portage to Oneida Lake, down the Oswego River to Lake Ontario, thence to Lewiston, from Lewiston to Batavia by wagon.

The name Batavia is another name for Holland, and was so given because it was the headquarters of the Holland Purchase.

Through Morris the old building recalls the Revolution, and it has been associated with all the great history of the intervening period. It recalls the struggles of the pioneers who were helped to independence within its walls, and who looked upon it as their citadel and seignorial castle.

The barony in the wilderness has become the scene of a most striking civilization. The old castle would fain hide its diminished head in the glare of modern wealth and prosperity. But its history gives it a value that modern wealth cannot buy. It stands for the Revolutionary patriot, the Revolutionary soldier, and the sturdy pioneer. It is as much an oddity as would be a cocked hat and a blue coat with with brass buttons walking down Broadway. But such oddities are precious ; they recall the debt that we owe to a past age. Morris, Ellicott, Otto, Evans, Van Hall, Redfield, Smith, and Lay sum up in a sense the history of the United States. It was all represented in their careers and largely formed by them.

(Batavia Daily News.)

Joseph Ellicott's grandparents came to this country from Wales in 1731. He had three brothers—Andrew, older, and Benjamin and David, younger—and five sisters, three of whom married brothers named Evans. Andrew Ellicott became an eminent surveyor, was at one time Surveyor General of the United States, and at the time of his death was professor of mathematics at West Point. Benjamin Ellicott also was a surveyor, and for several years was in the service of the Holland Company as an assistant to his brother Joseph. He was once a Member of Congress (1817-19). He was a bachelor and died a resident of Williamsville, Erie county, in 1827. The youngest brother, David, who likewise was once a surveyor on the Purchase, was erratic. He went South, and no tidings ever came of him. Andrew Ellicott had three sons—Andrew O., who died in Shelby, Orleans county; Joseph, who died in Batavia in 1839, and John B. Ellicott, whose death occurred in Batavia on August 27, 1872, at his home which stood on Main street, between Jackson and Center streets, the house he occupied now standing in the rear of G. D. Williamson's store.

The descendants of the Ellicott family now residing in Batavia are Mrs. Mary J. Smith, daughter of John B. Ellicott, son of Andrew Ellicott, and her niece, Miss Eva Collamer; Miss Mary L. Douglass, daughter of David B. Douglass and Ann E. Ellicott, a daughter of Andrew Ellicott, and her niece, Miss Annie Jarvis; Mrs. Pierson and her sister, Miss Maria Heston, daughters of Samuel Heston, the son of Joseph Heston and Ann Evans, whose mother was Letitia Ellicott, a sister of Joseph Ellicott; Mrs. Martha Potter, who resides in the western part of the town, and who is also a descendant of Letitia Ellicott. Other descendants of the Ellicott and Evans families are scattered throughout the country.

Joseph Ellicott, of Holland Purchase fame, was only fourteen years of age when his father moved from Bucks county, Pa., to Maryland, and he enjoyed no other facilities for an education than the common schools of the

ON THE LINE OF MARCH—THE LAND OFFICE VISTA.

country afforded. His early lessons in surveying were given him by his brother Andrew, whom he assisted in the survey of the city of Washington soon after the site had been selected for the National Capital. In 1791 he was appointed by Timothy Pickering, then Secretary of War, to run the boundary line between Georgia and the Creek Indians. Subsequently, as previously told, he entered the services of the Holland company, continuing as its representative until 1821, for many years of his association with it being in full charge of its affairs hereabouts, with his headquarters in the old Land Office that to-day, with ceremonials, was dedicated to the purposes of the Holland Purchase Historical Society.

"In person," says Turner's History, "Mr. Ellicott was rather above the midling size six feet three inches in height. In youth he was of spare habits, but about the age of forty became corpulent. He had a strong constitution, capable of much endurance, and enjoyed for the greater portion of his life uninterrupted health.

Joseph Ellicott's death occurred on August 19, 1826, when he was 66 years old, and his remains lie in the Batavia Cemetery, a monument marking the spot. On its face, or west side, this monument bears an inscription chiseled in memory of Joseph Ellicott, but the greater part of this inscription has been effaced by the action of the elements. On the north side is an inscription in better condition in memory of Benjamin Ellicott, and beneath it is the announcement that the monument was erected by the twin sister of Benjamin, Rachel Evans, in May, 1849. North of the monument, but within the iron fence that surrounds it, are two graves marked by a double headstone, those of Benjamin Ellicott and his sister, Mrs. Evans. South of the monument is an unmarked grave, presumably that of Joseph Ellicott. The monument is 32 feet high, its main shaft being 16½ feet, and it was erected by B. and J. Carpenter of Lockport, the material coming from their quarry of limestones. Its condition shows the ravages of time.

(Buffalo Express.)

In the office of the Secretary of State there is to be found a large wooden box, marked on the lid, "Holland Land Papers." This box, which is of about the size of a carpenter's tool-chest, and is preserved with the greatest care, is full of interesting relics of the settlement of Western New York, which would have added much to the exhibition made at the centennial celebration in Batavia.

Within the box are many deeds and other legal instruments. The most important of them are these: A deed of the 1,500,000-acre tract, dated December, 1792, from Robert Morris and Mary, his wife, to Herman Le Roy and John Lincklaen; an agreement bearing the same date, between the same parties, by which the grantors may convert the contract of sale into a loan of money, in which case the conveyance is to serve as a mortgage; a notice, dated December, 1795, given by Le Roy and Lincklaen to Morris, of their election to consider the contract as a sale, and the conveyance as absolute and not by way of mortgage; and a deed of the Sheriff of Ontario County, dated May, 1800, to Thomas Ogden, for land taken as the property of Robert Morris at the suit of William Talbot and William Allum. These papers, together with many others, are classified as "Deductions of Titles" to the 1,500,000-acre tract. Similar deductions also appear for the tracts containing respectively 1,000,000, 800,000, 300,000, and 40,000 acres.

Then there are numerous small books, of pocket size, that contain the field notes of the surveyors of 1798–9. All of these lead up to 15 books, of almost ledger size, bound in thick sheep-skin, each of which is devoted to a "range," whether it is filled or not. The number of the range is printed on red leather on the back. Within each book are given the exact boundaries of the townships into which the range was divided. The boundaries are, for the most part, either trees or posts, the name of the wood being given in every case. Stone boundaries are noted at very rare intervals. Aside from the boundaries, the physical features of each township are described, and the whole is signed: "Joseph Ellicott, surveyor for the Holland Land Company." The authenticity of the 15 range books was certified to by Samuel Nelson, Chief Justice of the Supreme Court of Judicature, on April 12, 1841. They were deposited with the Secretary of State, for safe keeping, by an act of the Legislature passed in 1839. The Secretary, John C. Spencer, acknowledges the receipt of the books, and also of the deeds and other papers, from J. J. Vander Kemp, general agent of the Holland Company.

But most interesting of all is the original map of the Holland Company's tract. It is about eight feet square, on heavy paper backed with cloth. Time and use have not dealt kindly with it, but much of it is still legible. The scale seems to be about half an inch to the mile. The eastern boundary known as "the transit line," was run in 1798. It started on the Pennsylvania line, at the southeast corner of the Willing purchase, and ran directly north-

A FIRE PLACE IN THE LAND OFFICE.

ward, crossing the Genesee River " at 21 miles going northwest and at 33 miles going northeast," and reached Lake Ontario at a place known as " The Devil's Nose." The ranges, averaging about six miles in width, have boundaries parallel with the transit line. They begin six miles west of that line, and they are numbered to the westward from 1 to 15, inclusive. The townships run from south to north, beginning at the Pennsylvania line, and they average six miles square. No range has more than 16 townships, and when the western end of the State is reached (in Chautauqua County, as it is now), the fifteenth range is only three townships high. The city of Buffalo was the 10th and 11th townships of range 15, and the city of Niagara Falls was in township 15 of the same range.

Between the seventh and eighth ranges a strip about two miles wide runs from the Pennsylvania line northward to Lake Ontario. It pierces the present counties of Cattaraugus, Erie and Niagara; and it is marked as the property of Wilhelm and Jan Willink. The same persons are also credited with 10 townships in the eastern and southern parts of the present Allegany County. Between the first range and the transit line is a strip, about six miles wide, running from Pennsylvania to Lake Ontario. This is assigned, with the respective number of acres named, to the following: J. Sterrett, 5,000; A. Hamilton, 100,000; Cattinger, 39,784; Ogden, 32,784; Cragie, 3,375, and Watson Cragie, 100,000. The lands of Sterrett and Hamilton are in the present county of Allegany; those of Cattinger and Ogden in Wyoming, that of Craigie in Genesee, and that of Watson Cragie in Orleans. There are two parcels of land to the eastward of the transit line. The first, in the present Allegany county, has 150,000 acres, credited to S. Sterrett, the second is a triangle, of 76,173 acres, assigned to Le Roy, Bayard, and McEvers. The northern boundary of the triangle is Lake Ontario, the western the transit line, and the third a diagonal beginning at the intersection of the southern line of the Phelps and Gorman purchase with the transit line, near the present village of Le Roy, and running northeasterly till it reaches Lake Ontario. The slanting boundaries of the eastern townships of Genesee County, and of the western townships of Monroe County, are laid along this diagonal line. All that part of the State was known to the province of New York as Tryon county, but, after 1784, it was called Montgomery County. All to the west of the "pre-emption line" was made into Ontario County in 1788; and the present western counties have been taken from the original territory of Ontario County since that date. Steuben was taken in 1796, Genesee in 1802, and Yates in 1823. Livingston and Monroe were formed from parts of Ontario and Livingston in 1821. Genesee, as originally constituted in 1802, embraced all of the Holland tract, but from its territory counties were carved as follows: Allegany, 1806; Cattaraugus, Chautauqua and Niagara, 1808; Orleans, 1824; and Wyoming in 1841. Erie was taken from Niagara in 1821.

Much confusion has arisen in the minds of average readers as to "the Genesee Country," and a word of explanation may be of interest. All through the Revolutionary war, and as late as 1789, that part of the State to the west of a line drawn north from about the site of the present city of Elmira, was known as the Genesee Country. The lands were claimed by both New York and Massachusetts, and over both of the claimants, the British forts at Oswego and Niagara held a constant menace long after the close of the Revolution. Simcoe, Governor of Upper Canada, protested against the settlement of the country "during the inexecution of the treaty that terminated the Revolutionary War." It was, indeed, a time of doubtful allegiances when the United States troops at Pittsburg were furnished with blankets by the British traders at the mouth of the Cuyahoga (Cleveland); and when, at the latter place, American farmers sold flour to the British posts along the Great Lakes. The British considered the treaty of 1783 a mere truce, to be followed by the speedy failure of the young republic and the restoration of the Colonies to England. There were, also, enough unfriendly Indians to make the life of a settler miserable. So bad was the reputation of the region that when apprentices were bound, or slaves sold, it was expressly stipulated that they should not be taken to the Genesee Country. When Oliver Phelps, in 1788, left Connecticut to look after his claim, he was called a fool, and the more religiously inclined followed him to the town limits with prayers and tears.

Phelps, together with Daniel Gorham, also of Connecticut, had bought the entire tract west of "the pre-emption line," from Massachusetts for $1,000,000, or about 11 cents an acre for the 7,000,000 acres. This line ran northward from the 82d milestone on the Pennsylvania border until it met the waters of Lake Ontario. By later and more accurate surveys, it proved to be almost the exact meridian of Washington. Massachusetts had resigned to New York all political jurisdiction over the territory to the west of this line, and situated within the State of New York; but she reserved the pre-emptive right, so far as the Indians were concerned. In 1788 Phelps held a council

THE OLD ARSENAL.

with the representatives of the Six Nations on the site of the present village of Canandaigua, and he bought their right to 2,500,000 acres in the tract, the Massachusetts title of which had already been vested in himself and Gorham. He then opened, in Canandaigua, the first land office in America for the sale of wild lands to actual settlers; and his methods have since been adopted throughout the country. Meeting with financial difficulties, Phelps and Gorham were obliged to surrender all of the tract to which the Indian title had not been extinguished, and the greater part of it became the purchase of the Holland Company.

The original Genesee Country, therefore, was a generic term that included the tract eventually known by that name, as well as the Holland tract and other tracts. What was finally known as the Genesee Country, after the failure of Phelps and Gorham, had an area of 2,200,000 acres. It was bounded by the pre-emption line on the east, and on the west by a line drawn through the "Big Elm" at the junction of Canaseraga Creek with the Genesee River, near the present village of Mount Morris. This line met the Pennsylvania line at the south. Two miles to the north of Canawagus (Avon), it turned at a right angle to the westward, and then followed the course of the Genesee River, at a distance of 12 miles, until it reached Lake Ontario.

(*E. L. Willard.*)

COUDERSPORT, Pa., Dec. 16, 1894.

Through the kind courtesy of Mr. H. P. Woodward I am informed as to the objects and successes of your honorable Society. In return I state what I shall be able to furnish, although I have not them all collected in form to forward. This place being only a temporary staying place for me, I must repeat largely from memory until such time as I shall return to my home and office in Elmira. The papers I have are some of them the originals, and others copies of some which can not be acquired, except for the purpose of copying.

Owing to the laws of Pennsylvania, the Company was unable to take lands in that state as a corporation or society, but they purchased under the separate names as follows (from memory): Wilhelm Willink, Ruter Jan Scheimmelpfennig, Hendrick Vallenhoven, Nicholas Von Stapherst, Jan Van Eaghen, and Christian Van Eaghen. There were also some lands purchased by "Heman Le Roy and Jan Lincklean, A. Z.," of Amsterdam, which were patented to "William Willink" and others.

On or about the 2d of February, 1792, these gentlemen purchased and paid for in part 1,132 tracts of 970 acres each, or about one million, one hundred and twenty-one thousand acres of land, all lying north and west of the Susquehanna River, the Tia lightem Creek and the Conewango River, in that part of Pennsylvania purchased from the Indians in 1782, and first opened for settlement in 1785, but immediately closed again until 1792, at which time this purchase was made. These tracts are situated in all parts of this territory described above. There were many litigations in regard to portions of the purchase, in the trial of which many important and interesting facts appear, and which I shall be able to transmit copies to you.

A curious fact (of which proof is negative, however, and consequently difficult to transmit) is that the gentlemen name I authorized one Paul Busti to act as their agent, and empowered him to act for them, but to this instrument so empowering him, the signatures of only three of the six appear affixed. It is presumed that the other three are dead, and were at the time of the execution of the instrument, but no statement is made to that effect therein. Consequently, all the titles to this one million acres, derived from the Holland Company, are defective as to one undivided one-half interest. The Courts, however, are seldom compelled to take cognizance of this, but it has been adduced in evidence twice to my memory. The Company, immediately after the date of their purchase, caused surveys to be made of the entire tracts, and took possession, leaving, however, part of the purchase money unpaid, and a part of this money is due and unpaid at the present day. This debt has long since become a lien against the land, collectable at any time since the 1st of June, 1868, by the Attorney General. This is a little known fact, even to the present owners of the land against which the debt is a lien, and I believe no attempt has ever been made to collect any part of the same, although in several cases particular parts of the purchase have been paid for and exempted. In my many years search of the titles and location of these tracts, I have frequently, I might say in hundreds of cases, gone upon the ground where these locations were made, to discover the marks made by the several surveyors in locating and marking each 990 acre tract. I find by counting the growths of the trees, which have long since grown over the marks there made, that these surveys were made, and the marks put upon the trees in 1793 and 1794. By the papers in my possession I am enabled to state that these surveyors

THE LAND OFFICE IN WINTER.

were William Ellis of Muncy, John Brodhead, James Hunter, Samuel Stewart, Joseph Eaton, William P. Brady, and Colonel Canan.

With regard to the date of the erection of the office in Batavia, I have no papers that I know of which have any bearing on the subject, but may be able to assist you in the search for the same. I can say, however, that in addition to the surveys made in 1793 and 1794, that in 1805 there were surveys made over the whole of the purchase in both States, which I believe to have been made by Mr. Andrew Ellicott of Ellicottville. This gentleman completed the surveys in New York State in the spring of 1805, and entered Pennsylvania and re-surveyed the lands of the Company in this State. At that time the Company had Mr. Busti for their agent, and were extensively oper ating on these lands, building roads, etc. I presume they must have had the office at Batavia at that date. Mr. Ellicott did not return to return to New York, but became a prominent citizen of this State, and continued to act in the interest of the Holland Company.

I will go to see some persons who will be able to tell me more of this office than I now know, and will send you whatever they may have.

I have in my possession many pieces of trees taken as sections showing the notches made by the original surveyors at the corners of the tracts in the purchase, and showing the one hundred and one growths or rings since that time, as well as the mark made at that time.

If this would be of interest I will forward you one or two, with the papers relating to the tracts from which the block is taken. I may say that the pa-

REPOSE ON THE TONAWANDA.

pers relating to each 990 acres are separate from those relating to each other 990 acres, a practice differing from that of your own State.

The surveys of 1805 have always been more or less of a mystery to those versed in the combined history and wood craft of this state, on account of the scarcity of papers showing the object of the extensive work. There is a volume of history connected with each of the one thousand tracts, but one of the most interesting is that relating to the litigation of the Company with George Meade, and of the same versus Robert Morris and John Nicholson; also the objections of sundry citizens of Pennsylvania against the policy of allowing the great purchase to be consummated.

These are some of the points of history covered by my information. If you see anything in these facts or the papers relating to them that is of interest to you. I shall be glad to aid you in securing the original papers verifying the facts. Many of the papers are in the office of the Secretary of Internal Affairs, who furnishes certified copies of the originals.

If these would be of interest, in the absence of the originals, I should be happy to be allowed to pay the Secretary the fees for the copies, and present the same to the Society, as verifying any points which may be dimly proven without them.

Hoping that my earnest good wishes, added to what little I can do, may be appreciated, I remain respectfully yours.

(Edward F. De Lancey.)

I have deferred answering your invitation to attend as a guest the dedi-

SIXTY MILES AN HOUR ON THE TONAWANDA.

cation of the old Land Office at Batavia on the 13th of this month, in the hope that I might be present. Unfortunately I find I cannot be absent from this city at that time. I deeply regret that I cannot therefore accept your very polite invitation. I rejoice that the old building and its invaluable records will be preserved, to show the beginnings and settlement of that immense tract, which form so large a portion of the western half of this State.

Having known, as a youth, some of Robert Morris's friends in Philadelphia, and his confidential clerk during the Revolution, and friend and agent in Western New York, the late James Rees of Geneva, from whom I learned much of interest concerning him, his estate and misfortunes, to say nothing of many of his grandchildren and great-grandchildren being among my own friends, I am extremely sorry that I am prevented from being with you on this important occasion.

(*L. W. Ledyard.*)

Will you kindly send me by return mail a program of the intended celebration, as I may feel an interest in attending. I am now the only person living that was connected with the Cazenovia establishment, although the concern passed into my father's ownership. He was the adopted son of Jan Van Lincklean, who came to this agency in 1792-3, and opened the lands in 1822.

(*Hon. Cuthbert W. Pound.*)

On my return from New York yesterday I found your very kind invitation to myself and Mrs. Ponnd to attend the dedication of the old Land Office of the Holland Purchase to-day.

I extremely regret that my engagements do not permit that we should accept the invitation. It is, however, with no small degree of interest, that I congratulate your Society upon its successful efforts to secure the preservation of this old land-mark. My grandfather was an early settler here, and on my father's knee I learned to regard Turner's " History of the Holland Purchase " as a local classic. This memorial, so frought with recollections of the long struggle with nature which redeemed the Holland Purchase from the wilderness, is particularly significant to the children of those pioneers.

I heartily wish your society and its undertakings a full measure of success.

(*Hon. James O. Putnam.*)

I had not the pleasure of meeting you on Saturday, when I could, in person, have given you my congratulations on the great success of the Morris memorial enterprise. You can fairly say of it: *Magna pars fui*.

Its conception was original and not without an element of courage.

Additional to the local virtue of the Morris memorial at Batavia, I believe its moral influence will lead to acts of National justice to a long, almost criminally, neglected character.

Even Philadelphia must now feel her own honor is in question, and be moved to do justice to the memory of her great citizen.

(*W. H. Samson.*)

After the close of the Revolutionary war and the successful establishment of the independence of the colonies, there was a serious dispute between New York and Massachusetts regarding the land in what is now Western New York. Massachusetts claimed the title by virtue of a grant from James I. to the Plymouth company, made November 3, 1620, and New York claimed it by virtue of the grant of Charles II. to the Duke of York, dated March 12, 1664, and the voluntary submission of the Iroquois to the crown in 1684.

Happily this dispute was amicably adjusted. By a compact dated December 16, 1786, signed by the commissioners representing the two States, New York secured the sovereignty and jurisdiction and Massachusetts the right to buy from the native Indians.

* * * * * * * *

Soon after making the purchase from Massachusetts, Mr. Morris resolved to settle his son Thomas in the Genesee country, "as an evidence of his faith in its value and prospects." Thomas Morris was 20 years of age. He had been educated at Geneva and Leipsic and was then reading law. In obedience to the wishes of his father, he left Philadelphia in the early summer of 1791, and coming by way of Wilkesbarre and what was called "Sullivan's path," reached Newtown, where he attended Pickering's council and received from the Indians the name of O-te-ti-ana, which Red Jacket had borne in his younger days. Proceeding on his journey, Mr. Morris visited Niagara Falls. On his return, he passed through Canandaigua. The aspect of the little frontier village pleased him and he resolved to make the place his home. Arranging his affairs in the East, he left New York in March, 1792, and went to

A REMINDER OF THE PIONEERS—THE HISTORICAL MUSEUM AT SILVER LAKE.

Canandaigua. In 1793 he built a framed house, filled in with brick—one of the two framed houses in the state, west of Whitesboro. Mr. Morris was admitted to the bar, and in 1794 attended the first court held at Canandaigua. He devoted much of his time to the care of his father's property and the settlement and development of Western New York, and was honored and esteemed by the pioneers. In 1794, 1795 and 1796 he was a member of Assembly from Ontario county. For five years, beginning with 1796, he was a Senator of the State of New York, and from December, 1801, till March, 1803, he was a Member of Congress—the first representative in Congress from that portion of the State of New York lying west of Seneca Lake. He shared in the financial reverses of his father and in 1804 appointed John Greig his attorney and removed to New York city, where he practiced law until his death in 1848.

Though Robert Morris desired a speedy settlement of his speculations with the Hollanders, it was not until 1796 that he asked President Washington to order a treaty and appoint a commissioner to represent the United States. The delay in the application was very creditable, for it was due entirely to motives of public consideration. Morris's letter was as follows:

PHILADELPHIA, August 25, 1796.

SIR—In the year 1791 I purchased from the State of Massachusetts a tract of country lying within the boundaries of the State of New York, which had been ceded by the latter to the former State, under the sanction and with the concurrence of the Congress of the United States. This tract of land is bounded to the east by the Genesee River, to the north by Lake Ontario, to the west partly by Lake Erie and partly by the boundary line of the Pennsylvania triangle, and to the south by the north boundary line of the State of Pennsylvania. A printed brief of the title I take the liberty to transmit herewith. To perfect this title it is necessary to purchase of the Seneca nation of Indians their native right, which I should have done soon after the purchase was made of the State of Massachusetts, but that I felt myself restrained from doing so by motives of public consideration. The war between the Western Indian nations and the United States did not extend to the Six Nations, of which the Seneca nation is one; and, as I apprehended that, if this nation should sell its rights during the existence of that war, they might the more readily be induced to join the enemies of our country, I was determined not to make the purchase whilst the war lasted.

When peace was made with the Indian nations I turned my thoughts towards the purchase, which is to me an object very interesting; but upon it being represented that a little longer patience, until the Western posts should be delivered up by the British government, might be public utility, I concluded to wait for that event also, which is now happily accomplished, and there seems no obstacle to restrain me from making the purchase, especially as I have reason to believe the Indians are desirous of making the sale.

The delays which have already taken place and that arose solely from the considerations above mentioned, have been extremely detrimental to my private affairs; but, still being desirous to comply with formalities prescribed by certain laws of the United States, although those laws probably do not reach my case, I now make application to the President of the United States and request that he will nominate and appoint a commissioner to be present and preside at a treaty, which he will be pleased to authorize to be held with the Seneca nation, for the purpose of enabling me to make a purchase in conformity with the formalities required by law, of the tract of country for which I have already paid a very large sum of money. My right to pre-emption is unequivocal, and the land is become so necessary to the growing population and surrounding settlements that it is with difficulty that the white people can be restrained from squattering or settling down upon these lands, which if they should do, it may probably bring on contentions with the Six Nations. This will be prevented by a timely, fair, and honorable purchase.

This proposed treaty ought to be held immediately before the hunting season, or another year will be lost, as the Indians cannot be collected during that season The loss of another year, under the payments thus made for these lands, would be ruinous to my affairs, and as I have paid so great deference to public considerations whilst they did exist, I expect and hope that my request will be readily granted now, when there can be no cause for delay, especially if the Indians are willing to sell, which will be tested by the offer to buy.

With the most perfect esteem and respect, I am, sir, your most obedient and most humble servant, ROBERT MORRIS.

George Washington, Esq., President of the United States.

President Washington appointed a member of Congress from New Jersey, named Isaac Smith, as the commissioner. But having been subsequently appointed a judge of the Supreme court of his State, Mr. Smith found that

THE EVANS MANSION—THE RIGHT WING OF THE BUILDING IS THE ORIGINAL HOLLAND LAND OFFICE.

his judicial duties would prevent his attendance at the treaty; accordingly he declined, and Colonel Jeremiah Wadsworth, who had been a distinguished member of Congress from Connecticut, was appointed in his place.

Unable himself to take part in the treaty, Robert Morris appointed his son Thomas and Charles Williamson as his attorneys; but Captain Williamson, busy with his affairs at Bath, declined to act, and so the responsibility for conducting the difficult and delicate negotiations fell entirely upon the younger Morris.

It was resolved to hold the treaty at Big Tree, near the settlement which afterwards became Geneseo.

In meadow lands within the corporate limits of the village of Geneseo, southwest from the park, about a quarter of a mile above the Erie railroad, and about the same distance west of the Mt. Morris road, is a cobblestone house ; on the site of this building there stood, 100 years ago, a small dwelling erected by William and James Wadsworth. This was rented by Thomas Morris for the entertainment of the principal persons at the treaty. He also caused a large council house to be erected, covered with boughs and branches of trees. Doty's "History of Livingston County" says that the Indian village of Big Tree was west of the Genesee river, and that the big tree itself stood on the eastern bank. Some Geneseo antiquarians of to-day declare that the village was east of the Genesee. Both are correct, the explanation being that the village was moved. At the time of the treaty, however, the village was west of the Genesee. It not only appears so on the first map of the region made from actual surveys, but the treaty as agreed upon declared that the reservation of Big Tree should embrace the village, and Ellicott's map of 1804 shows the reservation to be west of the river. In 1805 the village was moved, and on the map showing the Phelps and Gorham purchase in 1806, Big Tree village appears east of the Genesee. The probability is that the council house was erected on the eastern bank and Charles Jones, who derived his information from his father, Horatio Jones, who attended the treaty and took a prominent part in the negotiations, thinks it stood 500 feet northwest of the Wadsworth dwelling.

The Indians began to arrive at Big Tree late in August, not the Senecas alone, but groups from the other nations—attracted, doubtless, by the hope of presents and the possibility of good living. Fifty-two Indians signed the treaty. Many of them were famous in Indian annals. Young King, Chief Warrior, Handsome Lake, the Prophet ; Farmer's Brother, Red Jacket, Little Billy, Pollard, the Infant, Cornplanter, Destroy Town, Little Beard, Blacksnake—these were the leaders of the Senecas at Big Tree, interesting men, all of them. Time will not permit me to give biographies. It seems necessary, however, to explain that there were two Indians known to the whites as Big Tree.

Ga-on-dah-go-waah, called sometimes Big Tree and sometimes Great Tree, was a full-blooded Seneca of the Hawk clan and resided for many years at Big Tree village. He attended the Buffalo treaty of July 8, 1788, when Phelps and Gorham made their purchase, and went to Philadelphia in the winter of 1790 with Cornplanter and Half Town to protest against what they regarded an unjust treatment from Phelps and his associates. He was there again with Red Jacket in 1792 and died in that city in April of that year. Consequently he did not attend the Big Tree treaty. This chief's daughter had a son whose father was a Niagara trader named Pollard. The boy grew up in the Indian village and became in time a famous chief. His name was Ga-on-do-wau-na, which also meant Big Tree. He made himself conspicuous in border warfare, and was at the massacre of Wyoming. He it was who signed the Big Tree treaty. As an orator he was but little inferior to Red Jacket, and his character was finer. After the death of Cornplanter he was, perhaps, the noblest of the Senecas. He was among the first Indians on the Buffalo Creek reservation to embrace the truths of Christianity, and thereafter his life was singularly blameless and beneficent. He was sometimes called Colonel John Pollard. He died on the reservation April 10, 1841, and was buried in the old Mission cemetery.

Thomas Morris reached the Genesee on August 22d. The commissioners arrived four days later, Colonel Jeremiah Wadsworth to represent the United States and General William Shepherd to represent the commonwealth of Massachusetts. Captain Israel Chapin, who had succeeded his father, General Israel Chapin, as superintendent of Indian affairs, attended; James Rees, subsequently of Geneva, was there and acted as secretary, and among other white men who attended, and were greatly interested in the negotiations, were William Bayard of New York, the agent of the Holland Land Company; two young gentlemen from Holland named Van Staphorst,

THE REDFIELD RESIDENCE.

near relatives of the Van Staphorst who was one of the principal members of the Holland Company, Nathaniel W. Howell, Jasper Parrish, and Horatio Jones.

  * * * * * * * * *

The council was formally opened at 1 o'clock on the afternoon of August 28, 1797. Cornplanter spoke first. Turning to Thomas Morris, he acknowledged the speech of invitation conveyed by Jasper Parrish and Horatio Jones, and returned the string of wampum that had reached him with the invitation to the treaty. Then the commissioners from the United States and Massachusetts presented their credentials and addressed the assembly, assuring the Indians that their interests would be duly guarded and that no injustice would be done.

* * * * * * * * *

Within a short time an agreement was reached, and the Indian lands west of the Genesee, excepting ten reservations embracing 337 square miles, were sold to Robert Morris for $100,000, to be invested in the stock of the Bank of the United States, and held in the name of the President for the benefit of the Indians. The treaty was signed on September 15, 1797.

(*W. B. Turpin.*)

Is the "Society of the War of 1812" to be represented in your forthcoming celebration? Being a member of that Society and a descendant of a participant in that war who was quartered in the old Land Office after the retreat from the Niagara frontier, I should be glad to attend the dedication of the historic building as a representative of the Society of 1812.

(*General William H. Seward.*)

I feel much complimented by your kind invitation to be present at the celebration of the Holland Purchase Historical Society, and regret deeply my inability to attend, especially as my father was so closely connected in business interests with one of its largest tracts of land in this State, while he acted as agent for Messrs. Cary, Lay, and Schermerhorn, who bought the Chautauqua County lands from the Holland Company and sent my father, during the disturbing times of 1836, to Chautauqua to look after their interests.

I do not think he was ever the attorney for the Holland Land Company, as you suggest; and as I have found several letters written by himself at the time which graphically describe the condition at that time and his connection with the lands in Chautauqua County, I take the liberty of quoting to you portions of the letters, which I trust will be of interest to you and possibly to others of the Historical Society.

In response to a request of Messrs. Cary, Lay, and Schermerhorn, to undertake the settlement of their affairs in connection with the lands they had purchased from the Holland Company in Chautauqua, my father went to Batavia, where he arrived on the 28th of June, 1836, where he met his clients and Mr. Evans, the general agent of the Holland Land Company, whose principal office was in Batavia. Writing home on the following day, he described the condition of affairs found at Batavia as follows:

"I have seen enough of the affairs which call me here to know that they are much more deranged than I supposed, or than is understood by my employers. The whole tract of the Holland Land Company's lands, comprising seven counties, is in a state of great excitement. The disorganizing spirit is abroad, and men indulge fearful thoughts and dangerous purposes.

"There is a sub-Land Office in each county, and the general Land Office here. These offices contain the records and contracts. A desperate party have heretofore dared to seek the destruction of all the records and contracts, and, through that means, to relieve their lands from the debts which encumber them. The Chautauqua office has long since been burned, with all its valuable papers. The agent is here, driven from his post by terror. The Land Office here has been fortified. It is full of arms, and armed men keep guard. A block house is erected on each side of it. Conventions of the people are held, almost weekly, in the different counties, in opposition to the company. This, however, is the dark side. If I read aright the conditions around me, the excitement is passing off, and men will return to a more tranquil state.

"The village is small, although there are some rich families. Mr. Evans and his family have a fine house and extensive garden and grounds. They are, in virtue of his great wealth and his great office, "General Agent of the

A CORNER ON THE LINE OF MARCH.

"Towers and battlements it sees,
Bosomed high in tufted trees."

Holland Land Company," at the head of the society. He is an unassuming, intelligent, and worthy man. Both he and Mrs. Evans grace their position by native modesty and the absence of all affectation."

A few days later, on July 3d, and after he had had time to examine into the condition of affairs in Batavia more thoroughly, he again writes, describing the nature of his clients' interest which he is to look after, as follows:

"As I anticipated, I have found the condition of things in regard to my agency here quite confused. The true state of them is about as follows:

Messrs. Cary and Lay made a verbal agreement with Mr. Van der Kamp, at Philadelphia, the general agent of the Holland Land Company, for the purchase of all the interest and estate of the company in Chautauqua at about a million dollars.

"The purchase of the interest of the company in the other counties about the same time by other purchasers made a great excitement. All the other purchasers first, and Cary and Lay after them, undertook to raise the price by demanding a per acre advance upon forfeited contracts. This produced that commotion which has pervaded the whole country, and the outbreakings of which were seen in the destruction of the land office at Mayville, and the irruption into this place for the purpose of destroying the land office here. During the year 1835, the settlers paid largely and freely upon their lands. Almost a quarter of Cary's and Lay's debt was actually paid by the settlers. But the excitement put an end to these payments; and a set of demagogues and agrarians, taking advantage of the excited state of the public mind, have endeavored to induce the settlers to go in for an acquisition of their lands without payment for them. This was to be accomplished on the ground that the Holland Land Company had no title, and the means to be used were to nullify the judgments of the courts and destroy the records of the conveyances and contracts.

"In the mean time, Cary and Lay had not executed their contract with the Holland Land Company, although they have paid fifty thousand dollars out of their private funds, which, together with the payments derived from the lands, exceeds the first payment on their agreement.

"The indications are believed to be that the excitement is subsiding. A county convention has been held in Chautauqua, and has resolved that the proprietors be requested to re-establish their office there. It was my intention to do so to-morrow, but I find it necessary now to have copies made of the books relating to the Chautauqua lands kept in this office, all the books having been destroyed with the office in Chautauqua. I have procured an extra force to be employed upon the books, and we hope to get them ready so that I can go next week to Mayville."

Three weeks later my father left Batavia for Chautauqua County, taking the necessary books and papers prepared to enter upon his duties after selecting the proper place in the county to open a new land office in place of the one which had been burned by a mob at Mayville. From Westfield, after a short trip to Mayville in response to earnest requests of the citizens there to re-establish the old office at Mayville, he writes as follows:

"At 4 o'clock on Friday, we passed over to Mayville, the county town, and the locality of the old office. It lies at the head of Chautauqua Lake. That lake is seven hundred feet above the level of Lake Erie, and sends its waters into the Ohio through the Alleghany River. The road to Mayville crosses the ridge, which rises about four miles from the shore of Lake Erie, and stretches along the whole length of the southern shore. Nature has few more beautiful scenes than that which is displayed on this road. The lake is twenty miles long, and seems to rest in the bosom of a valley, formed by high hills, covered with forests on all sides. The village of Mayville contains scarcely more than fifty houses. We found a tavern and stores, a good court house and clerk's office, and the ruins of the old Land Office as they were left by the mob. Birdsall was very glad to see us, showed us the rooms in the Court House he had selected for my office, and the house in which I was to board. Neither he nor the other inhabitants of Mayville seem to have suspected that the office could be established elsewhere. My observation of Mayville resulted in the conviction that it would be a most uncomfortable residence, that it was an unprofitable place for the sale of lands, that its secluded position subjected it to the control of turbulent spirits who lived in the hills around it, and that, if I meant to be independent of the dictation of those who assume to direct the land agency by popular votes, I must avoid placing myself within their power.

"After hearing all that could be urged against these views, I decided to

ON THE LINE OF MARCH -EAST MAIN STREET FROM THE HOTEL RICHMOND.

return to Westfield. It was a sad blow to Mayville, for the land office was the principal source of its importance and business. Birdsall regarded it in a proper light, and behaves, as he always does, with magnanimity. Some of the other citizens were gloomy and excited. They warned me of consequences which they intended to produce. They assured me that I must be prepared for "agitation." They are to call conventions, and submit the question to the people, and procure resolutions to be passed that they will pay no money into the office until it is established at Mayville. Of course, these threats only confirm my conviction of the correctness of the determination I had made; nor did I find that conviction shaken by the menace that my office should not stand here two months."

Having decided to locate the land office at Westfield, he immediately commenced business there, and on July 29th, in a letter home, briefly described the feeling existing against him for this determination as follows:

"What with the solicitude I have felt from the indications around me for the result of the bold undertaking to restore peace in this excited country, and my preparation for future duties, I have suffered delay in writing to you.

"I wrote you that I had located here. This greatly grieved the people of Mayville; they became very much excited; and although they had sustained the laws and denounced the riots while the office was among them, they now appealed to the passions of the people, threatened every obstruction to our business, and courted disorder and outrage. Birdsall's excellent good sense and valuable influence have aided me much in allaying this storm. I went yesterday to Mayville, and thence by steamboat on Chautauqua Lake to Jamestown, and have seen most of the respectable and influential men in the county, besides many of the debtors, and I do not now apprehend difficulties."

He found his labors at Westfield engrossed nearly all his time, but evidently enjoyed the excitement, as his letter of September 10th shows:

"At the close of a very laborious week I am still surrounded by garrulous people, who distract me while I try to write. I have had experience enough this week in my new calling to learn that while it lasts, I am to enjoy little of that rest that I might have anticipated. From seven, and often from six, in the morning, until eight, or nine, or ten o'clock in the evening, we are constantly transacting business in a crowd; and my own cares of superintendence of our financial concerns, with other labors, engross all my hours except the few devoted to sleep. Nevertheless, I like it thus far better than the perplexed life I led at home. Our business is simple; it involves no intricate study, and is attended with none of that consuming solicitude that has rendered my profession a constant slavery.

"My health continues good; and I feel that, if I derive no other advantage from the change, I am abundantly repaid. The excitement is fast subsiding around me; and, if you could see me among the people here, you would almost suppose that I had always lived happily among them.

"Among my visitors to-day was one poor fellow, who spent an hour in deploring (to the infinite edification of a promiscuous audience) the error of marrying a widow, two children, and one hundred and ninety-five acres of land; the wife caring, as he says, all for the children and none for him, and the children claiming and taking all the land."

Although the excitement in the county had greatly subsided, there were frequent rumors of outbreaks, and it took some time for the dissatisfaction of the settlers to subside, as shown in his letter of September 20th which describes a rumored outbreak that was feared at the date of the annual military parade, as follows:

"I am to amuse you now with the adventures of an eventful season. On Sunday night, Bradley, being alone with me, told me of terrific insinuations and menaces uttered in the office on Saturday; and, among other things, that a person came from Ripley expressly to warn me that to-night or to-day a mob was to come to destroy the office. I discovered that they were both alarmed, but soothed their fears, and passed on. Yesterday morning, James Jackson a merchant of great respectability in Ripley, called me out of bed at six o'clock to warn me that a mob was to come to-night from Gerry to destroy my office and shoot me. He recommended the suspension of all business to-day, and that I should take shelter in his house five miles distant. I grieved him by resolving to stay and be killed, which he said, truly, would be a dreadful thing. Having learned from him that the storm that he feared was to come from Gerry, I procured yesterday a confidential person to reconnoiter there last night. I secured the attendance of the sheriff through the day, and at an early hour this morning caused all the most valuable papers and books to be transferred from the office to my private room. On opening the office this morning, two men came fraught with the news of the

ON THE LINE OF MARCH—COURT HOUSE PARK AND HOTEL RICHMOND

intended assault. The militia assembled, and not less than a thousand people, apparently to witness the parade. Business pressed us all day, for the people availed themselves of the occasion to transact it. My messenger returned from Gerry, and reported that all was quiet and the people all satisfied. The crowd have dispersed, and Haight and Bradley have forgotten their fears in a sound sleep, as I shall do after having told you the perils of the day."

By October 7th, the affairs in Chautauqua County had become fairly settled, so that he could then see that his undertaking was approaching its completion, and so wrote on that day.

"Order begins to come out of the confusion into which the land office has been plunged. The murmurs of discontent are dying away, and I think another month or two will bring the whole estate into a manageable condition. After that there will be no great cause for solicitude, and I shall be able to be more at home with you. Even now I am able commonly to leave the office at dark and spend the evening here."

Early in November he had completed the settlement of the affairs for his clients in Chautauqua County and was able to return home.

Trumbull Cary was a life-long friend of my father's, and during over thirty years they were intimately connected in politics and business. There are any number of letters written by my father which speak of the delightful entertainment he has received from Mr. Cary and at his home in Batavia, aside from those which have reference to his connection with the Holland Land Company. Mr Cary was probably the most important man of that part of the state at the time my father went there in 1836; and while enjoying the hospitality of his house then and afterwards, my father's acquaintance at Batavia included nearly all of the old families that were residents there at that time; and had I time to look through all his letters, I know I should find many relating to that and his other visits at Batavia. It is on that account that I am the more sorry that I cannot attend the celebration and meet the members of the old families who were his friends in those days and whom I have often heard mentioned by him.

*

(*Leander Mix.*)

In 1835 a mob of the settlers of the Holland Company's lands came to the conclusion that by destroying the records of the Land Office they would get their lands free. They tore down the Land Office at Mayville, Chautauqua county, N. Y., but after destroying the records found out that the originals were in the Land Office at Batavia. In the winter of 1835 and 1836 the agent at Batavia had the books and papers packed and taken to Rochester and stored in a stone warehouse on the canal. Before spring R. W. Lowber, H. L. Glowacki and Leander Mix transferred them back to the office. On the 13th of May, 1836, a mob from Allegany, Cattaraugus, Chautauqua and Erie counties organized for the purpose of destroying the Land Office and papers at Batavia. The agent being informed on the night of the 12th that they were coming notified the sheriff, Nathan Townsend. He ordered out the militia and had them stationed at the old Court House and jail. There were about thirty men at the Land Office on duty at the same time. The planks in the old bridge were taken up as the mob was coming in on the Alexander road. Just before daylight the planks were put down and a committee was formed to go up the road and see where they were. I was with the committee in a hack. Just as we got across the bridge we heard parties coming on horseback. I raised up my musket and called out, "stop, or I will fire." A reply came, "don't fire, it is I, Mr. Moulton come to tell you the mob is coming." He then came up and said the men were in Fargo's Tavern helping themselves to liquors, food and tobacco. He had heard them say that they were going to have David E. Evans', agent, and Ebenezer Mix's pluck, to grease their muskets with before they went back, as Mr. Mix carried all the details of the Land Office in his head. We returned to the Land Office and planked the lower doors and windows with three-inch planks and then placed six men at each window with muskets. I was at one of the front windows.

Shortly after daylight about three hundred men marched across the bridge and came down in front of the Office and halted. The Sheriff, accompanied by his posse, at once stepped in front of the mob and informed them that they stood on dangerous ground and were in imminent danger of getting hurt. His words were so impressive that the leaders of the mob marched their men down below the Oak Orchard road, where, after holding a parley, the army disbanded and mixed with the Batavia citizens. The Sheriff at once arrested many of the men and placed them in the jail. Guards were also formed to protect village property as well as the Land Office, and it was

BRISBANE CURVE—AT THE JUNCTION OF THE INDIAN TRAILS—SITE OF THE OLD FRONTIER HOUSE—THE LAND OFFICE IN THE DISTANCE.

many days before these guards were relieved. I stayed at the Land Office night and day until the agent had two block houses built, one on the northeast corner, and the other on the southwest corner. He then hired guards to protect the property. Altogether I was employed in the Land Office for about thirteen years, and I think that of all the old clerks H. L. Glowacki and myself are the only ones living.

(*George H. Holden.*)

The day of the mob was a thrilling one. There was a prospect of much bloodshed. But great preparation and firmness in the crisis brought about a peaceful ending. I think I was the only one hit. But I was hit hard. In fact, I got the worst licking that I ever received in my life for running away from school with a lot of other check-aproned urchins to see a little history made.

The first part of the battle-field I visited was the court house park. It was one mass of artillery and military. There were four or five six pounders, and one long twelve pounder. The long Tom had first been planted down by the bridge, but was subsequently brought up to the rest.

The men were expecting immediate action, and were busily loading their muskets. Augustus Cowdin had but one leg, and balancing himself on his crutch, he hastily shoved a cartridge into his musket, but he forgot to bite off the paper. In those days a man could not be a soldier unless he had good teeth. Augustus forgot that he had put in a cartridge, so he put in another in just the same way. As he shoved in the third one I called out to him that he was not loading his gun right. He turned on me a look of disgust and said: "Young fellow, what do you know about it?"

The invaders were down at the bridge; and like a young simpleton I went down to look them over. But my rashness was nothing to that of Dr. Cary. He was riding around on one of his favorite black horses, and he rode over the bridge and right into the midst of the raiders. I trembled for him; but they spared him. I was right by when their commander, "One eyed Hill," as we called him, gave the order to load guns. And they did it in downright earnest. I was impressed with the steadiness with which they formed their lines and marched across the bridge. The oldest veteran soldiers could not have improved upon it. Those fellows meant to fight, and would have done it if there had been a ghost of a chance for them. As they marched along with such an appearance of determination a man right at my side, who happened to recognize one of them, called out: "What did you come here for, John?" "I have come here to get old David Evans's gullet to grease my gun with."

I rushed on up to the Land Office. The troops were drawn up in two lines, extending from the creek across the road. As the mob came up I saw the guns come down to a level, the guns of the rear rank pointing between the necks of the men in front. Other muskets were sticking out of the Land Office in all directions. It seemed as though there was not two inches of space anywhere without a musket. Had they fired, the slaughter would have been simply awful. The mob halted as the muskets came down; and after a moment I saw Hill give a signal to bear around to the right. The order to recover arms was given, and the bloodless battle was over. I followed the defeated army. They went out West Main street to the green in front of the old arsenal, and lay down for awhile. They then arose and dispersed.

The civil power now appeared on the scene; constables were making arrests right and left. I saw the great Hill arrested. He and another one were riding along in a wagon. Constable Moore arrested them, and tried in vain to get them out of the wagon. Just then Jerome Clark happened along, and Moore appealed to him to help him with his prisoners. Clark grabbed them both at once, and, bracing himself against the wagon, pulled them both to the ground. He then led them away chop-fallen to the justice, who committed them. Clark's son, Delancey, was one of the class of '94 of

the high school, who raised the money that bought the old Land Office
I then went home and got my licking. And the whole thing made such
a striking impression on my mind that I can see it all to-day as vividly as I
did that day that I was galavanting around in my check apron.

(*Simeon D. Lewis.*)

From the time of Joseph Ellicott's appointment as the local agent of the
Holland Company in 1800, to his resignation in 1821, he was uniformly very
lenient in his treatment of the purchasers of the company's lands. Numerous instances could be cited to show where contracts were extended or renewed upon terms regardless of accumulations of unpaid interest, and a
general policy of aid and encouragement toward the pioneers was adopted

A SIDE GLIMPSE FROM THE LINE OF MARCH—NORTH FROM TONAWANDA BRIDGE.

and practised, in the administration of his trust. This liberal policy was
continued by his successors, Jacob S. Otto and David E. Evans. In one respect Mr. Otto organized still a new plan to aid the settlers, by accepting at
a stated price, cattle and grain in payment on contracts and mortgages, thus
enabling the debtors of the company to make their payments, when there
was no cash market for the products of their farms. I think that I am correct in saying that this practice was continued by his successor, Mr. Evans.

One of the results of this liberal policy seems to have been that many of
the settlers came to claim as a right what had for years been thus granted
as a generous concession.

In December, 1808, the Holland Company contracted to sell to Heman J.

Redfield and Jacob Le Roy, all of their unsold lands, and January 9, 1836 Messrs. Redfield and Le Roy assigned this contract to the Farmers' Loan and Trust Company of New York.

October 10, 1836, the Holland Land Company executed a tripartite deed, conveying these lands to Redfield and Le Roy, parties of the second part, and the Farmers' Loan and Trust Company, parties of the the third part.

Soon after this contract was made by the Holland company, and before the execution of this deed, baseless rumors began to be circulated, stating that the new company intended to adopt a more stringent policy than that which had formerly prevailed, and that no more renewals or extensions of contract would be made without the payment of a certain stipulated sum.

In every community, even now, one can easily find people who seem to take great pleasure in circulating unwelcome news; and in the case under consideration, there was no lack of men who, from motives of mischief or malice, circulated this rumor industriously. It is safe also to assume that it lost nothing in being repeated. We must remember that at the time under consideration there were no telegraphs or telephones. What is now the New York Central Railroad did not reach Batavia even, until later in this year 1836. Mails were infrequent and irregular, and comparatively few newspapers were in circulation. Indeed, means of communication were far from what we now possess. Perhaps it is not strange, therefore, that the circulation of these rumors should have produced great excitement in parts of the Purchase somewhat remote from the Batavia office; and the number of what were termed nullifiers increased rapidly, despite the wiser counsels of cooler and more intelligent citizens.

The first open outbreak was made February 6, 1836, when a mob made a raid on the branch office at Mayville, Chautauqua county, seized the records and burned them in the public highway. Afterwards a plan was arranged, more formidable in proportions, to loot the main office at Batavia. About May 13th of this same year, something like seven hundred armed men marched to Batavia "breathing threatenings and slaughter." In the meantime Mr. Evans, the company's agent, had not been sleeping. He was a bold, determined, energetic man, and had kept himself thoroughly posted as to the situation. When, therefore, this company reached Batavia, they found the Land Office well fortified and fifty armed men within. They also found that the Sheriff had called out the militia, and had them drawn up in line on the opposite side of the street. When they saw the preparations to give them a warm reception, they seemed to think "discretion the better part of valor," and doubtless believing that,

> " He who fights and runs away,
> May live to fight some other day,"

they marched back home again without offering any violence. Some fifty or sixty arrests were made of men who were supposed to be the ring-leaders of this party, but most of them were discharged without prosecution. When we consider the intense excitement that prevailed, it is not strange that some persons were arrested who were entirely innocent of any part in the matter.

Mutual explanations soon corrected the misunderstandings that had prevailed. Most of the citizens were convinced that the extravagant stories which had been circulated had been unfounded, and became satisfied that they had acted hastily and without reason. There were exceptions, however, to this, and ten or twelve years later, when I was sent out collecting for the Farmers' Loan and Trust Company, it was no unusual thing to find men along the border of Holland and Sardinia, in Erie county, who pretended to dispute the validity of the title of the company to their lands, and many of whom politely informed me that their rifle was a good enough deed of their farm. I think it very doubtful whether such a person could now be found, and history, which finally gives justice to all, must record the indisputable fact, that the policy of the Holland Land Company and their successors, was liberal, and their treatment of the pioneers considerate and generous; that in fact, in many instances, it may well be characterized as merciful.

ACROSS THE STREET FROM THE LAND OFFICE AREA—THE WATSON RESIDENCE.

(*Contributed*)

OLD GENESEE.

(Tune of A Thousand Years.)

During a hundred years, what changes,
Where the red monarch roamed so free,
Holding his birth-right undisputed,
In the dark wilds of Genesee.

A hundred years what wondrous changes,
From the wild forests now made free,
Rich golden fields, and flying chariots,
Crown the broad lands of Genesee.

During a hundred years, what changes,
  Where the beasts held their jubilee;
Ranging the forests unmolested,
  Wild hunting grounds no more we see;
Long have the buck and roe been strangers,
  In the woodlands of Genesee.

During a hundred years, what changes,
  Pioneer hands have wrought we see;
Turning to fruitful fields, wild forests,
  Fountains of wealth in Genesee.

Walls of a hundred years are standing.
  Kept as an ancient landmark free;
Long may they be an honored relic.
  Safe in the heart of Genesee.

NEAR THE SPEAKER'S STAND.

PHILADELPHIA, December 30, 1776.

"SIR—I have just received your favor of this day, and sent to Gen. Putnam to detain the express until I collected the hard money you want, which you may depend shall be sent in one specie or other with this letter, and a list thereof shall be enclosed herein. I had long since parted with very considerable sums of hard money to Congress, and therefore must collect from others —and as matters now stand, it is no easy thing. I mean to borrow silver and promise payment in gold, and then collect the gold the best way I can. . . .
I am dear sir, yours, etc.,
ROBERT MORRIS."

When Washington re-crossed the Delaware for the second time, in Dec., 1776, the time of service of nearly all the eastern troops had expired. To induce them to engage for another six weeks, he promised a bounty of $10 each; and for the necessary funds applied to Mr. Morris. In the answer of Mr. Morris, accompanying the sum of fifty thousand dollars, he congratulates the commander-in-chief upon his success in retaining the men, and assures him that if "farther occasional supplies of money are wanted, you may depend on my exertions either in a public or private capacity."

In 1781 (a period of despair), in addition to other contributions of money and credit, Mr. Morris supplied the almost famishing troops with several thousand barrels of flour. This timely aid came when it was seriously contemplated to authorize the seizure of provisions wherever they could be found,

NEAR THE SPEAKER'S STAND.

a measure which would have been unpopular with the whole country, and probably turned back the tide of public feeling flowing in favor of the Revolution.

There is upon record a long catalogue of transactions similar to those which have been related. Not only the commander-in-chief but generals of divisions, found Mr. Morris the dernier resort when money and provisions were wanted. In financial negotiations, with him to will a thing was to do it. —O. *Turner*.

(*George H. Holden*)

My grandfather, Capt. James Holden, came to Batavia with his family in 1803. He lived in a white house just across the creek from the land office.

He had been in the Revolutionary war. Was present at the Battle of Bunker Hill. I have heard him describe that battle many times. It was very amusing to hear him describe the battle. He always got intensely excited when describing that struggle. His eyes would glitter, and he would prance around the room. "Our powder gave out; but, confound them! we clubbed our muskets and made it as warm for them as we could." He had nine sons and three daughters. Five of the sons were out in the war of 1812. One morning my father saw a man rush out of the woods west of our house without hat, coat, vest, or shoes. When the excited individual came up, he found that it was his own brother, who had run all the way from the Niagara river to give the alarm that the British were coming. The inhabitants all fled to Canandaigua. Our folks buried their silver when they fled; but it was found by

THE RICHMOND MEMORIAL LIBRARY.

some recruits that were passing through to the front, and was all taken but one spoon, which I now have in my possession. The spoon seems to have been made by hammering. My grandfather on my mother's side, General Towner, thought he would not run with the rest of them. He gathered together some militia, and took a stand northwest of Batavia to protect the town. But the British did not come.

As my father was only fifteen they thought he had better stay at home. But the war got him. In 1813 he was hauling stone for the old arsenal when General Scott's officers came along and impressed his team and him. He was sent to Albany to bring on supplies. He got a land warrant for eighty acres of land for this involuntary service. He said that was the only time that lightning ever struck him.

One of my father's brothers became accidentally a hero at Black Rock. The Americans were keeping a sharp watch day and night against surprise. One evening my uncle was in a squad that was reconnoitering with lanterns near the edge of the cliff. The officer decided to send some of the men down to the water's edge. My uncle, in moving forward, lost his footing, and tumbled down to the bottom. He almost fell upon three British soldiers. Taking in the situation at once, he shouted, "Here they are, men, come on." The poor Britishers begged permission to surrender; and he took the three of them back to camp. When they asked him how he captured them, he said, "O, I surrounded them."

I have heard John B. Ellicott describe the coming over of the British. They had a long line of boats filled with soldiers. Directly in front of him an

A SIDE GLIMPSE FROM THE LINE OF MARCH.—SOME QUIET HOMES OF BATAVIA.

officer was standing in the bow of a boat giving orders. Ellicott drew a bead on him; but his heart failed him, and he didn't shoot. Again he took a sight on him; but again he could not prevail upon himself to kill that man. The third time he let her fly. "Did you hit him?" "I don't know. Somebody hit him; but by the time I shot there was a crash all along the line."

Ellicott would also tell of a funny panic that once took place among the troops at Black Rock. They were posted on the bluff; and one evening a violent clatter was heard down by the water's edge. A panic seized the detachment, and they fled with their arms in their hands. Pretty soon some one stumbled, and down went his bayonet into the fellow ahead of him. Then began a general stumbling, and a general bayoneting of the poor fellows that chanced to be ahead. "And what did you do?" "Why, I ran with the rest of them." When they came to investigate the cause of their terror and bloodshed, they found that an old blind horse was fumbling and stumbling around in the narrow passageway.

Grandfather died at the age of 88. His death was hastened, I think, by a fall he received on the bridge when he slipped on the ice. None of his children died under 80, except one who died of cholera in 1834.

The bears were very familiar in the early days in Batavia. My grandfather had a pig pen eight rails high just back of his house. In that pen they were fattening a lusty porker that had reached dimensions that would gratify the eye of Phil. Armour. One evening, when my father and grandmother were the sole occupants of the house the big piggy gave forth notes of positive

OLD BATAVIA—THE TRACY RESIDENCE—ON THE SITE OF THE PRESENT WIARD RESIDENCE.

distress. Peering out they saw a monstrous black bear depositing chaff on the outside of that eight rail fence, without disturbing a rail. And they decided not to interfere with the proceedings. The eight rail pen knew chaff no more forever.

I regret to say that my last encounter with my excellent old grandfather was of such a nature as to leave our relations a little strained. I was a very frequent visitor at his residence, and always had the run of the house. One day as I was roaming through the upper chambers, to my inexpressible delight, I chanced upon a violin and bow. I had never taken lessons from Paganini, but what I lacked in skill I made up in energy. I sawed and sawed until I was red in the face; and I certainly succeeded in making my self heard. In fact I thought that the remotest settler could not fail to catch my dulcet strains. I have said that my grandfather was not in robust health after his fall on the bridge, so he was not in a condition to enjoy my music.

ON THE LINE OF MARCH.—NEW BATAVIA.

I heard a very wrathful voice at the foot of the stairs; and when I tremblingly responded to its call I found my grandfather in such a rage that his wrath at the Britishers at Bunker Hill might in comparison be called amiability itself. I shrank home, and never had the courage to enter his home again.

though he lived several years longer. But I used to see him at a safe distance strolling up the street every day to get his mail.

The Batavia bar has always been strong. But the early bar of Batavia was exceedingly strong. There were Daniel H. Chandler, Albert Smith, Isaac H. Verplank, John B. Skinner, Ethan B. Allen, John H. Martindale, Edgar C. Dibble, Moses Taggart, Phineas Tracy, George W. Lay, Glen Carpenter, and Seth Wakeman. These were strong men.

We (the Board of War) had exhausted all the lead accessible to us; having caused even the spouts of houses to be melted; and had unsuccessfully offered the equivalent of two shillings specie (25 cents) per pound for lead. I went on the evening of the day in which I received a letter from the army, to

NEW BATAVIA—THE DORIC.

a splendid entertainment given by Don Mirailles, the Spanish minister. My heart was sad, but I had the faculty of brightening my countenance even under the most gloomy disasters; yet it seems not then with sufficient adroitness, for Mr. Morris, who was one of the guests, and knew me well, discovered some casual trait of depression. He accosted me in his usual frank and ingenuous manner, saying: "I see some clouds passing accross the sunny countenance you assume; what is the matter?" After some hesitation I showed him the General's letter which I had brought from the office, with the intention of placing it at home in a private cabinet. He played with my anxiety, which he did not relieve for some time. At length, with good and sincere delight, he called me aside and told me that the Holker privateer had just arrived at the wharf with ninety tons of lead which she had brought as ballast. "You shall have, said Mr. Morris, "my half of this fortunate supply; there are the owners of the other half" (indicating gentlemen in the department). The other half was obtained. Before morning a supply of cartridges was ready and sent off to the army.—*Judge Peters*.

(*John F. Lay.*)

Batavia figured in the War of 1812 as a sort of rendezvous for the troops assembling from different parts of the interior of the State on their way to the front, and as a city of refuge for the wounded and fugitives. Batavia had at that time a very unique character in the person of Judge Stevens. The

NEW BATAVIA—THE CORINTHIAN

Judge had served for a time on the staff of General Porter, as his adjutant-general. Among the duties of his position was the locating and setting up of the headquarters tent. On one occasion the enemy seemed disposed to disturb the ordinarily peaceful procedure of going into camp. The discreet limb of the law rode back to his general and made the following report. "General, the bullets are flying over there; it is positively dangerous to proceed with the setting up of that tent; I shall surely be killed if I tarry in that locality." The irate general at once discharged the full vial of his wrath upon the head of his cautious penman and mouthpiece: "Go back, immediately, sir, and proceed with your duties; it is your duty to direct the setting up of that tent." But the Judge had not studied law in vain; he had very clear notions of the imitations of jurisdictions, prerogatives, duties, vested rights, inalienable privileges, and other world-controlling abstractions and distinctions. Though prudent and discreet in regard to the enemies bullets, he was nevertheless a very lion where his own rights seemed to be trenched upon. Drawing himself up with great dignity he proceeded to lay down the law of the matter to the very face of his testy commander: "General Porter, sir, I would have you to understand that I am your *writing* aid, not your *fighting* aid."

The unfailing prudence and discretion of the worthy adjutant-general enabled him to avoid disagreeable contact with the ill-mannered bullets and to return with an unbroken skin to his chosen Batavia. Thenceforth his prowess in arms gave an added interest to a character that was never lacking in unique attractions.

> "As driftwood spars, that meet and pass
> Upon the boundless ocean's plain,
> So in the sea of life, alas!
> Man meets man ; meets and quits again."

The Judge was destined to give to literature and history another dash of genius. He had his residence on the south side of the creek, on the site of the present famous Law Mansion. On the Tonawanda bridge, which was afterwards the scene of such thrilling doings in the Land Office war, the history of the old world and the new came together. It is well known that after the battle of Waterloo the air of France was not congenial to the tardy Marshal Grouchy. He was seized with a desire to see foreign lands. Wrapped in his own reflections and his military cloak he seemed to stalk abroad like a restless ghost. In due time he appeared in the quiet frontier hamlet of Batavia, a solitary, contemplative, undisturbed figure. As the Marshal was strolling in solitary pensiveness across the Tonawanda bridge in the gloaming, another solitary figure was approaching from the opposite direction. Sympathy often springs forth like an electric thrill; he who was behind time at Waterloo could not fail to awaken an interest in him who was behind the lines at Lundy's Lane and Queenstown, and Fort Niagara. The Judge, being on his native heath, felt that the initiative rested with him. Stopping short in front of the silent, gliding exile, and with his characteristic abruptness, he said: "You, I believe, are Marshal Grouchy. I am Judge Stevens of Batavia." It was not exactly the manner of the French capital, so for a moment the Marshal's sensibilities were thrown into a chaotic condition. But, quickly collecting himself, it is said that a gleam of intellectual illumination came over his countenance; and just at that point tradition is silent.

The Judge was for many years a clerk in the Land Office. His assistant was Junius A. Smith. The statements were made quarterly; and it often required commendable diligence to get them ready on time. The burden fell largely upon the shoulders of the faithful Junius. The Judge, being really a kind-hearted man, felt like cheering his toiling Achates: "Now, Junius, when we get off these reports we will take some recreation." Junius brightened at the idea like an overtaxed race-horse that has had a word of encouragement come into his ear. The reports were ready in good season; and, the benevolent Judge, true to his word, said: "Now, Junius, we will proceed to take some recreation." The pair strolled together across the bridge to the Judge's house, where, to the surprise of the laborious assistant, his host produced a bottle of "recreation." "Well, Junius, *dum vivamus vivamus.*" Having thus taken the "recreation," they at once returned to the Land Office and the new records.

The Judge was very slow in adding. This was noticed by his observant assistant, Junius. The latter, after footing up a vast array of columns, complacently appended a little memorandum: "I have footed up these columns in just one hour. J. A. S." The Judge, having no confidence in such expedition, went over the whole matter in his usual laborious, careful, and slow manner, after which he appended the following supplementary memorandum: "And in doing so you have made fifteen mistakes. J. W. S."

In Philadelphia, before coming to Batavia, Judge Stevens wrote for the newspapers a series of articles over the signature of "Peter Porcupine," replying to Cobbett.

PARADING UNDER DIFFICULTIES.—THE INDUSTRIAL FLOATS AFLOAT.

Ellicott criticized Stevens to the effect that in his first view of things he got everything wrong side up, confused and mixed, but in the end he got them clarified, and brought them out all straight.

A story of hotel independence in the olden time is told in connection with the old "Frontier House" in Batavia. It was situated on Brisbane Place, almost on the site of the present Brisbane mansion, and was kept by a man by the name of Keyes. Mrs. Keyes was a very tidy and capable body, and was the moving spirit of the hotel. It was General Scott's fortune to come twice to Batavia, each time under very interesting circumstances, and once in the broad light of history. When he fell wounded at Lundy's Lane, his first field of fame, he was brought with other mangled sufferers to Batavia for care and treatment. There is a tradition that the Land Office was, for a time, his hospital. Here he was nursed back into health for the making of other great pages in history. But about the first history he made was a brilliant marriage, the bride of the hero of Lundy's Lane being a bud or blossom of one of the first families of Virginia. The distinguished bridal party appeared in Batavia on their way to Niagara Falls and the old battlefields, and sought accommodations at the old Frontier Hotel. Business was very brisk, and the old Frontier House had heavy demands upon its accommodations. The quarters assigned to the bridal party seemed to the Belle of the old Dominion utterly unworthy of such guests, and she spoke very freely of what she thought was due to General Scott, and Mrs. General Scott, and Mrs. General Scott's sister. The reply of the sturdy Mrs. Keyes has come down to us: "I told Mrs. General Scott and Mrs. General Scott's sister that my house was of as good standing as any in the country, and if they did not like my accommodations they might go elsewhere."

The imperious Mrs. Scott had been a Miss Mayo, the reigning beauty of Richmond. When Captain Scott attempted to storm the citadel of her heart, he was told that it was "impossible; not to be thought of." When *Colonel* Scott attempted the same bold enterprise, he was assured that it was "somewhat more reasonable." But when *General* Scott came crowned with the laurels of Lundy's Lane, he was pronounced "irresistible," and the fortress at once surrendered at discretion.

The agents were all subjected to assaults to secure their removal. But they all came out unscathed.

They were all men of note and influence. All distinguished guests were entertained by them with an easy and ample hospitality. They were the center of a very high society. Mr. Wadsworth of Geneseo and John Gregg of Canandaigua maintained the most intimate social relations with the incumbents of the Land Office.

Mr. Ellicott was an active promoter of the Erie canal, and was freely consulted in regard to all that pertained to it. The grade was too high to Batavia; but he got a feeder from Alabama to drain his swamp lands.

The agency was first offered to Andrew Ellicott, a brother of Joseph. Andrew was a very eminent surveyor, and had a national reputation. It was for this reason that the Hollanders offered him the agency. He ran the boundary lines on the lakes and in Louisiana, and laid out the city of Washington.

Joseph never married. Among the descendents of Andrew Ellicott, now resident in Batavia, are: Miss Douglass, daughter of Professor Douglass of West Point, and later of Geneva College, who married a daughter of Andrew Ellicott, and Mrs. N. T. Smith, a daughter of John B. Ellicott, who was the son of Andrew.

Goods came from New York by way of Rome and Oswego to Lewiston, and were carried thence to Batavia in wagons. The great boatman of the Mohawk was Eli Lasher. Another character in the Mohawk valley whose fame came with the goods to Batavia, was the interesting and very original Mr. Spraker of Spraker's Basin. When the church was struck by lightning

Spraker would not rebuild it. He said stubbornly: "If God chooses to strike His own house, why should I build it up again for Him?"

Ebenezer Mix, the great surveyor and mathematician, was originally a mason by trade. He wandered into Batavia by mere chance. His calculation of the plastering on Mr. Ellicott's house so impressed the latter that he put him in charge of all the mathematical calculations of the office. When the raiders planned the destruction of the Land Office in order to destroy the records, they intended also to kill Mix, as they feared that he would restore everything from memory.

He wrote and published a work on mathematics.

In trying an ejectment suit, Daniel H. Chandler said: "Now we'll bring on Ebenezer Mix, who has the Holland Land Company's land mapped on his

THE FIRST ON THE GROUND—THE OLD AND THE YOUNG CONTINENTALS—THE DRUMS OF BUNKER HILL.

brain." One of Mr. Chandler's sons became the distinguished Admiral Chandler of the United States navy. The well-known writer, Bessie Chandler, is his granddaughter, and daughter of the Admiral. She resides in Batavia.

Red Jacket appeared frequently on the streets in Batavia. He could understand English very well; but he disdained to speak it except in extreme necessity. When addressed in English he would answer in Indian. His illustrious descendant, General Eli Parker of General Grant's staff, had a silver medal given by Wellington to Red Jacket. General Parker was one of the invited guests to the dedication of the Land Office. By a remarkable coincidence his death occurred on the day of the dedication. Bishop Coxe made a feeling allusion to him as "The Last of the Iroquois."

The anti-Mason excitement was the means of bringing out a number of men into permanent prominence. Some rode upon the wave into the history of the nation. Among those were Millard Filmore, William H. Seward, and Thurlow Weed. It gave great prominence to my uncle, Phineas Tracy; it sent my father to Congress; and it brought out Thomas C. Love of Buffalo, Albert H. Tracy of Buffalo, Gideon Hard of Albion, and Frederick Whittlesey of Rochester.

A body was found in the Lake; and it was brought forward as Morgan's. There was a little discrepancy, however, in the whiskers; the face of the corpse had stub side-whiskers, whereas Morgan's face was smooth-shaven to the top. The story is told told that Thurlow Weed took hold of the stub whisker and it parted from the face. "There," he said, "that is a good enough Morgan till after election."

The Holland Purchase touches the Revolution, through Morris who transferred it to the Hollanders, and through the Hollanders themselves who were Morris's Revolutionary creditors.

But it seems that the Land Office was destined to be mixed up in some way with every great convulsion of the United States. If it can be said that it gave Lincoln to history, then it must be conceded that it had an important relation to the Civil War. That it caused the nomination of Lincoln I think can be established beyond dispute.

In 1860 Mr. Seward was the logical candidate of the Republicans. His pronunciamento of the "irrepressable conflict" voiced the coming struggle. Men looked to him as the prophet and the Moses of the hour. He came very near getting the nomination for president, and would have obtained it had he not been stricken down at the last moment by Horace Greeley at Chicago.

Greeley's animosity had its origin in the Land Office. Albert Brisbane of Batavia had become the great apostle of Fourierism, in which Greeley took some interest. This led to very friendly relations. Through the influence of Brisbane the columns of the *Tribune* were opened to a series of articles from Batavia reflecting upon the administration of Redfield and Pringle, who were acting as agents for the Farmers' Loan and Trust Company, the last owners of the interests of the Hollanders in the Purchase.

Mr. Redfield brought suit for libel; and William H. Seward was appointed referee. Mr. Seward decided against the *Tribune*, and adjudged it to pay a fine of five hundred dollars and to retract the libelous statements. Greeley did not mind the five hundred dollars much; but the retraction stung him to the quick. He became thenceforth a bitter, unrelenting enemy of Mr. Seward. He said that his time would come; and it came—at Chicago. By stating these cold facts we do not necessarily imply any regret that the great Lincoln came on to the stage of action for which he seemed providentially destined. But the facts show what great results may flow from very small causes. Mr. Seward was a high-minded man, and a patriot; and he faithfully co-operated with Mr. Lincoln in carrying forward to a successful issue one of the greatest struggles in history. He did what he thought was right in the Land Office matter; and I think that he could say with Clay that he "would rather be right than be President."

In a private interview with Washington the subject of an attack on New

York was broached. Mr. Morris dissented; assuming that it would be at too great a sacrifice of men and money; that the success of the measure was doubtful, that even if successful the triumph as to results would be a barren one; the enemy having command of the sea could at any time land fresh troops and retake it, etc. Assenting to these objections, the commander-in-chief said: "What am I to do? The country calls on me for action; and moreover my army cannot be kept together unless some bold enterprise is undertaken." To this Mr. Morris replied: "Why not lead your forces to Yorktown? there Cornwallis may be hemmed in by the French fleet by sea, and the American and French armies by land, and will ultimately be compelled to surrender." "Lead my troops to Yorktown!" said Washington, appearing surprised at the suggestion. "How am I to get them there? One

RELICS IN THE LAND OFFICE.

of my difficulties about attacking New York arises from the want of funds to transport my troops thither. How then can I muster the means that will be requisite to enable them to march to Yorktown?" "You must look to me for funds," rejoined Mr. Morris. "And how are you to provide them?" said Washington. "That," said Mr. Morris, "I am unable at this time to tell you; but I will answer with my head, that if you will put your army in motion, I will supply the means of their reaching Yorktown." After a few minutes' reflection, Washington said: "On this assurance of yours, Mr. Morris, such is my confidence in your ability to perform any engagement you make, I will adopt your suggestion."—*O. Turner.*

(*Joseph Edwin Wilford.*)

My Grandfather McRillus, on my mother's side, came to the Holland Purchase in 1808, and took up the McRillus place, one mile east of the present village of Oakfield. The property is still in the hands of his descendants, after the lapse of 86 years. He came from Madison County, in this State. His wife was a daughter of Dr. Cleveland, a third cousin of President Cleveland.

Mother was but four years of age when the family arrived here ; but to the day of her death at 82, she had a most distinct remembrance of the coming into the Genesee country, and of all the events that transpired subsequently. I was her home boy, and she lived with me to the day of her death. To the last her memory was a luminous storehouse of the history of this region, " all of which she saw and part of which she was ;" and she was constantly pouring it out to my not unwilling ear. They stopped in Batavia the first night, and then started to drive seven miles to Oakfield. It took two days to make the trip, which is now just one hour's delightful drive along one of the finest thoroughfares and among the noblest farm steads in the world. The two days were consumed in cutting away trees to let the wagon pass through. They stopped over night midway at Dusenbury's, at Dusenbury Hill. She was impressed with the superabundance of peaches and the scarcity of apples. The children were told to eat all the peaches they pleased, but to spare the apples. It is now just the reverse : the apple orchards are like sturdy forests on every farm ; but the raising of peaches is not a success. She accounted for the abundance of peaches by supposing that the Indians must have cultivated them.

The first white child born in Oakfield was born on the adjoining farm, a daughter of Aaron Waite. She married Harvey Fisher, a man somewhat prominent and well known in this region. When the war of 1812 swept all the men away, Aaron White went with the rest. In the report of the killed, wounded and missing, it was Aaron's fortune to be reported among the last. He never returned and no trace of him was ever obtained. No infant settlement ever had a more dismal start. There was but one man left, and he was left because he was both old and feeble. So the women and children had to do the best they could while wars and rumors of wars filled the neighborhood with distress, anxiety, and panic. Buffalo was burned by the British and Indians acting together. Battles and reverses came on the breeze ; the Americans were preparing for a retreat on Batavia, there to make a last desperate stand. At length the dreadful tidings came that the red-coats were coming, and the frightened women and children fled away through the woods, most of them passing entirely beyond the Genesee River. Others found shelter away up at Caledonia. Caledonia had been started early on account of its facilities for milling.

The very few who did not flee gathered together in one house, and my mother's family were among them. There they awaited, like frightened lambs, for the coming of the wolves. And the terrible red-coats came in earnest. But they came without arms in their hands, and they came between armed files of the blue-coated soldiery. They were prisoners of war taken at Lundy's Lane. The Americans had at last gained a great victory, and the time of extreme distress was past.

My father came in 1811, just in time to be swept away by the war. He lay out all night before Buffalo while it was burning, and in the struggle that occurred there he received a desperate wound in the leg. Three days later he arrived at Batavia with his wound still undressed, and in a horrible condition. The kindly Doctor McCracken took him to his house. But when Mrs. McCracken saw the condition of the man she positively insisted that that horrible looking soldier should be taken somewhere else. When the Doctor told her that it was one of their own neighbor boys, and who he was, she not only relented, but took him in and cared for him as a mother.

My father, John C. Wilford, came from Vermont. He drove through with a stock of hardware, which sold well. The family were originally Connecticut people, the ancestors of all arriving there about 1635.

NEAR THE SPEAKER'S STAND.

My father was one of the first, and, I think, the very first justice of the the peace in the town of Elba. In those days the justice was appointed by the Governor, and he was required to be a freeholder. In order to qualify himself my father bought a lot containing two acres of land. This little estate was never restored to the farm it was taken from, but became incorporated into the adjoining farm; and that farm to-day bears witness of the property qualification required in the olden time.

The old settlers thought it very important to let their boys see and hear great men. Daniel Webster once delivered an address in Batavia; and father took us boys to hear him. He spoke from the Court House steps and made a deep impression on me. He was received at the station and brought to the Court House in a carriage drawn by four black horses. Such things made a deep impression on boys.

The old people had very strict notions inherited from New England. General Erastus Cleveland, of Madison County, was a brother of my grandmother. Albert H. Tracy, a very distinguished lawyer of Buffalo, wanted to marry his daughter; but Mrs. Cleveland opposed the match on the ground that lawyers cannot enter heaven; and she carried her point. Mr. Tracy's brother, Phineas L. Tracy, was one of Batavia's distinguished citizens.

I was always a great admirer of Dean Richmond. He was a public-spirited man, a patriot, and a good citizen in every respect. It was Dean Richmond who got the State Institution for the Education of the Blind located here. He did much for Batavia. During his life every train on the Central had to stop at Batavia. He was a man of great force of character, and his influence was felt throughout the entire United States. Samuel J. Tilden said that Richmond could have had the nomination for President and could have been elected. His value to the State and nation during the Rebellion was incalculable The country owes much to the patriotism of such men as Richmond and Heman J. Redfield.

Since his death his excellent wife and family have been most active and liberal in all matters of public interest, and in public and private charities. As a consequence the name is and always will be dear to the people of this vicinity.

Among the dangers of the olden time was that of getting lost in the woods. One of Joseph Holmes's sisters was lost in the woods and died before she was found.

[The above modest narrative omits some important facts in regard to the Wilford family. The following significant quotation is from Beers's Gazetteer of Genesee County. It connects well with the story of Robert Morris. "Joseph Wilford, a native of Conecticut, was a soldier in the Revolutionary army. The British offered a bounty of 300 sovereigns for his body. He spent $40,000 of his private fortune to aid our government He afterwards went to Vermont, and from there came to Batavia (now Oakfield). John C. Wilford, his son, was born in Rutland, Vt., in 1787, and came to Oakfield in 1811. His education was liberal, and he taught several terms." This passage would bear much comment. -K.]

(*F. B. Redfield.*)

My grandfather, Peleg Redfield, came to the Genesee country from Sheffield, Connecticut, in 1799, and took a soldier's claim in the town of Manchester, Ontario county, a few miles from Clifton Springs. He had served throughout the Revolutionary War, was with Washington at Valley Forge, and shared in all the horrors of that winter encampment. He had two peculiarly bitter experiences that winter on the top of all the other troubles. He was taken down with small pox and narrowly escaped with his life While out on a scout with another soldier, they were espied and chased by a detachment of Hessian cavalry. The fugitives turned in at a farm-house to run across a field to some woods beyond. In passing the barn the other soldier slipped around to an over-turned sleigh and got in under the box. Grandfather ran on, and was half across the field before he realized that the other soldier was not with him. He halted a moment, and saw the Hessians tearing down the bars and rushing through the yard. They quickly located the poor soldier by his tracks in the snow. Grandfather saw them order him out from under the box and cut him down without a moments grace. He then ran for his life to the woods, and succeeded in eluding his pursuers. He passed the whole night in the woods. It was bitterly cold, and both his feet were frozen. They were never entirely right afterward. He was with Washington all through the war; on Long Island, at White Plains, on the retreat through the Jerseys, at Trenton and Princeton, at Brandywine, Germantown, Valley Forge, Monmouth, and Yorktown. He witnessed the execution of Major Andre, and always spoke of his fate with sympathy and re-

THE CLASS OF '94.

gret. He told of the horrible destitution of the army when a year's pay in paper money would hardly buy a meal of victuals. We have a piece of the Continental scrip which he received at Valley Forge. But he used to describe vividly the change that took place in their comforts, when Robert Morris came to their assistance. The soldiers revered Morris as their savior.

After all his sufferings in the Revolution he was ready for a struggle with the wilderness; and he fought out the battle of pioneering for nearly fifty years longer. My father used to say that if privations did not kill them, you could not kill those old fellows with a club.

My grandfather lived to be 91, and was a hale and lively old gentleman to the last. He stayed to the last on the farm which he took up in 1799. He retired, of course, from active business in his later life, and turned his farm over to one of his sons, with whom he continued to live. He kept for his own use a white mare and a buggy. The well-preserved old Continental and his unique little turn-out, were quite an interesting sight in the neighborhood. When my father would go to visit him in his last years the old gentleman would meet him at Clifton Springs with his little white mare and his little buggy and carry him out to the farm. On one occasion, on reaching the house, he bounded to the ground like an India-rubber ball, and began to pull down some steps, saying slyly to his son : "Heman, here are some steps that I have fixed for the comfort of the women folks."

It was his fate to die a sort of violent death after all. A boy came into

THE MACEDONIAN PHALANX SURROUNDING THE SPEAKER WITH SHIELD AND BUCKLER
—THE OLD GUARD NEVER SURRENDERS.

the neighborhood suffering with small-pox. No one would go near him. Grandfather said that the boy must have care, and, as he had had the small-pox at Valley Forge, he claimed that he was small-pox proof, and would attend the boy. He was warned of the peril ; but he said that the poor boy must have care. He went to the pest house, took the small-pox, and died. By a curious coincidence the figures were just reversed ; he was just 19 when he was stricken with the disease at Valley Forge ; he was just 91 when he died of it in the Genesee country.

His was a long life of unremitting service ; but it was throughout a life of spotless purity and integrity.

The pioneers were always kind and helpful to each other but what they did they did as a matter of course, and never said anything about it. The gates of my grandfather's silence, however, were once broken open in the midst of a spectacular and amusing scene. My father served in the State Senate in the early twenties. He was one of the "seventeen" who successfully resisted the attempt to change the law relating to the election of Presidential electors. For this they were for a time intensely unpopular, though the reaction afterwards came, and they were then known as the "glorious seventeen." But they were all burned in effigy, and were threatened with personal violence. Coffin handbills were sent to them, and "King Caucus" was denounced as "over riding the will of the people." Father found a placard posted on a wooden horse and left near his door. No pio-

THE OLD GUARD AT CLOSE RANGE.

neer needed any explanation of the hint intended to be conveyed by the wooden horse. In order to have some help in case of violence he had his law clerk sleep in his house.

In the midst of these troubles he paid a visit to grandfather. As the evening was wearing on they were suddenly astonished by a great illumination in the yard. Looking out they saw my father's effigy yielding to the devouring flames in the presence of a great crowd. My father was rather amused than otherwise, and stood gazing through the window at the martyrdom of his own poor image. Suddenly an apparition darted into the midst of the glare. It was that of an old man in his shirt sleeves with a pitchfork in his hands, and his white hair flying in the breeze, as he charged upon the nearest squad of the disturbers, and drove them off into the darkness. Then returning to another squad, he drove them off pell-mell in another direction. And as they rallied Old '76 would give them again and again the charge of Trenton, and Stony Point, and Yorktown, until he stood in victorious possession of the evacuated field. And he accompanied every vicious lunge with an objurgation : " Insult my son, will you, you worthless wretches? I'll teach you your manners, if you've never learned them before. Was it for this that I sheltered your families when you came into the wilderness?" And the murderous fork came gleaming into the faces of his quondam proteges. " Was it for this that I gave you a cow?" And where there were once bowels of mercy, there was now a raging fury, seeking with his pitchfork the bowels that had once digested his food. I have heard it said that people can tell when a man means to hit. This was the only occasion when my grandfather ever alluded to his benefactions ; and this was the only collision he ever had with his neighbors. It was the one solitary outburst of violence in half a century of quiet attention to duty.

My grandfather and his boys came to be possessed of a very comfortable competence. But they started in a very humble way. After filing on his claim he went back to Connecticut and brought his family out the next year, 1800. They came in a sleigh, and fed their horses the last day on brown bread. My father assisted in building the house that stands there today, and in doing so he fell and cut off his finger. They made the brick for the chimney by hand, and those bricks are still in their place. Some of the apple trees planted by them nearly a century ago are still standing.

The typical pioneer was ready for any emergency. After leaving the army my grandfather worked for a time at making shoes. His neighbors availed themselves freely of this skill. When one came with a pair of shoes to be cobbled he would hand him the axe and tell him to go on chopping while he did the cobbling. And when the job was finished the accounts were always squared. One pair of shoes a year was the rule ; and no one could break over it. If any one's shoes went to pieces before the end of the year he would have to tie them up with birch bark and hobble along to the appointed limit.

When our people came to the Genesee country they were guided by blazed trees in the woods.

The wolves would come right into the door-yard. One Sunday, while all the rest of the family were away at church, a very fine deer came into the yard ; and my father took down the gun and shot it. The neighborhood was very much scandalized by this desecration of the Sabbath, and my father was under a cloud for quite awhile. One evening while out looking for the cows he saw a gigantic bear sitting up on his haunches on the opposite side of a creek. He beat a retreat for home, and left the cows out that night.

Speaking of the shoes, the settlers tanned their own hides, and supplied about all their own wants at first hand.

When a man got into the nineties they began to look upon him as a little old. Delos Dodgson, however, says that his uncle was a good squirrel hunter at 98, and did not die till he was 103.

My grandfather drew a soldier's pension. He gave it all away in charity, and much more with it. He was always ready to leave anything that he was doing and go berrying with the children.

My father taught school and boarded around. He said that he always preferred the houses where the pretty girls were.

He served in the war of 1812. Was in the battle of Queenstown Heights. He rode through Buffalo soon after it was burned and saw just one house standing.

He studied law with John C. Spencer at Canandaigua and hung out his shingle at Le Roy. When he selected Batavia he thought that on the whole it promised to be a larger town than Buffalo.

He was in the Legislature in 1824, and was collector of the port of New York under Pierce. He came to Batavia to take charge of the Lan

THE "BLUE DOMES OF WYOMING'S HILLS" REFLECTED IN SILVER LAKE, THE "JEWELL OF THE GENESEE."

My brothers were in the war of the Rebellion. We had no one in Mexico. That is the one break in our military history.

[The following additional information in regard to Heman J. Redfield is from Beers's Gazetteer of Genesee County. "He was in the battle of Queenstown Heights, and was with General Harrison at Fort George, where he received a brevet from the commanding general for gallant services.

. . . He soon became distinguished as a lawyer. When arrangements were made for the trial of those accused of abducting William Morgan he was offered the position of special counsel to assist the attorney-gener-

. . In 1835 he also declined the office of circuit judge tendered

Governor Marcy. . . . It was highly creditable to him that, when he rendered his accounts as collector of the port of New York, involving the large sum of $143,493,957, they were promptly settled exactly as he rendered them. . . . In all the perils to which our country has been exposed, he has ever been on the side of the government. He sustained Mr. Polk throughout the Mexican war, and exerted himself on the side of the Government during the late war. . . . His first wife was Abby Noyes Gould, whom he married at Canandaigua, Ontario county, January 27, 1817. She died at Batavia on the 11th of February, 1841, in the 44th year of her age. The following children only survive them both: Elizabeth Gould, wife of Robert W. Lowber, of Bald Mountain, Washington county; Mary Judd, wife of Major Henry I. Glowacki, residing at Batavia; Jane, wife of Lawrence

SILVER LAKE EMERGING.

Turnure, of New York City; Cornelia, the widow of Rear Admiral Ralph Chandler, U. S. N., lately in command of the Asiatic station, at present residing at Yokohama, Japan; and Anna M., the widow of George Evans, of Albany, N. Y. In 1846 he married for his second wife Constance C. Bolles, of Newark, N. J., of English and French ancestry, who survives him, and by whom he had four children, as follows: Frank B. Redfield, Abby L. Sunderland, Una Clark (Mrs. Daniel W. Tomlinson), all of whom reside at Batavia, and Martha Evans, wife of Lieut. Rodman, U. S. N., now stationed at Newport, R. I."]

John Hancock, President of Congress, writing to Mr. Morris in a severe crisis of the Revolution, says — "I know, however, you will put things in a proper way, all things depend upon you, and you have my hearty thanks for your unremitting labor."

Paul Jones made Mr. Morris his executor, and bequeathed him as a token of his high regard, the sword he had received from the King of France. Mr. Morris gave it to Commodore Barry, with a request that it should fall successively into the hands of the oldest commander of the American Navy.—O. Turner.

(W. C. Watson.)

The tardy honors to Robert Morris, at last accorded by his much indebted but strangely-forgetful country, have my fullest approval and my most

SILVER LAKE EMERGED.

heartfelt sympathy. I am proud that it has fallen to the lot of our little city to take the lead in rectifying the great injustice done by America to her greatest benefactor and perhaps her greatest man. Certainly never before did the burden of nation-making fall more fully upon one pair of shoulders; and never before was the burden more triumphantly sustained. Never before was the burden borne with greater meekness or less of self-seeking, and never before was power more readily surrendered when the need of its exercise was past. The return of Solon, Cincinnatus, and Washington to private stations did not exceed in grace that of Robert Morris. Never before nor since did a man enter the public service with a more exalted motive; never before nor since did a man exhibit greater abilities or achieve greater results in that service; never before nor since have greater sacrifices been made by an individual for the public weal; and never before nor since has a man stepped more quickly aside the moment he could be spared. Never before nor since has a man been more reticent about his public service; never before nor since has a man shown more fully his conviction that a consciousness of duty performed is its own best and sufficient reward. Viewed from every point of view the man is simply colossal. That he has disappeared from American histories is the strangest phenomenon of our first century. But if he has disappeared from American histories he has not disappeared from American history; he is there forever; and any honest gropings after fundamental causes will find him every time. The enthusiasm which gathered about our recent celebration and which came up from all parts of the land, shows that the American peo-

THE RIVER CHICKSS.

ple do not want to be unjust, and that they will not be when they are once correctly informed. I am sure that I see in this movement the emergence of Robert Morris to his true place in American history and in the affections of the American people. And among all our great ones none can command higher admiration; none is more fitted to call forth the warmest love. He is the true protagonist of America; and I feel sure that he will be one of her most cherished idols.

But I feel that this occasion should not be permitted to pass by without appropriate recognition of another great American character. This celebration has been stimulated, perhaps brought to a successful issue, by the great name, the name of Richmond. The names of Morris and

Richmond are well met in American history. There is a remarkable parallel between the careers of the two men. Both were men of Titanic powers; both achieved extraordinary success in business; both were statesmen of the broadest outlook, and both were patriots of the most burning zeal. As Morris stood with his millions behind the war for American independence, so did Richmond stand with his millions behind the war for the preservation of the American Union. As furious as was Morris's determination to make the Revolution win, just so furious was Richmond's determination to make the war for the Union win. At his call regiments sprang up as it were from the ground; at his word the freights were side-tracked and those regiments were rushed forward to the front to fight for the life of the nation. His patriotism burned high above all considerations of party; he turned upon the party asso-

THE RIVER BREAKS

ciates of a lifetime and gave his loyal support to a president elected from the ranks of the opposition. Who will say how far this turned the tide of civil war? A Richmond was keeping the war from becoming one of parties, an internecine struggle between factions. The Richmonds were making the rear secure; the Richmonds were nerving the arms of the Grants, the Thomases, the Logans, the Slocums, and the Farraguts. The historians of the war must do as Mr. Lincoln did, give great credit to the Richmonds.

But the mightiest Richmond of them all was Dean Richmond of Batavia. His service and his influence in that great convulsion make him a national and historical character, and they place him in the high ranks of disinterested patriots. I lived beside him all my life. I felt the intensity of his zeal, I felt the power of his mighty influence. I think he ought to be regarded as one of America's strong and national characters, as one of her truest patriots. He had the history-making instinct, and the history-making force; and I hope to see him recognized as a historical character.

(Contributed.)

Among the celebrities that visited this region in the early day was the poet Moore. He came in 1804 to a country that had already quite a little history, but almost no literature. After singing the Dismal Swamp, the Potomac, the Schuylkill, and the Delaware into immortality, he at last came singing into the wilderness.

The Mohawk caught a noble ode:

WHAT THE WASHINGTON PARTY HEARD THAT NIGHT.

From rise of morn till set of sun,
I've seen the mighty Mohawk run;
And as I marked the woods of pine
Along his mirror darkly shine,
Like tall and gloomy forms that pass
Before the wizard's midnight glass;
And as I viewed the hurrying pace
With which he ran his turbid race,
Rushing, alike untired and wild,
Through shades that frowned and flowers that smiled,
Flying by every green recess
That wooed him to its calm caress,
Yet, sometimes turning with the wind,
As if to leave one look behind!
It! I have thought, and thinking sighed—

—189—

How like to thee, thou restless tide
May be the lot, the life of him,
Who roams along thy water's brim?
Through what alternate shades of woe
And flowers of joy my path may go
How many an humble, still retreat

WHAT THEY SAW THE NEXT MORNING.

May rise to court my weary feet,
While still pursuing, still unblest,
I wander on, nor dare to rest?
But, urgent as the doom that calls
Thy water to its destined falls,
I see the world's bewildering force

> Hurry my heart's devoted course
> From lapse to lapse, till life be done,
> And the lost current cease to run !
> Oh ! may my falls be bright as thine !
> May Heaven's forgiving rainbow shine
> Upon the mist that circles me,
> As soft as now it hangs o'er thee !

The voice is coming this way. Will the Tonawanda catch a note? Yes, the finest gem of all was dropped upon our stream. Tradition locates the spot about one mile west of Batavia. The singer arrived here in his best mood. As if prophetic of the peace and plenty which now smile all over the Genesee country, he left us the most exquisite little idyl that was ever dropped from poet's pen:

> I knew by the smoke, that so gracefully curled
>   Above the green elms, that a cottage was near ;
> And I said, 'If there's peace to be found in the world,
>   A heart that was humble might hope for it here."
>
> It was noon, and on flowers that languished around
>   In silence reposed the voluptuous bee ;
> Every leaf was at rest, and I heard not a sound
>   But the woodpecker tapping the hollow beech-tree.
>
> And ' Here in this lone little wood,' I exclaimed,
>   'With a maid who was lovely to soul and to eye,
> Who would blush when I praised her, and weep if I blamed,
>   How blest could I live, and how calm could I die !
>
> 'By the shade of yon sumach, whose red berry dips
>   In the gush of the fountain, how sweet to recline,
> And to know that I sighed upon innocent lips,
>   Which had never been sighed on by any but mine :"

But when he struck the undrained swamps as he wended his toilsome way westward, a cloud began to settle upon his spirits, and his song partakes of the spirit of the scene:

> Now the vapour, hot and damp,
> Shed by day's expiring lamp,
> Through the misty ether spreads
> Every ill the white man dreads ;
> Fiery fever's thirsty thrill,
> Fitful ague's shivering chill !
>
> Hark ! I hear the traveler's song,
> As he winds the woods along :
> Christian ! 'tis the song of fear ;
> Wolves are round thee, night is near,;
> And the wild thou dar'st to roam—
> Oh ! 'twas once the Indian's home.
>   *   *   *   *   *

At last footsore, lame from an accident, sick and discouraged, he arrived the shores of Lake Erie, and poured out his suffering and homesickness in a Jeremiade. It was the one brief cloud.

But here, alas! by Erie's stormy lake,
As far from thee my lonely course I take,
No bright remembrance o'er the fancy plays,
No classic dream, no star of other days,
Has left that visionary glory here,
That relic of its light, so soft so dear,
Which gilds and hallows even the rudest scene,
The humblest shed, where genius once has been!

All that creation's varying mass assumes
Of grand or lovely here aspires and blooms;
Cold rise the mountains, rich the gardens glow,
Bright lakes expand, and conquering rivers flow;
Mind, mind alone, without whose quickening ray,
The world's a wilderness, and man but clay,
Mind, mind alone, in barren, still repose,
Nor ideons nor rises nor expands nor flows.

A TITAN IN HARNESS

The despondent poet forgot for the moment that a people must make their epic before they can sing it. The heroic age of American history was sending up its notes from the woods; and he misunderstood the note.

But his depression was not of long duration. His recovery, physical and mental, was rapid. Buoyant as ever, he reached Niagara, and there poured forth his highest notes of triumph, worthy to mingle forever with the sounds of the mighty cataract.

I dreamed not then, that ere the rolling year
Had filled its circle, I should wander here
In musing awe; should tread this wondrous world,
See all its store of inland waters hurled
In one vast volume down Niagara's steep.

* * * * *

Now the voice is receding down the St. Lawrence River catching the romantic notes of the Canadian boatman's song.

Faintly as tolls the evening chime,
Our voices keep tune and our oars keep time,
Soon as the woods on shore look dim,
We'll sing at St. Ann's our parting hymn.
Row, brothers, row, the stream runs fast,
The Rapids are near and the daylight's past!

Why should we yet our sail unfurl:
There is not a breath the blue wave to curl.
But when the wind blows off the shore,
Oh! sweetly we'll rest our weary oar.
Blow, breezes, blow, the stream runs fast,
The Rapids are near, and the daylight's past!

Utawas' tide, this trembling moon
Shall see us float over thy surges soon.
Saint of this green Isle! hear our prayers,
Oh! grant us cool heavens and favoring airs.
Blow, breezes, blow, the stream runs fast,
The Rapids are near, and the daylight's past!

Up from distant and lonely Labrador come the solemn notes of the dirge by Dead Man's Isle.

See you, beneath yon cloud so dark,
Fast gliding along, a gloomy bark!
Her sails are full, though the wind is still,
And there blows not a breath her sails to fill!

Oh! what doth that vessel of darkness bear?
The silent calm of the grave is there,
Save now and again a death-knell rung,
And the flap of the sails with night fog hung!

There lieth a wreck on the dismal shore
Of cold and pitiless Labrador;
Where, under the moon, upon mounts of frost,
Full many a mariner's bones are tossed!

Yon shadowy bark hath been to that wreck,
And the dim blue fire that lights her deck
Doth play on as pale and livid a crew,
As ever yet drank the churchyard dew!

To Deadman's Isle, in the eye of the blast,
To Deadman's Isle she speeds her fast;
By skeleton shapes her sails are furled,
And the hand that steers is not of this world!

Oh! hurry thee on—oh! hurry thee on,
Thou terrible bark! ere the night be gone,
Nor let morning look on so foul a sight
As would blanch for ever her rosy light!

* * * * *

Last of all we have his half-sorrowful, wholly-joyful, outburst, as he ascends the vessel that is to bear him home:

> "Farewell to the few—though we never may meet,
> On this planet again, it is soothing and sweet
> To think that, whenever my song, or my name
> Shall recur to their ear, they'll recall me the same
> I have been to them now, young, unthoughtful, and blest,
> Ere hope had deceived me or sorrow depressed.
>   *   *   *   *   *
> But see!—the bent top-sails are ready to swell!—
> To the boat—I am with thee—Columbia, farewell!"

The region has had its Iliad of horrors. It has been girdled by fire, and war, and desolation, while struggling forward to its present prosperity. But in the midst of its greatest trials came that beautiful and never-to-be forgotten episode, that sweet girdle of song.

> Thou, too, sail on, O ship of state!
> Sail on, O Union, strong and great!
> Humanity, with all its fears,
> With all the hopes of future years,
> Is hanging breathless on thy fate!
>
> We know what Master laid thy keel,
> What Workman wrought thy ribs of steel,
> Who made each mast, and sail, and rope,
> What anvils rang, what hammers beat,
> In what a forge and what a heat,
> Were shaped the anchors of thy hope!
>
> Fear not each sudden sound and shock,
> 'Tis of the wave and not the rock
> 'Tis but the flapping of the sail,
> And not a rent made by the gale!
> In spite of rock and tempest's roar,
> In spite of false lights on the shore,
> Sail on, nor fear to breast the sea!
> Our hearts, our hopes, are all with thee;
> Our hearts, our hopes, our prayers, our tears,
> Our faith triumphant o'er our fears,
> Are all with thee,—are all with thee!—*Longfellow.*

This is the point at which Robert Morris performed his greatest public service. *It was known that the army would rebel if an attempt was made to disband it without pay. No one knew how to make any provision for paying it, unless Robert Morris would do it.* For the moment he was indispensable. If those notes had been simple certificates of indebtedness of the United States, it appears that *nothing would have been done to redeem them. It was his name and credit that made them available.*—*Wm. G. Sumner.*

In his person [as now conducted] he was of nearly six feet [in stature], of large, full, well-formed, vigorous frame, with clear, smooth, handsome visage. His loose, gray hair was unpowdered, his eyes were gray, of middle size, uncommonly brilliant. He wore, as was common at that day, a broadcloth of the same color, and of light mixture. His manners were gracious and simple, and free from the formality which generally prevails. He was very affable, and mingled in common conversation, even with the young. —*Sullivan.*

Frank, generous and manly mortal.—*John Adams.*

Upon him had devolved the financiering for our country in a period of peril and embarrassment. When the army of Washington, unpaid, were lacking food and raiment; murmuring as they well might be; *it was his purse and credit that more than once prevented its dispersion, and the failure of the glorious achievement of Independence. His ships were upon the ocean, his notes of hand forming a currency, his drafts honored everywhere among capitalists in his own country, and in many of the marts of commerce in Europe.*

A reverse of fortune, saddening to those who are now enjoying the blessings to which he so eminently contributed—who wish that no cloud had gathered around the close of his useful life—intervened between the dates of the two letters.—*O. Turner.*

(*Buffalo Express.*)

Maybe this credit was fictitious; but maybe fiction doesn't come pretty close to the fact when for eighteen years men and banks and nations loan money on it without question! *The fact remains that he associated himself with the government a rich man, and emerged in a debtor's prison.*

Mr. Morris began to notice the decline of his credit in 1793 or '94, while in the midst of colossal land speculations for the purpose of meeting his never-ending obligations.

In 1796 his new house on Chestnut street, Philadelphia, was sold under the hammer before its completion. When at last the financial crash came to Mr. Morris, *there was for him no pity but in words, no seeming memory of what he had been and achieved, no second great-hearted Morris to save him from a debtors prison as he had saved his country from oppression.* Washington came to see him and Hamilton wrote dunning letters; but he was not released, not until the law allowed.

My ships have all miscarried, my creditors grow cruel, my estate is very low, my bond is forfeit.—*Shakespeare.*

I oft delivered from his forfeitures
Many that at times made moan to me.—*Ibid.*

But if you know to whom you show this honor,
How true a gentleman you send relief,
* * * * *
I know you would be prouder of the work
Than customary bounty can enforce you.—*Ibid.*

Glancing an eye of pity on his losses,
That have of late so huddled on his back,
Enow to press a royal merchant down
And pluck commiseration of his state
From brassy bosoms and rough hearts of flint,
From stubborn Turks and Tartars, never train'd
To offices of tender courtesy.—*Ibid.*

Therefore I beseech you
'Make no further offers, use no further means,
But with all brief and plain consistency
Let me have judgment.—*Ibid*

The weakest kind of fruit
Drops earliest to the ground ; and so let me :
You cannot be better employ'd, Bassanio,
Than to live and write mine epitaph.—*Ibid*.

Grieve not that I am fallen to this for you ;
* * * * *
Say how I loved you, speak me fair in death.—*Ibid*

And be repents not that he paid your debt.—*Ibid*

Gaoler, look to him ; tell not me of mercy :
This is the fool that lent out money gratis :
Gaoler, look to him.—*Ibid*.

These griefs and losses have so bated me.
That I shall hardly spare a pound of flesh
Tomorrow to my bloody creditor,
Well, gaoler, on.—*Ibid*.

But since he stands obdurate
And that no lawful means can carry me
Out of his envy's reach, I do oppose
My patience to his fury, and am arm'd
To suffer, with a quietness of spirit,
The very tyranny and rage of his,—*Ibid*

In the course of justice none of us
Should see salvation; we do pray for mercy;
And that same prayer doth teach us all to render
The deeds of mercy. I have spoke this much
To mitigate the justice of thy plea;
Which if thou follow, this strict court of Venice
Must needs give sentence 'gainst the merchant here.—*Ibid*

Come, merchant have you anything to say?
But little: I am armed and well prepared.—*Ibid*.

The Age its latest decade shows,
The wondrous century nears its close,
Revealing in its fateful span
Unwonted ways of good to man

Imprisoned vapor speeds its course,
Files, quick with life, th' electric force
Nature's dæmonic mysteries
Are angels now, that aid and please.

But dearer far to human ken
The record of illustrious men,
The gifts conveyed in measures wrought.
Of noble purpose and high thought.
* * * * *
Still battling on the field of Life,
We break from the unequal strife,
From task or pastime hasten all
As at a vanished leader's call.
* * * * *

No gift whose precious bloom can fade,
No holocaust on false shrine laid ;
A legacy of good untold,
August as oracles of old,
The winged word that cannot die,
The world-transcending prophecy.
—*Mrs. Julia Ward Howe.*

On this green bank, by this soft stream,
 We set to day a votive stone ;
That Memory may her dead redeem,
 When, like our sires, our sons are gone.

Spirit, that made those heroes dare
 To die and leave their children free,
Bid Time and Nature gently spare
 The shaft we raised to them and thee. —*Emerson.*

www.ingramcontent.com/pod-product-compliance
Lightning Source LLC
Chambersburg PA
CBHW020237170426
43202CB00008B/115